# In the Presence of Master

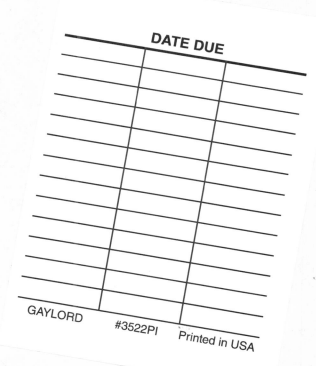

**DATE DUE**

GAYLORD          #3522PI          Printed in USA

# *In the* PRESENCE *of* MASTERS

Wisdom from
30 Contemporary
Tibetan Buddhist
Teachers

EDITED BY
REGINALD A. RAY

*Shambhala*
BOSTON & LONDON → 2004

*To Sakyong Mipham Rinpoche,*
*Shambhala Lineage Holder and Dharma King*

SHAMBHALA PUBLICATIONS, INC.
HORTICULTURAL HALL
300 MASSACHUSETTS AVENUE
BOSTON, MASSACHUSETTS 02115
*www.shambhala.com*

©2004 by Reginald A. Ray

Please see pages 273–290 for a continuation of the copyright page.

9 8 7 6 5 4 3 2 1

First Edition

Printed in the United States of America

⊗ This edition is printed on acid-free paper that meets the
American National Standards Institute z39.48 Standard.

Distributed in the United States by Random House, Inc.,
and in Canada by Random House of Canada Ltd

Library of Congress Cataloging-in-Publication Data
In the presence of masters: wisdom from 30 contemporary
Tibetan buddhist teachers / edited by Reginald A. Ray.
p.   cm.
ISBN 1-57062-849-1 (pbk.: alk. paper)
1. Buddhism.   2. Buddhism—China—Tibet.   I. Ray, Reginald A.
BQ4016 .I5   2004
294.3'923—dc22
2003026575

# CONTENTS

# Part Four   *Vajrayana*   153

# Part Five   *Conclusion*   233

# PREFACE

This volume contains instructions on meditation and the spiritual life by contemporary Tibetan lamas of the "practice lineages," primarily of the Nyingma and Kagyü. The teachers represented here include both those trained in Tibet who were part of the original diaspora that occurred in the late 1950s and the 1960s as well as lamas of the second and even third generation, brought up and educated in refugee communities in Asia and elsewhere.

All of these instructions were originally given orally to Western students or adapted from those teachings. In assembling this collection, I have drawn both upon unpublished transcripts of talks and discussions and also upon published materials (interviews, articles, and books). The thirty lamas represented here include many of the most energetic, creative, and eloquent Tibetan teachers working with Westerners in recent decades. In this collection I emphasize teachings of Nyingma and Kagyü lamas because it is these lineages that have historically defined themselves most comprehensively as meditative traditions, and it is the masters of these lineages who have been most active in promoting meditation practice in the West.

The fact that this volume is composed of teachings that were originally given orally deserves some comment. Oral teachings, and especially those composed for and addressed to particular listeners, occupy a distinctive and important place within Tibetan Buddhism and within Buddhism as a whole, both past and present. The Buddha instructed and educated his own disciples primarily by talking with them: he conversed with them about what was going on in their lives and their world, showing them, in each situation, the unassailable and often shocking nature of how things are. The early texts show him revealing, case by case, that the paltry ideas we humans habitually have about our lives are finally inapplicable; he also demonstrated how easily they vanish before an experience of reality itself. The Buddha addressed his disciples' immediate situation rather than quoting ancient texts because the experience of liberation can occur only as the epiphany of the present moment in all its fullness. And the depth and subtlety of the present is best unveiled—so Buddhism asserts—through the immediacy of the freshly spoken word, rather than something composed a long time ago.

It is interesting that, in spite of the existence of a huge written Buddhist canon and many thousands of books on Buddhism now in print in the West, the oral tradition continues to take precedence in the lives of individual, practicing Buddhists. When Buddhist practitioners think about how to approach life, they generally don't look to the books as the first and foremost reference point. Rather than quoting the the Bible as Christians might, Buddhists will quote the words of a teaching they received from their mentor that has struck them and remained in their minds.

The teachings presented in this book are, of course, written down. However, like the earliest Buddhist texts, they stand very close to the original oral teaching situation. In the Asian past of Buddhism, oral instructions given by accomplished teachers would be received only by the audiences actually present at the teachings. Others who were not present might hear about what was taught and very occasionally might see notes taken by someone who was there, but they would not have access to the full extent of what was said. With the recent invention of audio and video recording, the situation we face is different. Now, when a teacher gives an oral instruction, although we may not have been there, we may listen to, and perhaps also watch, a recording of it. Beyond that, as in the present instance, we may be able to read an edited transcription of what was said. This volume, then, enables us to see the situation that was addressed, the images that were used, something of the nuances of the presentation and the interactions between teacher and student. As we read these selections, we may feel that it is our own lives that are in question and our own situations that are being addressed. Because the modern world is so increasingly standardized, in a certain sense, this is an accurate impression.

As I have prepared this collection, I have been particularly struck by two things. First, I have been surprised that the voices of the various teachers have often seemed so markedly different from one another. It is not just that some lamas are more traditional in their style while others are more innovative and contemporary sounding. In addition, some are more formal while others are more conversational; some tend to present ideas while others make more use of imagery and stories. I invite the reader to appreciate this diversity.

Such diversity among teaching approaches and styles is not an incidental element in the transmission of Buddhism. Different kinds of students are able to "hear" and respond to different kinds of teachers in different ways. We are not talking here about better or worse dharma. It is similar to languages: if one person can understand French while another can understand Arabic, Swahili, or Korean, this does not mean that one language is "better" than another in some abstract sense. Similarly, given a specific teacher and student, meaning is best able to be conveyed in a particular way. It is one of the great strengths of Buddhism that such inevitable variability of idiom and presentation is appreciated and affirmed. In Buddhism, one size does not, and cannot, fit all.

At the same time—and this is something all the more clear given the context of the different styles of the teachers—one cannot help but be struck by the extent to which the message of dharma has a certain sameness throughout the different presentations. I suppose this is what is meant by a common "tradition"—a certain way of doing things that endures through individual variations and across time. One sees the belief in the importance of that kind of continuity in the Tibetan emphasis on rigorous training for its teachers and the great value placed on maintaining the integrity of individual lineages, practices, and teachings. Sensing such a high degree of underlying continuity across the span of our selections has left me with a certain reassurance. While the individual teachers may come and go, as long as a few authentic masters remain, one may have some confidence that the Tibetan dharma will survive.

The teachings contained herein are organized according to the three *yana*s, the standard, three-stage progression of the spiritual path as understood in Tibet: Hinayana ("the lesser vehicle"), Mahayana ("the greater vehicle"), and Vajrayana ("the indestructible vehicle"). Along with an introduction that concerns the Buddha and a conclusion that deals with Buddhism in the West, the book thus contains five major parts. All are divided into chapters on specific topics. Each chapter begins with its own introduction. The introductions provide not only an entry to the topic but also a precise geography of the terrain to be covered in each chapter. Each entry in the chapter is referred to by number; the introductions represent a summary of the passages such that each passage is discussed in the order in which it appears. When reading each introduction, readers will thus be able to see the logic of the order of passages. They also may use this numbering to look ahead to a specific selection of particular interest. And, when reading individual selections, they may look back at the introduction to see where that particular passage fits into the overall logic of that section.

I have arranged these passages as if they were each entries in a coherent conversation. The reader will notice that each passage, in a real sense, responds to the previous one. It is as if each teacher represented in a given chapter is party to a dialogue on the topic in question: one teacher makes an observation, a second teacher responds to the point just made, and each subsequent passage represents a further response as the topic unfolds and is explored to ever greater subtlety and depth. The book as a whole also possesses this same kind of unfolding, dialogical character wherein the path of dharma is explored from its fundamentals (Introduction), through its increasingly sophisticated and advanced levels (Hinayana, Mahayana, Vajrayana), to a conclusion that examines the implications of what has been discussed for Buddhism in the modern world.

Readers of this collection will no doubt hear and assimilate these selections in a great variety of ways. This, also, is fully in keeping with the ancient expectation of Buddhist tradition—that people come away from the same teachings with often vastly different experiences owing to their different temperaments, past experiences, and needs. An example may illustrate the fortuitous character of such variability. When an accomplished Tibetan lama gives a discourse, it is always striking how much variety there is in what different people experience. An individual who has never attended a teaching situation before may be struck by the atmosphere of the room, the presence of the lama, and the respectful and gentle behavior of the audience. Another, who is a new practitioner, may be struggling to make sense of conceptual content that he or she is hearing for the first time. For someone already quite familiar with the conceptual content, the teaching may offer contemplation of a well-known topic and the opportunity to arrive at a deeper understanding. A more experienced practitioner, perhaps one just recently come out of retreat, may be deeply moved by the compassion and blessings of the situation itself—that the dharma is being presented in such a world, in such a way, to such people. And, at a certain moment, another may glance up at the teacher and may find him- or herself gazing into the brilliant, endless space of reality itself. Such a moment may be, for that person, the fulfillment of a lifetime. But, oddly enough, others in attendance may feel that they also saw "what was occurring" and that they received what they came for, varied though their experiences may have been. As in the living situation, so may it be with the teachings contained in this volume.

# ACKNOWLEDGMENTS

I would like to acknowledge some of the many people and the organizations who have helped bring this collection to completion. Thanks to the Goldfarb Foundation and to Naropa University for grants underwriting some of the expenses of manuscript preparation. Special appreciation goes to Diana J. Mukpo for permission to quote from the works of Chögyam Trungpa Rinpoche. I want to express my gratitude to Matthieu Ricard for allowing me to include teachings of H. H. Khyentse Rinpoche found in *Journey to Enlightenment*. Thanks to Marcia and Erik Schmidt for permission to include instructions of Tulku Urgyen Rinpoche. Thanks also to Sakyong Mipham Rinpoche and to his editor, Emily Hilburn, for the unpublished teachings included here. Thanks also to the following lamas for use of their unpublished teachings and to their students who acted as advisers, intermediaries, and editors: to Thrangu Rinpoche and his student Clark Johnson; to Pönlop Rinpoche and his student Cindy Shelton; to Dzigar Kongtrul and his student Vern Mizner; to the Ven. Khandro Rinpoche and her student Karl Gross; to Ringu Tulku and his student Tharpa Lowry. And thanks to the other lamas quoted in these pages, and to their editors and publishers for giving permission to reprint them. I want to express my special appreciation to Beth Marvel for her extensive and computer-sophisticated editorial assistance in this project and for carrying through the sensitive task of obtaining the necessary permissions. Many thanks go to Bill Hulley for putting together the photographs in the book. Thanks also to Amelie Bracker for help with the biographies of the authors. And much gratitude goes to my wife, Lee, who provided indispensable advice and assistance at each stage of manuscript preparation down to reading and correcting the final proofs.

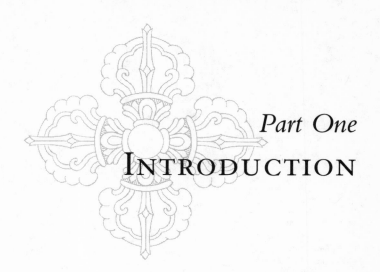

*Part One*

# INTRODUCTION

# → I

# The Buddha

## His Life, His Aspects, and His Legacy

SOMETIMES IT IS SAID that Shakyamuni Buddha plays a less prominent role in Tibetan tradition than in, for example, Theravada. The
reason given is that the Tibetans speak of several bodies of the Buddha,
of a larger array of teachings than the early schools, and of other celestial
buddhas and bodhisattvas who play important roles in meditative and
ritual life. It might be more accurate to say that, within Tibetan Buddhism, Shakyamuni Buddha is understood in a more expansive way
than in some other traditions.

As the following passages show, Tibetans consider the human person, Shakyamuni Buddha, with unparalleled reverence and devotion.
Tibetans might have had spontaneous visions of him (1.1) and felt his
ever ready availability (1.2). In Tibetan tradition, the Buddha is seen as
an exalted and inspiring example for all who aspire to realization. He
was an ordinary person who, unsatisfied with received or partial truths,
through his dedication and exertion, found a new way (1.3). He was,
in fact, a revolutionary who freed himself from what was conventionally
accepted and attained the pinnacle of enlightenment itself (1.4). His
attainment of the realization of egolessness (1.5) meant that he was utterly insignificant but, because of that, the "world enlightened one"

(1.6). From that point onward, the Buddha's sole purpose was to lead beings to that same awakening (1.7). The method he taught was meditation (1.8). Tibetan tradition emphasizes the Buddha's compassion: he was not trying to create a new "ism," but gave himself utterly to the world, teaching and showing others the solitary path that he had found to the full realization of what a human being can be (1.9).

One of the most interesting aspects of the practice lineage approach is its understanding of the Buddha's attainment and its relation to us. There is a strong sense that the Buddha's experience of the awakened state is accessible to us through the practice of meditation. While in some interpretations, the Buddha's awakening is considered so exalted and so far off as to be an object of devotion but not emulation, in the practice lineage, it is precisely that awakening that should be sought by meditators in this life. The great devotion felt toward the Buddha is not because he is different from us, but rather because he has shown us what we are and can be. He was the first to find this, the one whose attainment was complete and perfect, and the one who opened the door for the rest of us.

The object of devotion is not just the immediately manifest human Buddha, but rather the Buddha in his full reality, majesty, and humanity. These three aspects are known as the three bodies of the buddha. What made Gautama the Buddha was his discovery of an awareness within his own human experience that is beyond birth and death, beyond being and nonbeing. This "fundamental nature," as it is called, is the "ultimate body" (*dharmakaya*) of the Buddha. His corruptible form, his human body, is known as his "created body" (*nirmanakaya*). Because of his attainment, he was able to show himself to his disciples and later followers in a transcendent body, one made of form and light but not substance, known as the "body of enjoyment" (*sambhogakaya*). These "three bodies" are not really three, but three different aspects of the same person, Shakyamuni Buddha (1.10). The essence of this person (the *dharmakaya*) is beyond all manifestation, any kind of being or nonbeing (1.11, 1.12), and it is this that makes the human person what he is (*nirmanakaya*) and defines his glorious aspect (*sambhogakaya*). The three *kaya*s not only define Shakyamuni, but also represent our own enlightened nature that, again, becomes accessible to us through practice (1.13). And the three *kaya*s manifest in and through our own paths (as spaciousness, compassion, and skillful means) (1.14). While there is one *dharmakaya* that is the same for all buddhas, there are multiple human (*nirmanakaya*) and celestial (*sambhogakaya*) buddhas. In Tibet, the tradition knows much of these other buddhas and, as we shall see below, in the tantric practices, the celestial buddhas and bodhisattvas play an especially important role.

Tibetans hold that during the Buddha's lifetime, he gave three cycles of teachings known as the three turnings of the wheel of dharma. These all relate to "view," or the way in which one understands reality as one progresses along the path to awakening. The first turning concerns the individual's lack of a substantial "self," the second teaches the emptiness of individual self as well as all external phenomena, and the third outlines the doctrine of buddha-nature (1.15, 1.16). These three can be summarized in the phrase: "mind; there is no mind; mind is luminosity" (1.17). The Buddha also taught three bodies of increasingly subtle and advanced contemplative and meditative practices known as the three *yana*s, Hinayana (the lesser vehicle), Mahayana (the greater vehicle), and Vajrayana (the diamond vehicle), to be considered in the next section. A buddha appears and teaches us, not because he has to, but because of our needs and the vows he made prior to enlightenment (1.18). The Buddha's teachings on view and on practice were passed down from generation to generation in India and eventually came to Tibet beginning in the seventh century. It is this legacy of Buddha Shakyamuni, along with creative Tibetan amplifications and developments of that legacy, that makes up Tibetan Buddhism today (1.19).

## A VIVID MOMENT OF RECOLLECTION                                     1.1
When I was eight I [learned] . . . about the life of the Buddha. I could visualize him among his monks in their saffron robes, for one day I had had a vivid moment of recollection. When I read about the death of his mother, seven days after his birth, I seemed to share his loss.

*Chögyam Trungpa Rinpoche*


## THE BUDDHA IS READILY AVAILABLE                                    1.2
The Lord Buddha said, "I am always in front of the one who has faith."

*Dilgo Khyentse Rinpoche*

## THE BUDDHA WAS AN ORDINARY HUMAN BEING          1.3

Buddhism was founded by the Buddha about twenty-five hundred years ago. What we know about the Buddha is that he claimed to have seen the reality of things and to have gained enormous insight into the nature of the human condition. He did not claim to be an incarnation of some higher being nor to be a messenger of any kind. Neither did he say that he was an intermediary between some higher reality and human beings. He said that he was an ordinary human being who applied himself through the practice of meditation and was able to purify his own mind, so that insight was born in him, enabling him to see things as they are. And Buddha also said that this ability can be developed by anyone.

*Traleg Kyabgon Rinpoche*

## THE BUDDHA WAS A GREAT REVOLUTIONARY          1.4

[Gautama discovered] that wherever one is trying to learn, it is necessary to have firsthand experience, rather than learning from books or from teachers or by merely conforming to an already established pattern. That is what he found, and in that sense Buddha was a great revolutionary in his way of thinking. He even denied the existence of Brahma, or God, the creator of the world. He determined to accept nothing which he had not first discovered himself.

*Chögyam Trungpa Rinpoche*

## THE BUDDHA'S DISCOVERY          1.5

Buddha discovered that there is no such thing as "I," ego. Perhaps one should say there is no such thing as "am," "I am." He discovered that all these concepts, ideas, hopes, fears, emotions, and conclusions are created out of one's speculative thoughts and one's psychological inheritance from parents and upbringing and so on. We just tend to put them all together.

*Chögyam Trungpa Rinpoche*

## THE BUDDHA'S INSIGNIFICANCE          1.6

The Buddha had no ground, no territory. So much so that he was hardly an individual. He was just a grain of sand living in the vast desert.

Through his insignificance he became "the world enlightened one," because there was no battle involved.

*Chögyam Trungpa Rinpoche*

## THE BUDDHA'S SOLE PURPOSE    1.7

The Buddha's sole purpose for giving teachings is to enable us to recognize our empty, cognizant nature, to train in that and to attain stability.

*Tulku Urgyen Rinpoche*

## THE BUDDHA'S METHOD: MEDITATION    1.8

The method that the Buddha discovered is meditation. He discovered that struggling to find answers did not work. It was only when there were gaps in his struggle that insights came to him. He began to realize that there was a sane, awake quality within him which manifested itself only in the absence of struggle. So the practice of meditation involves "letting be."

*Chögyam Trungpa Rinpoche*

## THE BUDDHA DID NOT INTEND TO CREATE A NEW "ISM"    1.9

Buddha did not intend to create a new "ism." An intention to create a new system, a new faith, or a new philosophy would be contradictory to the discovery of absolute truth, which is the main emphasis and aim of Buddhism. The fruition of Buddhist meditation is realization of the absolute truth, which enables one to remove every stain of ignorance so that genuine kindness, genuine wisdom, genuine common sense, and a genuine human nature can be discovered and realized.

*Venerable Khandro Rinpoche*

## WHO IS THE BUDDHA? HIS THREE BODIES    1.10

At the Dharmakaya level, his mind is the vast expanse of omniscience which knows all things exactly as they are. At the Sambhogakaya level, which transcends birth and death, he continually turns the Wheel of

Dharma. At the Nirmanakaya level . . . he achieved complete Enlightenment near the Bodhi tree at Vajra Asana, India. He then turned the
Wheel of Dharma three times for the benefit of sentient beings.

*Dilgo Khyentse Rinpoche*


## THE BUDDHA IS BEYOND ETERNALISM
## AND NIHILISM                                           1.11

The Buddha is beyond eternalism and never remains in any elements.
The Buddha is beyond nihilism and never separates from any elements.
But sentient beings cannot recognize this, so we always trust either eternalism or nihilism and are always suffering and punishing ourselves in
the circle of death and rebirth.

*Thinley Norbu Rinpoche*


## THE BUDDHA'S OMNISCIENCE                              1.12

The Buddha sees everything because in Wisdom Mind there is no time
and no direction. Without time and direction, there is nothing more to
see. But if there is nothing more to see, how can the Buddha be a guide
and benefit sentient beings? If we think there is no time, how can the
Buddha predict time? If we think there is no direction, how can the
Buddha indicate direction?

The Buddha is omniscient: his mind is like the sky. He does not
show anything: what appears is a reflection. If sentient beings have direction, it is reflected. If sentient beings have a time, it is reflected.

*Thinley Norbu Rinpoche*


## THE THREE BUDDHA BODIES ARE OUR
## PRIMORDIAL MIND                                        1.13

Mind is primordially empty. It is original wakefulness that is empty in
essence, cognizant by nature, and all-pervasive in its capacity. This original wakefulness, *yeshe* [Skt. *jnana*, wisdom], is not a blank void; it is
cognizant. It has the ability to know. When we talk about the real, the
original, *this* is what it is. Original wakefulness empty in essence is the
*dharmakaya* of all buddhas. Original wakefulness cognizant by nature is

*Dilgo Khyentse Rinpoche*

the *sambhogakaya* of all buddhas. Original wakefulness is also all-pervasive in its capacity. The innate capacity in which being empty and cognizant are indivisible is called the *nirmanakaya* of all buddhas. These three *kayas* form a single indivisibility, the *svabhavikakaya*, which is our own mind. This original basic reality present in oneself—as opposed to the seeming—is exactly what we call buddha nature.

*Tulku Urgyen Rinpoche*


HOW THE THREE KAYAS MANIFEST ON OUR PATH           1.14

There is tremendous, living power within this path, and that living quality of the journey begins with *spaciousness*. If there is no sense of spaciousness, there is no way we can take a journey. We must have the fullness of space in front of us and the fullness of space around us. There is a fundamental sense of freedom within that notion of journey. Because of that basic freedom, we are able to take such a journey and are in the situation that makes it possible. There is a tremendous quality of possibility within that space. So the first, living quality of the journey of the path is spaciousness, freedom. This freedom is the primordial nature.

That basic space, which has tremendous possibilities, is the fundamental quality of our path. Within that possibility, within the space quality of the path, we have the second aspect of the path, which is *compassion*. Compassion manifests in the nature of clarity. We may have a strong sense of space, a great sense of freedom and of the path in front of us, but if there is no light, if there is no clarity, then we do not know where to walk, or where to go. [By itself,] freedom gives us no guidance. Freedom has no direction. The sense of direction, which makes it possible for freedom to totally manifest, comes from having true vision. With such vision and sight, we can exercise the full power of our liberty and freedom. The full power to exercise our freedom and innate sense of liberty only becomes possible with the light of compassion. So the second essential quality of the path is compassion.

When we have the possibility of manifesting our freedom, the basic space, in the light of compassion, that is the third aspect of the path, which is knowing how to direct our compassion, how to manifest this light, in union with the space. Tremendous expertise, or *skillful means*, is needed in order to unite the primordial space with the light of compassion, and to manifest freedom in that unification. This involves tremendous skill. That skill is the child, so to speak, of space and luminosity; it comes out of the primordial space and the total light of compassion. These three aspects or elements of the path are the true manifestation of Guru Padmasambhava.

*The Dzogchen Pönlop Rinpoche*

## THE THREE TURNINGS OF THE WHEEL OF DHARMA            1.15

In the early Hinayana teachings—referred to as the first turning of the Wheel of Dharma—the Buddha negated the existence of a permanent, substantial self, but did not go into an elaborate discussion of this in relation to emptiness. In the second turning of the Wheel of Dharma, the teachings of the emptiness of phenomena are introduced. Here there is both the idea of the nonsubstantiality or emptiness of the self and the emptiness of external phenomena. Then, in the third turning of the Wheel of Dharma, the idea of *tathagatagarbha* or Buddha-nature is introduced. In these teachings, the negation of an inherently existing self or ego or soul is integrated with an incorruptible spiritual principle called the *tathagatagarbha,* or Buddha-nature, that remains unstained by the passions and conceptual confusions of the mind.

*Traleg Kyabgon Rinpoche*

## THE THREE SUCCESSIVE STAGES OF TEACHING            1.16

In the first of three successive stages of teaching, referred to as the First Turning of the Wheel of Dharma, the Buddha taught the four noble truths: the truth of suffering, its origin, the path by which it is eradicated, and its cessation. In the Second Turning, he taught that the true nature of all phenomena is empty, signless, and aspirationless: the foundation nature is emptiness, the path is without signs, and the fruition is beyond aspiration. In the Third Turning of the wheel, he spoke of the full, infallible, resplendent qualities of mind's nature, the appearance of the clear light of wisdom.

*Chagdud Tulku Rinpoche*

## THE PURPOSE OF THE THREE TURNINGS                              1.17

The Buddha taught three different approaches on three separate occasions. These are known as the Three Turnings of the Wheel, but they can be summed up in a single phrase: "Mind; there is no mind; mind is luminosity."

The first, "Mind," refers to the first set of teachings and shows that the Buddha taught that there is a "mind." This was to dispel the nihilistic view that there is no heaven, no hell, no cause and effect. Then, when the Buddha said, "There is no mind," he meant that mind is just a concept and that there is no such thing as a truly existing mind. Finally, when he said, "Mind is luminous," he was referring to buddhanature, the undeluded or primordially existing wisdom.

The great commentator Nagarjuna said that the purpose of the first turning was to get rid of non-virtue. Where does the non-virtue come from? It comes from being either eternalist or nihilist. So in order to put an end to non-virtuous deeds and thoughts, the Buddha gave his first teaching. The second turning of the Dharma-wheel, when the Buddha spoke about emptiness, was presented in order to dispel clinging to a "truly existent self" and to "truly existent phenomena." Finally, the teachings of the third turning were given to dispel all views, even the view of no-self. The Buddha's three sets of teaching do not seek to introduce something new; their purpose is simply to clear away confusion.

*Dzongsar Khyentse Rinpoche*


## WHY DO THE BUDDHAS HELP US?                                    1.18

Space, within which the whole universe appears, does not need to show itself in any way to whatever is taking place within it. In the same way, the buddhas in their enlightened nature do not need to manifest in any way. Yet, through the links created by the powerful aspirations they conceived just before achieving enlightenment and by beings' prayers to them for blessings, the buddhas spontaneously appear in various ways to help beings according to their needs.

*Dilgo Khyentse Rinpoche*

## THE BUDDHA'S HERITAGE IN TIBET 1.19

When the teachings spread to Tibet, new lineages were named according to the varying periods of new transmission. The first was the Old School, called Nyingma. The subsequent seven lineages were called the New Schools. Altogether these different schools of teachings are known as the Eight Chariots of the Practice Lineage. They are Nyingma, Kadam, Sakya, and Karma Kagyü, then Shangpa Kagyü, Shijey an Chö, Jordruk, and Nyendrub. Today these are all included within the four schools of Tibetan Buddhism renowned as Nyingma, Kagyü, Geluk, and Sakya.

*Tulku Urgyen Rinpoche*

# → 2

# The Three Vehicles

ALL KNOWN BUDDHIST SCHOOLS describe a path to enlightenment made up of various graduated stages and associated practices. Within Tibetan tradition, the path is divided into three *yanas*, or vehicles: three major stages of practice, understanding, and realization (2.1). All are considered the authentic word of the Buddha (2.2). The Buddha, according to Tibetan Buddhism, first taught the initial stage, or Hinayana, then the intermediate stage, or Mahayana, and finally, the unexcelled stage of the Vajrayana. Each *yana* has its associated view, practice, and result. The view of Hinayana is defined by the first turning of the wheel of dharma or the four noble truths; the practice is meditation carried out to free oneself from suffering; and the result is freedom from the defiling emotions. The view of Mahayana is defined by the second and third turnings of the wheel of dharma, or the teachings on emptiness and buddha-nature; the practice is absolute bodhichitta (emptiness) and relative bodhichitta (compassion); and the result is, after three incalculable eons, buddhahood. The view of Vajrayana is the same as Mahayana, emptiness and buddha-nature; the practice is deity yoga, the inner yogas, and meditation on the nature of mind; and the result is enlightenment in the present lifetime (2.3).

The three *yanas* are an evolutionary process that arises naturally as the individual practitioner matures through his or her meditation (2.4).

The three *yana*s were taught to address individuals of lesser, medium, and advanced capacities (2.5). They provide various points of view and practices capable of addressing any of us, no matter what our level of development (2.6, 2.7). Within the three-*yana* framework, Hinayana is not to be understood in a pejorative way, but as the foundation for the subsequent *yana*s (2.8). The next selections highlight now one, now another aspect of the three *yana*s (2.9–2.12). Finally, within all three vehicles, we are not dealing with different enterprises, but with the single project of a progressively deeper and deeper understanding of reality, whether one wishes to speak in terms of what it is *not* (emptiness) (2.13) or in terms of what it *is* (unborn awareness) (2.14).

## THE THREE VEHICLES OF TIBETAN BUDDHISM                              2.1

Some say Tibetan Buddhism is the practice of Mahayana Buddhism. Others say that Tibetan Buddhism is actually the practice of Vajrayana Buddhism. Really one cannot say that Tibetan Buddhism is just Mahayana or just Vajrayana Buddhism. The teachings of dharma in Tibet are called the "three immutables" or the "threefold *vajra*," meaning that the dharma of Tibet contains the teachings of the Hinayana and the Mahayana as well as the Vajrayana. More specifically, Tibetan Buddhism has the outer practice of the Hinayana, the inner motivation or bodhicitta of the Mahayana, and the view and practice of the Vajrayana, known as the secret or essential view.

*Thrangu Rinpoche*

## ALL THREE YANAS ARE AUTHENTIC                                        2.2

All three yanas . . . are authentic teachings of Lord Buddha Shakyamuni; all of these are part and parcel of the Buddha dharma.

*Kalu Rinpoche*

## THE THREE DIVISIONS OF THE 84,000 METHODS
## TAUGHT BY THE BUDDHA                                                 2.3

The 84,000 methods taught by the Buddha Shakyamuni fall into three main categories. The first, the Hinayana path, is based on the understanding that samsara is permeated by suffering and difficulty, that whatever happiness can be found is impermanent. One who follows this path makes the firm decision to practice in order to find freedom beyond suffering. By applying the methods of the Hinayana, the practitioner develops the capacity to go beyond the cycles of suffering to an experience of joyousness and bliss.

In addition to this same view of suffering, in the Mahayana, the second category, we find, in addition to this same understanding of suffering, the teaching that everything—suffering and happiness, misfortune and fortune, all of which arise as the play of karma—is illusory, like a dream, a mirage, or the reflection of the moon in water. Basic to this path is the view of the inseparability of relative and absolute truth and one's aspiration to help all beings, not only oneself, find liberation. . . . We don't just wish for this to happen, but diligently apply the methods by which enlightenment can be attained. Through the practice of the six perfections, we develop the ability to go beyond samsara and nirvana, to find complete liberation. This is the bodhisattva path.

The third category of Buddhist practice is called the Vajrayana. That which is "vajra" has seven qualities: it cannot be cut by *maras*, obstacles to our enlightenment, nor grasped or separated by concepts; it cannot be destroyed by concepts which invest appearance with a truth they do not have; it is the pure truth in that there is nothing wrong within it; it has no substance that has been compiled and can break apart; it is not impermanent, and is therefore stable and unmovable; it is unstoppable in that it is all pervasive; and it is unconquerable in that it is more profound than everything else and thus fearless. These are the seven qualities of our own true nature.

*Chagdud Tulku Rinpoche*


## THE THREE YANAS ARE AN EVOLUTIONARY PROCESS    2.4

The whole development is regarded as a maturation process rather than something that is imposed on you. Nobody says to you, "Now you are finished with hinayana, you should change to second gear and do mahayana, then change to the top gear, which is tantra." You don't ever change that way. It's a gradual process of development that becomes tantra automatically when it reaches maturity.

*Chögyam Trungpa Rinpoche*

## THE BUDDHA TAUGHT THE THREE YANAS                    2.5

For those of lesser understanding, he taught that Samsara is a burning house and that the discipline of a monk is the proper method to escape the Wheel of Birth and Death [Hinayana]. For those of more advanced intellect, he taught that a compassionate intention towards all beings will liberate all of Samsara [Mahayana]. And to those most advanced, he taught the method of recognizing non-dual insight and obtaining Buddhahood in a single lifetime [Vajrayana].

*Tarthang Tulku Rinpoche*

## WHY ARE THERE THREE YANAS?                           2.6

One needs to understand that when the Buddha taught, he was not teaching as a great scholar who wanted to demonstrate a particular philosophical point of view or to teach for its own sake. His desire was to present the very essence of the deep and vast stages of realization. For this reason, he gave teaching which matched the abilities of his disciples. All the teachings he gave, some long and some short, were a direct and appropriate response to the development of the disciples who came to listen to him. Of course, people have very different capacities and different levels of understanding. They also have very different wishes and desires to learn and understand the dharma. If the Buddha had taught only the very essence of his own understanding of those vast and far-reaching teachings, then apart from a small number of disciples who had great intelligence and diligence, few people would have entered the path. The Buddha taught whatever allowed a person to develop spiritually and progress gradually towards liberation. When we analyze all the Buddha's teachings, we see that they fall into three main approaches or vehicles [Hinayana, Mahayana, and Vajrayana].

*Thrangu Rinpoche*

## BUDDHISM HAS MANY DIFFERENT TECHNIQUES              2.7

Buddhism has many different techniques or practices which apply to different situations and our different levels of consciousness. Some teachings stress self-help through disciplined inquiry and self-control [Hinayana]. Others emphasize compassion and understanding [Mahayana]. But just as you cannot talk to a breadmaker about the intricacies of sending a rocket to the moon, nothing can be understood properly or deeply without an initial experience of the teachings and a certain amount of practice and skill. Vajrayana has always been taught and understood as a path for the very strong, and this path involves complete openness to each experience.

*Tarthang Tulku Rinpoche*

## THE HINAYANA                                                         2.8

Of the three *yanas*, the first is the hinayana. *Hinayana* literally means "lesser vehicle." . . . It should be very clear that the term "lesser" is in no way a pejorative term. It provides the necessary foundation on which to build.

The fundamental teachings of the hinayana are the main subject matter of the first *dharmacakra* or *turning of the wheel of dharma*. These teachings were given mainly in India in the town of Varanasi. The main subject matter of these teachings is the four noble truths.

*Thrangu Rinpoche*

## THE SEQUENTIAL WAY OF BUDDHIST PRACTICE               2.9

There is a sequential way of approaching the Buddhist teachings. In the very beginning, we talk about the *sutrayana,* or Hinayana, tradition of Buddhist teachings, which is the basis or the ground level. The [Hinayana] emphasizes discipline. . . . [In the Hinayana] the emphasis is on understanding cause and effect in regard to the actions of body, speech, and mind that create emotions or activities that are harmful. Recognizing them to be harmful, one develops the attitude of refraining from such actions. The second or medium level is the Mahayana teaching, which joins compassion and discipline as the two main qualities to be practiced. [In this] approach, the Hinayana discipline of body, speech, and mind is further refined by generating genuine compassion. In the Vajrayana teachings, there is an emphasis on awareness and really understanding the wisdom quality inherent in each sentient being. Gathering these three *yanas*—Hinayana, Mahayana, and Vajrayana—one works with discipline, compassion, and generating genuine wisdom. This wisdom is not an interpretation of one's own understanding, but a genuine wisdom of knowing things as they truly are, and being able to remain within that.

*Venerable Khandro Rinpoche*

## KHYENTSE RINPOCHE ON THE THREE YANAS    2.10

The Buddhist teachings describe three fundamental attitudes, corresponding to the three paths, or *yanas* ("vehicles"), which can be practiced together as an integrated whole.

### The Basic Vehicle (Hinayana)

Renunciation, the foundation of the Basic Vehicle and therefore at the root of all subsequent stages of the path, implies the strong wish to free oneself not only from life's immediate sorrows but from the seemingly unending sufferings of samsara, the vicious cycle of conditioned existence. With it comes a heartfelt weariness and disillusionment with the endless quest for gratification, approval, profit, and status.

### The Great Vehicle (Mahayana)

Compassion, the driving force of the Great Vehicle, is born as one realizes that both the individual "self" and the appearance of the phenomenal world are actually devoid of any intrinsic, independent existence; one sees all the suffering that results from one's own and others' fundamental ignorance, which misconstrues the infinite display of illusory appearances as being composed of separate, permanently existing entities. An enlightened being—one who has understood this absence of any intrinsic, independent existence as the ultimate nature of all things—naturally acts from the boundless compassion he feels for those who, under the spell of ignorance, are wandering and suffering in samsara. Inspired by a similar compassion, the follower of the Great Vehicle does not aim for his own liberation alone, but vows to attain Buddhahood in order to attain the capacity to free all sentient beings from the suffering inherent in samsara.

### The Adamantine Vehicle (Vajrayana)

Pure perception, the extraordinary outlook of the Adamantine Vehicle, is to recognize the Buddha-nature in all sentient beings and to see primordial purity and perfection in all phenomena. Every sentient being is endowed with the essence of Buddhahood, just as oil pervades every sesame seed. Ignorance is simply to be unaware of this Buddha-nature, like a poor man who does not know that there is a pot of gold buried beneath his hovel. The journey to enlightenment is thus a rediscovery of this forgotten nature, like seeing the brilliant sun again as the clouds that have been hiding it are blown away.

*Dilgo Khyentse Rinpoche*

## FROM THE POINT OF VIEW OF INDIVIDUAL PRACTICE    2.11

[One] way of looking at the three *yana*s is from the point of view of our individual practice. The outer element, our particular lifestyle, pertains to Hinayana individual liberation vows. The inner motivation of our practice is the Bodhisattva attitude of the Mahayana. The secret or hidden aspect of our practice is the experience that we develop through tantric practice, through Vajrayana techniques and our *samaya* or commitment to that practice.

*Kalu Rinpoche*

## THE YANAS IN A NUTSHELL    2.12

According to the Hinayana system, the point of view is egolessness. According to the Mahayana system, the point of view is egolessness, the insubstantiality of phenomena, and freedom from all mental activities. According to the Mahamudra system, the point of view is all-pervasive Wisdom Mind in existent and non-existent phenomena. According to the Mahasandhi [Dzogchen] system, the point of view is the beginningless liberation of Samanthabhadra's Wisdom Mind.

*Thinley Norbu Rinpoche*

## EMPTINESS IS THE OBJECT OF EACH OF
## THE NINE VEHICLES    2.13

The vital point of the view in each of the . . . vehicles is nothing other than emptiness. Each vehicle attempts to experience this empty nature of things and apply it in practice, in what each maintains is a flawless and correct fashion. . . . From the Hinayana vehicle on up, the concept of what mind actually is becomes increasingly refined and subtle.

*Tulku Urgyen Rinpoche*

## THE PATH IS PROGRESSIVELY DEEPER REALIZATION OF BUDDHA-NATURE 2.14

The buddha nature is precisely what is practiced in each of the . . . vehicles, but exactly how it is put into practice differs, because there is a refinement of understanding that becomes progressively more subtle through the vehicles.

*Tulku Urgyen Rinpoche*

# 3

# How to Study the Buddha's Legacy

WHEN WE WESTERNERS take an interest in studying the Buddha's legacy, the dharma, we come with the attitudes and preconceptions of our own upbringing and experience. Some of us want to abandon intellectual study altogether and simply meditate. Others want to apply their intellectual skills to the dharma, taking it as a new conceptual challenge to be mastered. As the passages in this section suggest, each of these approaches is considered one-sided and, in and of itself, ineffective. The study of the dharma is very different from conventional education in the West because it will involve every dimension of our being (3.1). In fact, words have little importance in and of themselves, without practice and realization (3.2).

Tibetan Buddhism recognizes the need for a gradually evolving depth of understanding that goes through three stages, the so-called three *prajna*s, or types of knowledge (3.3). First, we need to begin by studying the dharma's words and concepts in a very literal way ("hearing"). Next, we progress through an ever deepening reflection upon their meaning ("contemplation"). And, finally, through "meditation," we arrive at a nonconceptual realization of the nature of things (3.4). If any of the three *prajna*s are missing, we will lose our way (3.5). Hearing, the first *prajna*, lays a solid foundation for contemplating and meditating (3.6, 3.7). In hearing, we should not be indiscriminate but take precisely what we need (3.8). Hearing is, itself, practice (3.9). Through the second *prajna*, contemplation, we explore the actual, personal meaning of what we have heard or studied (3.10, 3.11). In contemplation, we look for the reality behind the concept we have learned (3.12). In the third *prajna*, meditation, we aim for a direct, intuitive experience of the nature of mind beyond words and images (3.13). It is not just the third *prajna*, but in a real sense all three that qualify as meditation (3.14).

There are two major ways in which one may study the dharma, through an exclusively scholarly method or through the way that leads to and culminates in meditation practice. The scholarly approach seeks to know what the Buddha said in the texts and to clarify that. This is "not the real dharma; the real dharma is the experience" (3.15). The scholar's way requires a comprehensive understanding of what the Buddha taught. The way of the simple meditator is to recognize mind's essence (3.16). The two approaches seem to be related to two different personality types, the first more intellectual, critical, and analytical, the second more intuitive, devoted, and experiential in their orientation (3.17).

### STUDYING THE DHARMA IS VERY DIFFERENT          3.1
Studying the Dharma is very different from studying at the University. If success is to be achieved, we must allow the teachings to touch all aspects of our lives. As our understanding deepens we will find we are becoming in many senses a wholly new person. But all this basically depends on our willingness to study seriously. The Dharma is no game; we can gain nothing if we only play at it.

*Tarthang Tulku Rinpoche*

### MERE WORDS THEMSELVES ARE OF
### LITTLE IMPORTANCE          3.2
Mere words themselves are of little importance. They are but signposts to a more profound wisdom. What is central to your education here is your own inner experience of dharma. You must experiment with the teachings you receive and see for yourself whether or not the dharma is

beneficial for your mind. If you do this conscientiously and open-mind-edly, liberation is easy. It all depends on how aware you are. The key to making the methods of dharma effective is always trying to see how the teachings fit in with your day-to-day life.

*Lama Thubten Yeshe Rinpoche and Zopa Rinpoche*


## WHEN THE DHARMA IS COMPLETE                                    3.3
One of the most important teachers in the Kagyü tradition, Lord Gam-popa, said, "The dharma is complete when one combines hearing, con-templation, and meditation in one's practice."

*The Dzogchen Pönlop Rinpoche*


## THE THREE APPROACHES                                          3.4
The first [approach] is studying, an act which does not have direct access to wisdom. We don't naturally know how to help wisdom develop, so we turn to the teachings of the Buddha. By studying the teachings, we begin to grasp the ways to the development of wisdom. Now, study in itself will not bring the growth of much wisdom. We need to go on to the second step, which is contemplation of the teachings, in which we think again and again about the meaning of what we have studied to really get to the heart of it. Even this won't bring about the highest, deepest, or ultimate benefit; we need to take the third approach, which is to meditate. It is through meditation that we actually attain the ulti-mate emergence of wisdom. Of the three main modes of developing wisdom, by far the most important one is the wisdom that emerges from our meditation.

*Thrangu Rinpoche*


## THE THREE PRAJNAS AND AN EXAMPLE                              3.5
It is necessary to get a solid foundation by correctly listening, reflecting, and meditating. We must begin by listening to the teachings, that is, to have some knowledge of them. We reflect on what we have studied until convinced of its validity. Finally, after having understood the meaning of the teachings, we meditate, taking them as the basis of our

meditation. When these three steps, listening, reflecting, and meditating, are correctly done, our practice automatically becomes efficient and beneficial. If we begin to practice Buddhism without listening, studying, or reflecting, we will have an insufficient and superficial comprehension that produces a practice that is not correct, authentic, or beneficial.

Let us take an example. The teachings of the Buddha inform us that the human existence is characterized by sufferings due to birth, sickness, old age, and death. From listening, we obtain some knowledge of this. We then reflect on these different types of suffering. Becoming aware of what they are, we begin to see that we have to live in a way to rid ourselves of them in this and future lives. We will decide to realize the nature of mind, beyond birth and death, beyond all suffering. Having passed this step of reflecting, we undertake the practice of meditation in order to reach liberation.

*Kalu Rinpoche*

## HEARING                                                                    3.6

The basic need for listening to and hearing the dharma is that all dharma practice, all aspects of the path of Buddhadharma, are included in the three steps of hearing, contemplation, and meditation. These three steps contain all the various aspects of the Buddhadharma. . . . Since there is a sequence to these steps, it is absolutely necessary to begin with the step of hearing or listening to the dharma. Jamgon Lodro Thaye compares it to the ground which is necessary for there to be crops. If there is no ground, nothing can grow. In the same way, if there is no initial hearing of the dharma, there can be no contemplation upon it. Without hearing and contemplation, there can be no practice of meditation. For that reason, it is important in the beginning to engage in impartial and wide hearing or study.

*The Dzogchen Pönlop Rinpoche*

## THE MANY ASPECTS OF "HEARING" THE DHARMA            3.7

There are many different aspects to hearing the dharma. There is literally hearing it in the presence of the *kalyanamitra* [spiritual friend], the

*The Dzogchen Pönlop Rinpoche*

presence of the teacher. But the term "hearing the dharma" includes all forms of study. It includes reading books of the Buddha's teachings and, given the examples of modern technology, it also includes receiving instruction by watching video tapes, listening to audiotapes, and so forth. All of this is genuine activity of hearing the dharma. All of it is very important.

*The Dzogchen Pönlop Rinpoche*

## LEARN WHAT IS GOING TO BE USEFUL    3.8

[In the first *prajna*, hearing,] what's recommended is to take the approach of the swan drinking milk out of water. There is a legend that if you pour milk into water, swans can get the milk out without drinking any water. When they are finished, you end up with just water. This signifies that within the massive amount of things one could learn, one has to prioritize and select what is actually going to be useful.

*The Dzogchen Pönlop Rinpoche*

## THE FIRST PRAJNA: HEARING OR STUDYING THE DHARMA    3.9

Hearing or studying is very much emphasized in the practice of the Buddhist path. Studying or hearing the dharma is regarded as practice. Generally, people have a slight misconception about the relationship between study and practice in Buddhadharma. They think that study is one thing and that then there's real practice, which is something else. They think that study isn't real practice, that real practice consists of things like visualizing deities and reciting mantras. Sometimes they think that study is all well and good, but that you need to accumulate a great deal of merit which can't be accomplished through study since study is merely intellectual. One of the reasons we tend to look at things this way is that we're sick of studying. We've spent our whole lives studying and we feel that it hasn't really benefited our minds. But the type of study involved in the study practice of Buddhadharma is the kind of study that increases your wisdom, your insight, and your understanding. Actually, there is no better way to gather the accumulation of merit.

*The Dzogchen Pönlop Rinpoche*

## CONTEMPLATION, THE SECOND PRAJNA                                    3.10

The second stage of the training in *prajna,* or knowledge, is called, literally, *thinking about what has been heard.* What "thinking" refers to in this
context is *analytical meditation.* The necessity for applying this method is
that "what has been heard" or learned through simply listening to the
dharma has not yet been mixed with your mind or applied to your
actual experience. Whereas thinking about it actually mixes it with your
mind and produces experience.

At the same time, as was said by Jetsun Milarepa in one of his songs:
*"Experiences are like mist. They will dissipate."* This refers to all the sorts
of experiences you could have in practice, experiences of bliss, clarity,
nonthought, and so forth. All such experiences will eventually dissipate
like mist in the morning.

In order to generate the *prajna* arising from this thinking or analysis,
one examines with rigorous reasoning again and again what has been
heard or what has been learned. The reason for this is that when you
think of something that you have heard the first time, you understand
it in one way. When you think of it again, you gain a different understanding, and when you think of it a third time you gain again a different and more profound understanding. If you think about things that
way, you will understand why experiences are like mist.

The training consists in analyzing repeatedly the contents of the
teachings of the Buddha and commentaries on his teachings to which
you have been exposed. This analysis produces the basis for the third
wisdom, which is *the prajna of meditation.*

*The Dzogchen Pönlop Rinpoche*

## IN CONTEMPLATION, WE INDIVIDUALIZE
## THE TEACHINGS                                                       3.11

In contemplation, we individualize what we have heard in the first
*prajna,* hearing or studying, and we contemplate its meaning. This is
critical to developing our understanding. Often, our mind is working at a very superficial level: we are at the edge, on top of the water.
Contemplation begins to penetrate beneath the surface of the water.
When we hear the dharma, we think about it, read about it, and go

over it. Then we contemplate. Can we contemplate while we are sitting? Sure. We can also contemplate during our everyday life.

*Sakyong Mipham Rinpoche*

## How to Practice Contemplation, the Second Prajna    3.12

Contemplative meditation involves thinking about something. We sit
there for ten minutes, twenty minutes, and we just think about whatever it is. When our mind strays, we bring it back to that thought. Most
of us are not used to meditating on a verse. We're used to practicing
*shamatha*, reducing thoughts. What we're doing now is saying that we
can use other objects of meditation besides the breath. We could meditate on suffering, impermanence, karma, or loving kindness and compassion for others.

When we meditate on suffering and impermanence, for example,
eventually we find ourselves able to look straight at it. It's a relief and
it's much easier, because usually we avoid looking at it. So when we sit
down and just look straight at it, there can be a quality of profound
shock, profound emotion, just as when somebody dies and we realize
the truth of death. That kind of experience affects how we see our body
and mind, our emotional state, how we look at the rest of our life. It's
like when we are sick and lying in bed, and we begin to think about
our life. If you have a relatively serious illness—it doesn't even have to
be life threatening—it begins to affect your whole approach to life. You
think about the body. You think about things you did before and how
precious that was. You think about what you've done in your life, what
you would like to do, and what you shouldn't have done. That is the
way in which contemplative meditation works. You reflect deeply and
it opens up your understanding in profound ways and that changes your
whole outlook.

*Sakyong Mipham Rinpoche*

## The Third Prajna, Meditation    3.13

[In contemplation] we receive instructions from a teacher, then we
study and practice them by reflecting on what has been taught and

comparing it with our personal experience in order to validate it or not. We examine and analyze at a conceptual level what we have been told in order to determine its correctness. This is very beneficial, but it does not yield an authentic experience of the nature of mind.

Thus there is a need for [meditation], an intuitive, immediate approach which entails perceiving the nature of mind without searching intellectually. Unlike the analytical approach, which has an objectifying nature—mind searching itself—this approach consists of abiding in the state of "bare awareness" in which the basic nature of mind reveals itself "from itself to itself." Rather than consciously searching for what mind is, we open ourselves to the immediate revelation of its nature. There is no one who searches and nothing to search; there is no subject or object, only a state of awareness in which mind's nature is revealed. At this level, we no longer observe mind as in analytical meditation, but instead we see it without looking and understand it without thinking.

*Kalu Rinpoche*

## All Three Prajnas Can Properly Be Called Meditation

3.14

The real and central method of the path is the generation of *prajna* and wisdom. This is achieved by means of the continual cultivation of hearing, contemplation, and meditation. The cultivation of these, in a developing continuity, brings about realization. It exposes a fundamental wisdom that produces realization, which in turn eradicates ignorance.

In actuality, all three stages of this path of hearing, contemplation, and meditation can properly be called meditation. In Tibetan, the word *cultivation* and the word *meditation* are very close. They are cognate in their etymology, and there are punlike references to this relationship. In a song by Milarepa, he says, "It is not 'meditation' but 'cultivation.' Cultivation is mastery."

In other words, when something is cultivated it becomes mastery. The meaning of this is beyond the mere etymology of the term. Since hearing, contemplation, and meditation are all equally stages in the cultivation of wisdom and *prajna*, they are, ultimately speaking, all aspects of meditation practice. From a Buddhist viewpoint, there is not that much difference between study and meditation.

*The Dzogchen Pönlop Rinpoche*

## THE SCRIPTURAL DHARMA AND THE DHARMA OF ACTUAL EXPERIENCE                                    3.15

The Dharma can be described in terms of two aspects: the teaching or scriptural Dharma and the Dharma of experience or realization. The teaching Dharma consists of the teachings, in the sutras and tantras, of the Buddha and other great masters. The Buddha gave his followers the guidance: "If you do this, you will get this result," and that's called the teaching Dharma, because it's a guide; it's the road map. But that's not the real Dharma; the real Dharma is the experience.

There's a difference between talking about something and actually experiencing it. The Dharma of experience has to depend on the teaching Dharma, maybe, but the teaching Dharma is not the whole of the Dharma. If we listen to and understand the teaching Dharma and then put it into practice, we will experience it, and that's the real Dharma which will transform us. The teaching Dharma alone doesn't transform us, and unless we're transformed we're not really practicing the Dharma.

*Ringu Tulku Rinpoche*


## TWO MAIN WAYS TO APPROACH THE BUDDHA-DHARMA                                    3.16

There are two main ways to approach the Buddhadharma: the way of a scholar or the *pandita*'s way, and the way of the *kusulu*, meaning a simple meditator. The scholar's way involves complete comprehension of what the Buddha taught, which requires a perspective on the whole body of teaching. Scholars need the details of everything in all of the nine vehicles, starting with the aggregate of form and continuing all the way up until the state of complete omniscience, the enlightened state. A scholar needs to gain complete comprehension about how everything works in relationship with cause and effect.

In contrast to this is the path of a *kusulu*, a simple meditator. For this type of person, the main point of the Buddha's teaching involves nothing more than understanding the difference between recognizing and not recognizing mind essence. Not recognizing is samsara, while recognizing is nirvana or liberation.

*Tulku Urgyen Rinpoche*

## THE TWO APPROACHES IN MORE DETAIL                           3.17

Within Buddhism there are traditionally two approaches to studying, reflecting upon, and practicing the sacred Dharma: the analytical approach of a scholar and the simple approach of a meditator.

The style of a scholar is to study numerous details and carefully reflect upon them, refining one's understanding through using the words of the Buddha, the statements of enlightened masters, and one's personal power of reasoning. By doing so, one can establish a clear understanding of the real state of things as they are, the profound emptiness that is the essence of the realization of all the buddhas. This is one type of approach and it is excellent.

Certain people, whose character is intellectually inclined, find it best to take this approach, and especially if they harbor many thoughts and doubts, or have a tendency toward nit-picking and suspiciousness. A person with a skeptical mentality finds it very difficult to trust a genuine master, even after having met him and received the revealing pith instructions. A strong fascination with critical questioning and analyzing prevents one from following the approach of a simple meditator and from gaining an immediate certainty about the profound nature of emptiness, the basic wakefulness that is the very heart of all the buddhas. Due to these reasons some people find greater benefit from the analytical approach of a scholar through which doubts and lack of understanding can be gradually cleared away.

Another type of person feels less inclined to study all the details of the words of the Buddha and the statements of enlightened masters, or to investigate them with the power of factual reasoning. Rather, they wish to focus directly on the very core of the awakened state—the wakefulness that perceives every possible aspect of knowledge exactly as it is—personally, within their own experience. Such people are not so interested in taking a long, winding, roundabout road through detailed studies and analytical speculations; rather, they want immediate and direct realization.

*Chökyi Nyima Rinpoche*

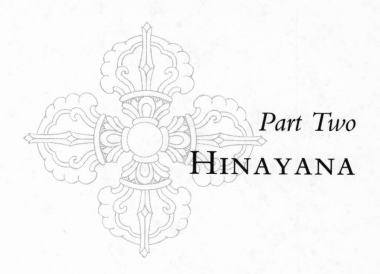

*Part Two*

# HINAYANA

# → 4

# The View of Hinayana

THE HINAYANA PRACTITIONER follows a basic threefold process, beginning with developing an accurate understanding or "view" of what he or she is doing; then progressing to the actual practice; and culminating in some maturity or accomplishment. As the following passages indicate, in the Hinayana, the view is defined by the "four reminders" or "four thoughts that turn the mind" toward the dharma: precious human birth, impermanence, karma, and the suffering of samsara. Through gaining an accurate "view" of these four, one is able to establish the basis of understanding necessary to actually follow the path and, equally important, unlock the springs of motivation within.

Without knowing what we were trying to accomplish or why, we would quickly become overwhelmed or confused by our experiences and lose track of our reasons for working on ourselves in the Buddhist way. Recalling the previous section, we can see that the view is developed through the first two *prajna*s, hearing and contemplating. Through hearing, we are reminded of the blessings of our human existence and its fragility, of the pattern of cause and effect that governs this state, and of the suffering that marks it so strongly. Through contemplation we reflect upon these facts and consider them deeply, until we see, in truth and reality, that this is our actual human condition. For these reasons, having a correct "view" or intellectual understanding is necessary right at the beginning, before we can pursue the path with success (4.1) and confidence (4.2).

The first of the four reminders points to our unique human situation. Rather than taking our lives for granted, we must recognize the blessings and possibilities of our current existence. In particular, we need to realize that this birth offers the opportunity for realizing our inherent wakefulness (4.3). This birth has occurred through many causes and conditions that may not be present in the future. Such a recognition creates a strong motivation for us not to fritter our time away and waste the opportunities that we have but to devote ourselves to practice (4.4). Sometimes, especially in the West, we can take the preciousness of our lives for granted. One antidote to this is to visit other places in the world where life is infinitely more difficult and troubled (4.5).

The second of the four thoughts calls us to contemplate the impermanence of all compounded things and especially the fragility and brevity of our own lives (4.6). As an emblem of impermanence, one may think of the utter destruction of Tibet, its temples, monasteries, and Buddhist culture, by the Chinese communists (4.7). The teaching on impermanence is not necessarily bad news (4.8). We should bring this recognition home to ourselves: every moment brings us closer to the unavoidable, inevitable moment of death (4.9). This isn't some personal twist of fate, but rather the common lot of all people and all of life (4.10). Usually, our understanding of death is relatively superficial. However, at certain moments it is brought starkly to our attention and can be utterly compelling and terrifying (4.11). Some people may feel that the Buddhist emphasis on the reality of death is unnecessarily negative. More accurately, however, it is a realistic assessment of our actual condition and one which, if contemplated deeply, can lead to serious spiritual engagement (4.12).

Having acknowledged our precious human life and how fleeting it is, the third reminder* bids us contemplate the nature of this life: more than anything, it is marked with dissatisfaction, frustration, and suffering. We struggle to escape from our pain, but the success rate of

---

*I am following the sequence of the four reminders found in *The Words of My Perfect Teacher* by Patrul Rinpoche. Sometimes karma is the third reminder and suffering is the fourth.

doing so is very low (4.13). Human relationships are a good example of just how pervasive our suffering is (4.14). Lest we believe that in the higher *yanas*, such as Vajrayana, we can escape the truth of suffering, we are reminded that tantra brings us right to the heart of a realization of pain (4.15).

The natural question raised by the fact of suffering is "Why do we suffer? What leads us to suffer as we do?" The fourth reminder, the teaching on karma, provides some answers. We can locate the cause of our suffering in desire, in wanting: we want things to be a certain way and we cannot accept what they are (4.16). It is not our desire per se that is the problem, but rather the fixations we develop in relation to our experience (4.17). It is our pattern of nonacceptance, our tendency to develop fixations, that creates karma (4.18). The concept of karma includes all intentional actions and their results (4.19). When we act, the imprint of that action is left on our fundamental consciousness where it grows, like a seed, to produce a later result (4.20). The doctrine of karma does not imply fatalism (4.21). Why is the teaching on karma so important for ourselves and others? Because our actions have such powerful effects on ourselves and others (4.22). The passages that follow provide a variety of ways of looking at karma: it is the result of our "taking refuge in samsara" (4.23); it leads to rebirth of a supposed "self," when in fact no self actually exists (4.24); and it can be compared to dust gathering on a mirror; it comes about when we do not realize the inherently enlightened nature of all phenomena (4.25); and it comes about from forgetting our own true nature (4.26). Finally, karma is valid not only for those who believe in it (i.e., Buddhists), but for everyone regardless of what they may think (4.27).

## THE IMPORTANCE OF VIEW                                    4.1

View is a critical element of the path. View means always knowing what we are doing. When we sit down on the cushion, we should completely understand why we are doing so and what the purpose is. View is very simple: it is understanding. It is having a feeling, a motivation, a desire to know which way and how we are going. For example, if we have a view from a hill, we can look and see where we are going. Then, as we walk, we are in a sense combining view and action. Similarly, when we sit in meditation, that is when we are actually walking. We are moving in a certain direction, in accord with our view.

*Sakyong Mipham Rinpoche*

## WE NEED TO UNDERSTAND THE "VIEW"                    4.2

We need to feel confident. The more confidence we have in our practice, the more confident we can be in handling any situation. . . . If we really understand the view, if we just meditate for twenty minutes and get up, then we feel completely okay—because we feel so certain that this is very much the view of all Hinayana, Mahayana, and Vajrayana practitioners. The more we know, the more confidence and understanding we can have at every stage of the path.

*Sakyong Mipham Rinpoche*

## OUR HUMAN LIVES ARE EXCEEDINGLY PRECIOUS            4.3

Our human lives are exceedingly precious because they offer us the possibility of discovering our inherent awakeness.

*Sakyong Mipham Rinpoche*

## PRECIOUS HUMAN BIRTH                                4.4

This [human birth] is like a precious jewel because it is very difficult to find. If we don't have a human existence, then it is impossible to practice the dharma. . . . Our precious human existence is the result of our previous good actions. To gather all the good conditions that make a human birth possible is quite difficult. It requires a great deal of good karma and the blessings of the Buddha. When a human birth occurs, it is indeed a very rare thing and is not guaranteed for future lifetimes. If we use this human life to practice properly, we will have the opportunity to reduce suffering, not just for ourselves but for all other beings. But if we don't use our human birth to practice the dharma, then most likely things will not be very good in the future for anyone.

*Thrangu Rinpoche*

## IT IS VERY HARD TO FIND A HUMAN BIRTH 4.5

From a Buddhist point of view, it is very hard to find a human birth. There is a story that describes a turtle swimming in an ocean that covers the whole planet. There is one turtle, and there is one hoop floating on the water, big enough for the turtle to stick his head through. This turtle swims around, and every one hundred years it sticks his head up. The chance of getting a human birth is the same as the chance of the turtle sticking his head through the hoop. Maybe there is numerical comfort in that; we have all sort of won the lottery. We need to contemplate our fortunate circumstances.

It is hard for that to have impact in America, where there is so much material comfort, particularly if you have never gone to a country that is very poor. But it is shocking if we travel to India, for example, where so many people will never have even the most basic things that we take for granted—all of a sudden we realize how precious our situation is. We realize that on our worst day, our worst, bad day when we do not get what we want, we are a hundred times better off than so many human beings. When you sit here, contemplating your precious human birth sounds almost like a joke, but when you go there it hits you so hard. You realize, "I'm really fortunate. I should stop complaining."

The same thing can happen if we get very sick and close to death. When we have been sick for a few weeks, all we want is to feel normal. Before, we wanted all sorts of things; and now, we would just like to be normal again. We would love even the most boring day, sitting reading a book, because now we feel terrible. So we appreciate what we had before on a very basic level.

*Sakyong Mipham Rinpoche*

## IMPERMANENCE 4.6

Every phenomenon we can think of is compounded, and therefore subject to impermanence. Certain aspects of impermanence, like the changing of the weather, we can accept easily, but there are equally obvious things that we don't accept. For instance, our body is visibly impermanent and getting older every day, and yet this is something we don't want to accept. Certain popular magazines that cater to youth and beauty exploit this attitude. In terms of view, meditation, and action, their readers might have a view—thinking in terms of not aging or escaping the aging process somehow. They contemplate this view of permanence, and their consequent action is to go to fitness centers and undergo plastic surgery and all sorts of other hassles. Enlightened beings would think that this is ridiculous and based on a wrong view. Regarding these different aspects of impermanence, getting old and dying, the changing of the weather, etc., Buddhists have a single statement, namely this first seal: phenomena are impermanent because they are compounded. Anything that is assembled will, sooner or later, come apart.

*Dzongsar Khytense Rinpoche*

## NOT ONE THING IS STABLE AND LASTING    4.7

Before the arrival of the Chinese Communists, how many monasteries were there in what used to be called Tibet, Land of Snow? How many temples and monasteries were there, like those in Lhasa, at Samye, and in Trandruk? How many precious objects were there, representations of the Buddha's Body, Speech, and Mind? Now not even a statue remains. All that is left of Samye is something the size of this tent, hardly bigger than a *stupa*. Everything was either looted, broken, or scattered, and all the great images were destroyed. These things have happened and this demonstrates impermanence. . . . There is not one thing in existence that is stable and lasts.

*Dilgo Khyentse Rinpoche*

## IS IMPERMANENCE A PESSIMISTIC TEACHING?    4.8

Some people think that Buddhists are pessimistic, always talking about death, impermanence, and aging. But that is not necessarily true. Impermanence is a relief! I don't have a BMW today and it is thanks to the impermanence of that fact that I might have one tomorrow. Without impermanence, I am stuck with the non-possession of a BMW, and I can never have one. I might feel severely depressed today and, thanks to impermanence, I might feel great tomorrow. Impermanence is not necessarily bad news; it depends on the way you understand it. Even if today your BMW gets scratched by a vandal, or your best friend lets you down, if you have a view of impermanence, you won't be so worried.

*Dzongsar Khyentse Rinpoche*

## RECOLLECTION OF DEATH

4.9

Just as every single thing is always moving inexorably closer to its ultimate dissolution, so also your own life, like a burning butter-lamp, will soon be consumed. It would be foolish to think that you can first finish all your work and then retire to spend the later stages of your life practicing Dharma. Can you be certain that you will live that long? Does death not strike the young as well as the old? No matter what you are doing, therefore, remember death and keep your mind focused on the Dharma.

*Dilgo Khyentse Rinpoche*

## THE BASIC LANDSCAPE WE'RE LIVING IN

4.10

We have to recognize the basic landscape we're living in. If our goal in life is giving "me" a good time, it won't work out. Why? Because the lay of the land is birth, aging, sickness, and death. That's the game plan for "me." And within that, we have pleasure that keeps changing into pain. There's no permanence or stability here, nor is there a solid self. Death comes, often without warning.

*Sakyong Mipham Rinpoche*

## WHEN SOMEONE CLOSE TO US DIES

4.11

When somebody close to us dies, we contemplate the notion of death. It is so near, so tactile, we cannot deny it. All our life we have heard about death and that we might die at any time—but now we are experiencing it. We feel the potency of what is happening, and we actually contemplate it. Our mind penetrates the subject of death, and it is very frightening. Suddenly it becomes very powerful and it dominates our whole life, because we truly realize, "Everybody could die. I could die." We may have heard the words before, but we had never thought about it all that deeply.

*Sakyong Mipham Rinpoche*

*Sakyong Mipham Rinpoche*

## PEOPLE SAY, "BUDDHISTS BELIEVE IN DEATH"   4.12

People say, "Buddhists believe in death, they believe in sickness, they believe in suffering," but we didn't make it up. It's not our fault. We're just looking at our basic predicament. We're simply contemplating it and thinking about it, trying to absorb the reality of the world we're living in. When we begin to do this, what comes out of it? Obviously we want to do something about it. We say, "What can I do about suffering, what can I do about death, what can I do about impermanence?" When we contemplate these things we're turning our mind toward the dharma, turning our mind toward the Buddha. . . . We have a friend who becomes very sick, who may die; or we almost get hit by a car, and we experience how momentary our own existence is. At that moment death feels like a real experience.

*Sakyong Mipham Rinpoche*

## THE SUCCESS RATE IS VERY LOW   4.13

Beings are in tremendous pain and suffering. It is so bad that sometimes it feels like when you put your foot in ice water or boiling water and you don't know whether it's freezing or boiling. Beings go through so much pain and suffering that they have no idea what's really happening. Even if they realize how much pain there is, they have no understanding of where their pain and suffering come from. They wonder, "What is happening to our minds? What is making us go through what we are going through? Could we do anything to make it be different? Is there any way to liberate ourselves from this pain and suffering? Or is there no hope?" We try in so many ways to escape from our misery. But the success rate of being able to reduce one's pain and suffering is very low. So the desperate feelings grow stronger. Sometimes, there is a moment or two, or a day or two, of a break. But that is a questionable break.

*Dzigar Kongtrul Rinpoche*

## EVEN INTIMATE RELATIONSHIPS ARE NOT RELIABLE   4.14

Love and care, kindness and compassion are found most naturally in our parents' minds. But when we take complete refuge in our parents, it is as said in *The Words of My Perfect Teacher*, "One's own parents are the best guides in directing us how to be reborn in the lower realms since they teach us how to cultivate this miserable suffering of samsara in accordance with their own views." In the end, it is often what *they* think is best that parents tend to enforce on their children rather than cherishing the children's own nature and wishes. This is shown to be true through the examples of the great teachers in the past. Even the Buddha's father wanted him to be king, to rule the kingdom and conquer the world, rather than cherishing his desire to be free of all ordinary concerns and to strive for the benefit of all beings' enlightenment. In this way there are always hooks and ties and strong attachments in our relationship to our parents.

Then, there is the relationship with our spouses. Even though we are married and sleeping in the same bed, eating off each other's plates, and constantly verbally engaged in the romantic expression of our feelings, in the core of our hearts there is much distrust of each other. There is never a sense of complete acceptance or of being completely unbiased and nonjudgmental toward each other. There is often not even a sense of honoring the vow of being married or committed to one another. When we take such a vow, we don't vow to stay together only during good times. But it often turns out to be only a "good-time vow." So, in that way, we are constantly thinking of our own interests: "I have thirty or forty years left of my life, maybe fifty years at the most, can I spend all my remaining time with this person? Can I actually sell all my freedom and all my sense of companionship to this person, or should I be looking for someone else? Should I find someone better? Should I find the happiness I long for somewhere else?" Much of this kind of thinking is present in all relationships. This is especially the case in modern times, where people take vows easily and give up their vows easily, saying to themselves, "This is my own individual freedom and choice." We justify ourselves and our actions in such ways.

Living in tight quarters, when you are confronted with life's troubles—combined with having children—it turns out you get much more irritated with your spouse, whom you are supposed to love the most. Your spouse irritates you more than anyone and you have so much aggression—even beyond your knowing—toward your spouse, along with a sense of resentment and pain because of your own dissatisfaction with life and the commitments and choices you have made. It often turns out that way, becoming the source of much difficulty and suffering.

Yet, these are the things we take refuge in; these are the things we cherish in samsara. They are supposed to be unfailing but they fail all the time. From this point of view, we can understand that human relationships do not ultimately fulfill us. Human relationships are mostly based on confusion, on our own attachment. Actually, in the first place, regardless of what we cherish, it is "I" that is the most important to us, and because of that "I," we cherish "Thee." From this point of view, there will never be a time when there is not a problem with "I," so there will always be problems with "Thee."

*Dzigar Kongtrul Rinpoche*

## TO UNDERSTAND PAIN IS THE GROUND OF TANTRA        4.15
You might say that it is very easy to understand or experience pain. Oh no. It takes a lot of understanding to realize pain. This level of understanding is what is necessary to prepare the ground for tantra. The tantric type of intelligence exists right at the beginning at the ordinary level, the level of pain. . . . Tantric intelligence is understanding, realizing, experiencing pain. . . . [Tantric methods] enable us to realize pain.

*Chögyam Trungpa Rinpoche*

## THE CAUSE OF SUFFERING IS OUR WAY OF PERCEIVING AND REACTING        4.16
If we can somehow change our way of being, our way of perceiving, if we can work on our habitual tendencies of being and perceiving and go beyond that to see exactly the way things are, and then work on that basis, maybe we can overcome the causes of our suffering. . . .

Whether I am happy or unhappy, whether I am in a joyful state or in a suffering state, that is my own experience. What is happening when I have an unpleasant experience? I am perceiving the experience as something bad; I don't like it; I have aversion to it. Any experience that I don't like becomes suffering; any experience that I fear becomes suffering. Therefore the root of all suffering is aversion and fear. And because of aversion and fear, there is also wanting. . . .

All our suffering and pain . . . [are] based on our not seeing clearly the actual way things are and who or what we are. From the Buddhist point of view, that's the cause of suffering: it lies in our way of perception and our way of reaction.

So if—and this is the crucial understanding—if we can somehow change our way of seeing and of reacting so that we don't have to keep running after or running away from things, if we can be without the fear and the aversion, then we will find peace.

*Ringu Tulku Rinpoche*

## DESIRE ITSELF IS NOT THE PROBLEM                    4.17
We do not really understand what desire means. In the West, desire seems to refer to sense gratification. However, in the Buddhist view, desire is not a craving of the sense, but the mental concepts and projections that we build up on an object, thereby bringing us problems. Desire misinterprets and distorts the object; we then hallucinate and drive ourselves crazy.

*Lama Thubten Yeshe Rinpoche*

## SUBJECT–OBJECT FIXATION                    4.18
Subject-object fixation is the cause for continuing in deluded samsaric existence, day and night, life after life. The fixation upon subject and object, the perceiving subject and the perceived object, is solidified again and again each moment and thus re-creates samsaric existence.

*Tulku Urgyen Rinpoche*

## KARMA IS CONDITIONED ACTIVITY                    4.19
*Karma* is a Sanskrit word that literally means "conditioned activity." This notion includes the entire gamut of activity, from the cause up to the consequence of an action. Karma is, therefore, activity understood as being the series of causes and results of actions.

*Kalu Rinpoche*

How the Process of Karma Works                    4.20

[Our] fundamental consciousness can be compared to a ground that receives imprints and seeds left by our actions. Once planted, these seeds remain in the ground of fundamental consciousness until the conditions for their germination and ripening have come together. In this way, they actualize their potential by producing the plants and fruits that are the various experiences of samsara. The traces that actions leave in the fundamental consciousness are causes that, when favorable conditions present themselves, then result in a particular state of individual consciousness accompanied by its own specific experiences. In general, the collection of imprints left in this fundamental awareness by past actions serves to condition all states and experiences of individual consciousness, that is, what we are and everything we experience. The linking of the different steps of this process, from the causes, the initial acts, up to their consequences, present and future experiences, is called karma, or causation of actions.

*Kalu Rinpoche*


Karma Does Not Imply Fatalism                    4.21

Within the concept of karma, there is no notion of destiny or fatalism; we only reap what we sow. We experience the results of our own actions.

*Kalu Rinpoche*


Why Is the Teaching on Karma So Important?        4.22

It is essential to understand clearly one's responsibility as a human being. If actions did not have any reactions, and did not create some kind of a force and fruition, then there would not be any problem. If one were to generate anger, and that anger did not affect someone else or oneself, if it didn't give rise to painful circumstances, then it would be all right. In that case, a person would not have to take care, or take responsibility, for the actions generated. But that is not the case. If we take time to reflect quietly within ourselves, we discover that each action has an effect.

As human beings, we continually bring about innumerable actions.

We have a body that moves constantly and creates actions. Each of these actions has the full potential of bearing results and having impact, on others as well as oneself. Our speech and our thoughts have the same impact, creating actions that have reactions. What we think has tremendous potential of becoming actions that have results. If we observe ourselves, our body movements create innumerable actions. Each of those has a full potential of an impact, which might be immediately felt by another being, such as the action of killing [an animal for food]. We take life just to sustain this body and to let it survive. We are careless in not respecting other life forms that are as precious as we are. Even as meditators we are not able to really be sensitive to this awareness. The awareness is not there; the body continues to move around and function, and because of this functioning, there are beings whose lives are affected. It could be a very disrespectful action that might hurt somebody else. It could be a physically aggressive action that might harm somebody else.

Even if no one else is apparently affected by one's activities, the ignorance and laziness of the body, its attachment to itself, build up a kind of sediment that settles down and becomes the attitude of a person. So the fruition not only affects someone else, but actually begins to form the ground basis of one's own character, personality, and attitude. That's an aspect of fruition, which in the moment may not necessarily turn into something immediately harmful, but as one's laziness begins to settle down, it often leads to a lazy character. Similarly, if we have only one episode of aggression or laziness per lifetime, then that is not a problem. But the repeated occurrence, that familiar or habitual tendency, begins to format one's personality. Aggression, even though we do not like it, is still there. It is still there because we have become familiar with it. It was never tamed, and we were never truly aware of it. We never trained ourselves in the awareness of how we may be physically hurting somebody. Even when there is regret later, there is always the lack of mindfulness in that action.

*Venerable Khandro Rinpoche*

## WHEN WE TAKE REFUGE IN SAMSARA GOALS    4.23

Ordinary refuges become much more pervasive in our lives and begin to "benefit" our own confusion, making it stronger. Our grasping toward reality continually goes astray and we become much more vulnerable to our own confusion and the pain that is produced by that confusion. All of this becomes unavoidable. In such a way we look for a relative refuge outside of our mind as ultimate. Since it cannot be ultimate if it's a relative thing, then we find ourselves having no refuge at all in the end.

*Dzigar Kongtrul Rinpoche*

## IF THERE IS NO "SELF," WHAT REINCARNATES? 4.24

Buddhism believes in a stream of consciousness that gets transferred from one birth to the next. This stream of consciousness is an instance of mental occurrence, arising due to its own internal momentum as well as external stimuli, all of which seemingly perpetuate its continuity over time. It thus serves as the basis for one's self-identity.

*Traleg Kyabgon Rinpoche*

## THE ORIGIN OF EGO FROM CLEAR SPACE 4.25

From beginningless time there are no habits in unconditioned, natural mind. Still we create habit by dividing phenomena from clear space. Inherently a mirror does not have any dust. Still it attracts and gathers dust, which obscures its natural clarity. In the same way, our pure Wisdom Mind becomes obscured by ego when we become attached to its pure phenomena's unobstructed display. If we can recognize our natural stainless mind, we will not become obscured through attachment, but if we do not recognize our pure natural mind, then our subtle elements' phenomena gather like dust on our clear mirror mind.

*Thinley Norbu Rinpoche*

## THE ABSOLUTE NATURE AND THE ARISING OF PHENOMENA 4.26

Beings have forgotten the absolute, their own true nature. The absolute nature is like the sun, and phenomena are like the rays of light that emanate from it. To recognize that all these rays of light, phenomena, come from the sun, the absolute nature itself, is to be totally enlightened at that very moment.

But unenlightened beings, not recognizing where the rays are coming from, turn their backs to the sun, and instead of looking at the light rays' source they look at where they fall. They start to create the notion of an object out there and a subject within. Then, when the fives senses connect the "object" to the "subject," craving and aversion arise; the seeds of samsara have been sown, and from them grow the three realms of existence. But at no point have the phenomena of delusion been separated from the nature of buddhahood, which always pervades each and every being, and all phenomena.

*Dilgo Khyentse Rinpoche*

## Is Karma Only for Buddhists?                           4.27
Some people might say, "Oh, karma is experienced only by those who believe in it. Those who don't believe in karma don't experience its effects." Many Westerners have given me this argument. This is a completely wrong conception. The law of karma applies whether you believe in it or not. If you act in a certain way, you are sure to experience the appropriate result, just as surely as taking poison will make you sick—even though you might think that it is medicine that you are swallowing. Once you've created the karma to experience a certain result, that's where you're headed.

*Lama Thubten Yeshe Rinpoche*

# ⇥ 5

# The Practice of Hinayana

## REFUGE IN THE THREE JEWELS

ONE ENTERS INTO THE HINAYANA and into the practice of the dharma altogether by taking refuge in the three jewels of Buddha, dharma, and sangha (5.1). In some ways, refuge is the most important and most advanced of all practices (5.2) as it involves abandoning the commitment to samsara (5.3). In refuge, we are able to open ourselves to the blessings and compassion of all the buddhas dwelling inherently, but in a hidden way, within us (5.4). The three jewels are incredibly important for us, because they help us understand our human situation. (5.5). Helpless and trapped as we are within the vicious cycle of confused existence, taking refuge in the three jewels helps us find the way out (5.6).

Taking refuge thus has the incomparable power to help us escape from "this indefinite imprisonment in samsara" (5.7). Through relying on the three jewels, we find a source of clarity, security, and comfort—not in the samsaric way of protecting our ego, but in the dharmic way of drawing on the enlightened aspects of openness, understanding, and perspective (5.8). The Buddha is the person who is truly free from suffering and confusion; the dharma is both the written and remembered teachings as well as the realization that study and practice lead to; and the sangha can refer variously to the bodhisattvas on the high *bhumis* [the ten stages that the bodhisattva must go through to attain buddha-hood], to the monastic sangha, and, most broadly, to all those who have dedicated their lives to the liberation of sentient beings (5.9, 5.10). Refuge does not mean giving up our independence, but only giving up our useless and self-destructive patterns (5.11).

Our commitment in taking refuge is to gradually eliminate the obscurations covering our own awakened nature, so we can radiate its qualities outward into the world (5.12). When we have learned how to take refuge properly and constantly, as taking refuge in the enlightened qualities within, we realize a state of being that is completely at peace (5.13). When we are the most lost and desperate can be the ideal moment for taking refuge (5.14). Finally, one can speak of the three jewels as having an outer, inner, and secret aspect, and, in so doing, make clear how taking refuge is, indeed, a practice that runs through all three *yana*s (5.15).

## THE CEREMONY FOR OFFICIALLY ENTERING THE
## PATH OF MEDITATION                                    5.1

Buddhists have a ceremony for officially entering the path of meditation. It's called "taking refuge," and it involves embracing the Buddha as an example, the Buddha's teachings as a guide, and the community of other Buddhists as helpful, supporting companions on the path. And what are we taking refuge *from* in such a ceremony? From this endless cycle of frustration—of seeking pleasure and trying to avoid pain. We recognize this approach, ironically, only brings more pain.

*Sakyong Mipham Rinpoche*

## REFUGE IS THE ESSENTIAL TEACHING                     5.2

Refuge is the essential teaching. . . . The only practice one needs is refuge; it contains everything. . . . Refuge is a very profound and very advanced practice. Indeed, it is the most important part of Buddhism. Unfortunately, many people think of it as a beginner's practice and do not believe it is necessary even to have it explained. However, it is the important first step on the Buddhist path and the source of all other practices.

*Lama Lodö*

THE COMMITMENT INVOLVED IN TAKING REFUGE   5.3

What does it mean to take [the refuge vow]? It means we acknowledge and renounce with conviction the cycle of suffering. It means that we give our allegiance to something worthwhile, something that we've found to be true and wholesome and good. We have decided to take this path because we recognize that it leads to a place where we can flourish. Making this declaration enables us to begin to break our negative patterns and to develop the helpful qualities that we all possess inherently.

*Sakyong Mipham Rinpoche*

IN TAKING REFUGE, ONE IS CREATING OPEN SPACE
IN ONE'S MIND   5.4

When one takes refuge in Buddha Shakyamuni, one is additionally taking refuge in his teachings, known as the Dharma, and in the close adherents practicing Buddhadharma, known as the sangha, or monastic community. These three sources of refuge, Buddha, Dharma, and Sangha, are termed the Three Jewels. One takes refuge with the basic confidence that the Three Jewels represent a source of blessing, of inspiration, and of spiritual development. . . . In taking refuge, one is creating the open space in one's mind so that the blessings and compassion of all the buddhas, which are inherently there, can be felt.

*Kalu Rinpoche*

NOTHING IS MORE PRECIOUS THAN THE
THREE JEWELS   5.5

When we are completely lost in the suffering of samsara, the three jewels provide a refuge. Through the Buddha as a guide, the dharma as a path, and the sangha as a companion, we can have some understanding of what's occurring. We can get some sense of what's happening and some ideas about what we can do. Therefore, there's really nothing in the whole world more precious than the Buddha, the dharma, and the sangha for us, the samsaric beings.

*Dzigar Kongtrul Rinpoche*

## WHY WE NEED REFUGE                                              5.6

We have been in this world numberless times and have not been able
to escape from the cycle of existence. We have tried many ways to
escape to freedom and happiness. We may hope to do this on our own
but we cannot succeed. We don't have the power to stand against the
habit of conflicting emotions and we don't have help from anyone.
This is why we need refuge.

*Lama Lodö*

## REFUGE IN THE THREE JEWELS IS THE ONLY WAY                    5.7

This indefinite imprisonment in samsara can and must be changed by
learning how to take refuge in the three jewels. Nobody could actually
be more kind to you than they. Many understand this intellectually,
but emotionally speaking, there are very few with clear understanding. There are very few who have this kind of appreciation of the
three jewels and completely feel it from their own experience rather
than from a textbook. Someone who has understood this always feels a
real sense of comfort because during the highs and lows, good times
and bad times, their eyes are open. They are not going to fall down
and injure themselves. They will know how, with open eyes, to take
refuge.

From that point of view, if you are a blind man and have to walk
for even ten yards, you will feel emotionally insecure and you will feel
a sense of danger in walking those ten yards. If you were blind and
vulnerable, you would find it difficult to even walk from one room to
another without any help. If you had to walk outside onto the street,
just think how difficult it would be emotionally. You have your feet, you
have your hands; you have everything except your eyes, because your
eyes are blind. You are a blind person. Imagine how hard it would be.

Now, if you have eyes, walking from one room to another or even
walking outside would just be taken for granted. This serves as an example of how different it is for one who has taken refuge in the three
jewels and learned to completely appreciate the three jewels from the
bottom of their heart compared to one who has not. There is this level
of security, this sense of comfort present in having the eyes of the three
jewels. We depend upon our eyes and other parts of our bodies; when

*Lama Lodö*

we have them, they serve us very well to do whatever we need to do in our lives. And when we don't have those parts of our bodies, it becomes very difficult to do many of the things we need to do. It is like that with the three jewels; when we have them, there is that much security and comfort in our lives. When we don't, there is no real sense of comfort or security.

*Dzigar Kongtrul Rinpoche*

## THE THREE JEWELS ARE THE ONLY SURE REFUGE          5.8

One who has learned how to take refuge from the bottom of one's heart—over the course of one's life and practice, and through many different ups and downs—arrives at a point where he or she feels that taking refuge in the three jewels never fails to bring complete security and a total sense of comfort. It is not that we want a false, unreal "reality" or an artificial kind of security and then we find those by taking refuge in the three jewels. These false, unfounded "realities" and artificial securities that we constantly seek in our human existence have nothing to do with the true sense of complete security that one finds in taking refuge in the three jewels.

What does it mean to take refuge in the three jewels and find a sense of complete and never-failing security and comfort? When one has completely taken refuge over the course of one's life and practice, through life's ups and downs, one finds a way to put all things in perspective. In this, there is a way to work with one's emotions and therefore there is a way to overcome the unnecessary fears that eat up our peace of mind most of the time. Having said that, what is required here most is a sense of faith in the Buddha as the guide, dharma as the path, and sangha as companion.

*Dzigar Kongtrul Rinpoche*

## THE THREE JEWELS IN MORE DETAIL          5.9

The Three Jewels in which we can take refuge are, first, the Buddha, an ordinary person who attained a completely transformative awakening; second, the Dharma, a practice which transforms our impurities and develops our wisdom; and third, the Sangha, the dedicated people and great Bodhisattvas who support our efforts to reach enlightenment. . . .

The first of the Three Jewels is the Buddha. The Buddha has completely purified conflicting emotions so his mind is free from suffering and calm like clear weather. . . . The second of the Three Jewels is the . . . Dharma. There is a Dharma of Precept and a Dharma of Realization. The Dharma of Precept consists of the scriptures, the teachings of the Buddha, which in Sanskrit are called "sutras." There are 84,000 of these. . . . The Dharma of Realization is seen when practicing. . . . As we read the scriptures and hear the teachings, our thinking is refined and doubt and hesitation are destroyed. We do the practices and learn to separate emotions from the nature of the mind. Then we can develop wisdom, the "truth of the path," and this is the Dharma of Realization. . . . From this practice we can receive the joy of bliss which we call freedom. . . . The Third Jewel is the Sangha. This can refer to the monastic order and also to anyone who dedicates his or her life to the liberation of all sentient beings. Sangha can also mean the glorious assembly of tenth-level Bodhisattvas.

*Lama Lodö*

## OUR THREE OBJECTS OF REFUGE                      5.10

The Buddha, our first object of refuge, traveled on the path of awakening and overcame all sorts of difficulties. He demonstrated that fixation on the self can be overcome. He was brave enough to take a stance against materialism and his own attachment to pleasure. If we emulate him, we are emulating a being whose mind and actions were in accord with reality, who was not simply following the endless cycle of samsara.

We call the Buddha's voice the dharma, our second object of refuge. He expressed his mind to others by showing them a practical way to achieve selflessness and to understand emptiness. He gave us instructions for realizing the profound meaning of every possible situation.

The community of people who study and practice the Buddha's teachings, the sangha, is our third object of refuge. As a group, the sangha keeps alive the instructions from the Buddha. Fortunately, because of the sangha, we don't have to be alone on our spiritual journey. None of us is perfect, but because we agree on the truth of the Buddha's teachings, we share a view of one another—and of all beings—as having basic goodness. In fact, we can see all beings as buddhas.

*Sakyong Mipham Rinpoche*


## REFUGE IS NOT GIVING UP INDEPENDENCE 5.11

Many people think that taking refuge means belonging to some group and giving up independence. This is not true. In reality, when we take refuge, we give up only what is useless and destructive in ourselves.

*Lama Lodö*


## OUR COMMITMENT IN TAKING REFUGE 5.12

We are making a commitment to discover that our own basic nature is the wisdom of the Buddha and to uncover this nature. We are making a commitment to work on the development of our basic potential of the Dharmakaya Buddha, which is always within our being, within all sentient beings. On the one hand, we possess the basic qualities of, and we ourselves *are*, the Buddha from beginningless time. On the other hand, this buddha-quality potential is covered by our defilements and our obscurations. The *klesha* mind and cognitive obscurations are covering our basic buddha qualities. Therefore, we make a commitment to work on clearing these obstacles and to generate our basic buddha quality to the extent that we can fully radiate this quality. That is the fundamental notion of taking refuge in the Buddha as being within our own nature.

*The Dzogchen Pönlop Rinpoche*


## THE TRUE REFUGE IS WITHIN 5.13

The only never-failing, constant refuge is not found outside of yourself, outside of your mind; it is only found within your own mind. If we are quite clear how to take refuge in the Buddha, Dharma, and Sangha that we have cherished so much in our mind, then we find that this refuge is constantly there.

Having the three jewels constantly with us in our mind means the mind is always at peace. There is no room for the mind to go astray.

The mind is imbued with the blessings of the three jewels. And through constant engagement in taking refuge—solely, whole-heartedly—we learn how to take refuge in the three jewels completely. We have to discover how to take refuge on all occasions, in every step of our lives. It means not looking outside ourselves for other alternatives.

If we are looking for alternatives outside of our mind without taking refuge solely in the three jewels, it shows that our faith in the three jewels is very questionable. It reveals what our sense of reality is. It shows that we believe the many problems we face to be real and outside our own minds. In such a mode, mind and phenomena do separate. Then the mind fails to take refuge in the mind with the complete confidence that the three jewels are found within. Hence, we look for what we ignorantly believe is something outside, toward causes and conditions from sources other than our mind. In this way, we fail to receive the actual benefit of having such a refuge. We begin to ignore our own three jewels that we have cultivated in our own mind, and our own mind as a source of strength and refuge. Therefore, we start to go astray. We start to look for material substances, material goods, and relationships that are limited in their ability to benefit us. We look to those as an alternative to the three jewels and begin to rely on them as an ultimate refuge. Then we are faced with a sense of constant disappointment—or, if not constant disappointment, then ultimately a sense of disappointment.

*Dzigar Kongtrul Rinpoche*

## WHEN WE ARE DESPERATE                                        5.14

When we are more desperate, we are in some ways more innocent as well. We can take advantage of the innocent mind [that is exposed] when we are completely overwhelmed by the confusion and pain of our own vulnerability, when we have lost all our control, when we are trying so hard to find some other means to strengthen ourselves, when we are trying to find other means of understanding. If at that moment we could simply turn our mind to the refuge prayer with this innocent mind, like the innocent mind of a child who is completely bewildered by a task he or she has not done before and who is utterly confused and vulnerable, we might actually discover the real benefit of taking refuge.

Because of the child's innocence and acceptance of guidance and benefit without reservation, he or she can be guided easily. It could be the same way for us.

*Dzigar Kongtrul Rinpoche*

## THE OUTER, INNER, AND SECRET ASPECTS OF
## THE THREE JEWELS                                           5.15

The outer three jewels are the Buddha, Dharma, and Sangha. The Three Jewels have an inner aspect, known as the Three Roots: the Guru (or Teacher), who is the root of blessings; the Yidam, who is the root of accomplishment; and the Dakini, who is the root of enlightened activity. Although the names are different, these three do not in any way differ from the Three Jewels. The Guru is the Budha, the Yidam is the Dharma, and the Dakinis and Protectors are the Sangha. And on the innermost level, the Dharmakaya is the Buddha, the Sambhogakaya is the Dharma, and the Nirmanakaya is the Sangha.

*Dilgo Khyentse Rinpoche*

## MEDITATION

The heart of Buddhism is the practice of sitting meditation. This was the method by which the Buddha attained enlightenment and, since his time, has been the core Buddhist methodology by which practitioners seek spiritual transformation. It is all well and good to study the teachings and contemplate them. But they only find their real point and fulfillment in the practice of meditation (5.16). Even if we are very successful Buddhists in other respects, if we do not carry out the practices that lead to a transformed, transcendent mind, then there isn't much point to any of it (5.17).

Because meditation is the core Buddhist methodology, much of what we have already considered in the preceding pertains directly to it. As we saw, the path of studying Buddhism leads from an external and fairly literal learning (hearing), through understanding the meaning of what one has learned (contemplation), and culminates in the practice of meditation. Again, an understanding of the four reminders shows us why one might want to practice meditation and rouses our motivation (5.18).

For example, through appreciating the principle of karma, we begin to realize that everything we do has an impact on our lives and on the situation in which we live. In other words, our actions of body, speech, and mind provide the conditions of our life, as they either help or hinder our spiritual practice. This is why a respect for karma and a commitment to ethical conduct or behavior (*shila*) is considered an essential preliminary and analog to the practice of meditation.

In fact, when Tibetan Buddhists talk about dharma training, they typically speak of a threefold process (*tri-shiksha*) composed of *shila* (ethical behavior), *samadhi* (meditation) and *prajna* (insight). In this view, *shila* provides the foundation for meditation; through meditation one takes the journey; and *prajna* is the fruition of meditation, in insight.

Within this framework, *shila* provides the critical foundation. When negative karma predominates, we will have difficulty at every stage— meeting an appropriate teacher, connecting with our own inspiration, and creating the conditions necessary to maintain a regular meditation practice. And, even if we manage to sit down to meditate, our mind may be so overburdened with distraction and negativity that no amount of effort with a technique will produce results. On the other hand, if positive karma is dominant, no matter what challenges may present themselves, we will seem to find a way through and be able to turn them into stepping stones on our path.

Of course, we can't do anything about the karma that we have created in the past. What's done is done. But the way we act now can be astonishingly powerful in terms of coloring our current situation. No matter how much negative karma we may have created in the past and no matter how abysmal our current circumstances, once we commit ourselves to abandoning harmful actions and to cultivating kindness to others, and once we begin to act on that commitment, we will discover our external situation becoming gradually—or even rather quickly— more workable. And we will find our mind beginning to settle down. The tremendous importance of ethical behavior for meditation practice explains why Tibetan masters, in teaching meditation to Westerners, typically emphasize the importance of *shila* as the foundation of the path.

*Shila* provides the ground for meditation practice, but it also exhibits the same insight-bearing and transformative functions of meditation itself. For example, *shila* in light of an understanding of karma can, in its impact, already be classified as meditation practice. Action in light of karma can often be even more powerful in developing mindfulness (*shamatha*) than focus on one-pointed concentration (*samadhi*) and insight (*vipashyana*) (5.19). The traditional Tibetan story of the "sweeper *arhat*," who was completely unlearned, illustrates how the practice of *shila* can create such positive karmic circumstances that it leads the practitioner to the verge of enlightenment itself (5.20).

Once the ground of ethical behavior has been established, we are ready to engage in the practice of sitting meditation, the heart of Buddhism. The remainder of the selections in this chapter reveal some important facets of this practice (5.21–5.53). Prominent in Tibetan Buddhism is the Mahayana viewpoint that one should practice meditation in order to be helpful to others (5.21) and so that one's own altruistic qualities may flourish (5.22). Beyond that, the goal of meditation itself is very simple: it is learning how to "just be" (5.23). Also to be noted are the facts of the importance of commitment (5.24), the perpetual challenge of meditation (5.25), and the fact that meditation is not therapy (5.26).

The foundation of all meditation practice is *shamatha*, the cultivation of calm abiding (5.27 and 5.28). *Shamatha* involves taking a stable and relaxed posture (5.29) and then using the breath in various ways to develop relaxation (5.30). One needs to carry out the practice in a focused way (5.31). As we practice, various thoughts will arise, and in such cases we should just return to the breath (5.32). We should not be discouraged if at first the thoughts seem overwhelming, for this is actually the beginning of the experience of stillness (5.33). As we continue our practice, more recognizable peace does begin to develop (5.34). The essential point is to keep the mind within and not let it wander about, outside (5.35).

*Vipashyana* (insight), which develops out of *shamatha*, is the first experience of egolessness (5.36). *Vipashyana* literally means higher or superior seeing, and indicates that we are penetrating into the heart of experience (5.37), the essential nature of things (5.38). It is critical to realize that, as practitioners, we ourselves can have an actual experience of *vipashyana* (5.39) in which our minds rest in a very large space (5.40), so large that we might almost call it absentmindedness (5.41). As *vipashyana* develops, we develop heightened curiosity about our experience in the largest sense (5.42). At a certain point, we discover the union of *shamatha* and *vipashyana* (5.43), which eradicates the causes of samsara (5.44). Although the ultimate nature transcends conceptual mind, the analytical mind has a role to play in its cultivation (5.45). At the Hinayana level, *vipashyana* leads to the realization that there is no "I," no "self" behind our experience (5.46, 5.47). Such awareness arrives simply on its own, without our intervention, if we are simply open to it (5.48). It may emerge in the context of great boredom (5.49, 5.50). Such awareness is not manufacturing anything, it is just being (5.51), though being as light, luminosity (5.52). In Tibetan tradition, the attainments of *vipashyana* are described as being of four different types, ascending in their ultimacy (5.53).

## WE NEED TO GET TO THE POINT                                        5.16

The dharma is as vast as the sky. There are volumes and volumes of teachings, and no one could master them all. Therefore, we have to get to the main point. Given our human situation, what *is* the main point? It is to do something with our minds, to make some change or difference in our minds. And how can we do that? Through hearing and contemplating the teachings, yes, but mainly, through realizing them through practicing [meditation]—through actually realizing whatever teachings are given. Just hearing and contemplating the teachings alone will not do anything for you at all. That alone has never done anything for anyone. But, if you practice and have a glimpse or some realization of the teachings, then perhaps, there will be some true benefit.

*Dzigar Kongtrul Rinpoche*

## ON THE NECESSITY OF MEDITATION PRACTICE                            5.17

Buddhism has experienced tremendous growth. I come from the East, where we have many monasteries, temples, retreats, and meditation centers. However, it is not so much the container but the contents that must be profound, and must be steeped within the essential teachings.

The outer growth and increase in number and size of meditation centers is one aspect, but it is more important that meditators actually practice the profound teachings. We talk about the dharma, the teachings of the Buddha, and all these instructions and methods of practices we can do and benefit from; there are methods of meditating, there are philosophies, and there are doctrines and logic. But in essence, to find dharma one has to look inward, not outward. One has to constantly exert effort in examining oneself and one's own mind. Within Buddhism, there is a tremendous treasure of teachings; nevertheless, everything is inherently contained within one's own mind.

The structures, the various formats and techniques, as well as the inspiration and guidance of teachers, Buddhas, and bodhisattvas, are supports that we can always benefit from. As long as we need that support, there is no end to it and it is always there. We meet great teachers and masters; we listen to the teachings; we study and reflect. Everyone tries to meditate in his or her own way. Nevertheless, as long as one relies on purely external supports and does not really work at the level of one's own mind and one's own heart, there is not much benefit. One could say: "This is the most profound path of practice; it is 2600 years old; Buddha Shakyamuni taught it in India and then it was transmitted to Tibet. We have all these great masters, His Holiness the Dalai Lama, the Karmapa, and Khyentse Rinpoche." We have all our teachers, but if we do not really take the essence of these teachers and their instructions to heart and actually practice by looking inward, then it doesn't really bring much benefit and it doesn't make much sense. You may have the most beautiful monastery and the strongest sangha, but if there is no evidence of a transformed and transcendent mind, then it doesn't make much sense.

*Venerable Khandro Rinpoche*


## WHY DO STUDY AND CONTEMPLATION
## COME FIRST?                                    5.18
The best and most effective method of cutting through bothersome sensations, odd thoughts, or even hallucinations during meditation is to strengthen the understanding of the importance of meditation. We need to take time to reflect upon our human situation, karma and its creation,

and the various experiences of sentient beings. Usually, meditation is begun with the intention of doing something good. However, we need to have a sound and strong foundation of really being aware of the whole reason why we need to be free from samsara. When that foundation is weak, various experiences will distract us. When the mind has matured and taken time to understand why one should meditate, when we genuinely understand what the teachings talk about—the renunciation of self and samsara—then the likelihood of being preoccupied with, and attached to, various experiences decreases. It is essential to first train the mind through hearing the teachings, contemplating, reflecting on, and examining them, so that one has a strong foundation of knowing why one should practice the path of seeking liberation from the sufferings of samsara. In that case, the mind will not be focused so much upon what one might experience in meditation. Instead, there will be an understanding that meditation is the only method of being free from the unceasing creation of ignorance and the entertainment of various kinds of experiences, which are nothing other than ignorance.

*Venerable Khandro Rinpoche*


## REFLECTION ON KARMA IS ALSO MEDITATION    5.19

[Reflection on karma] is a far better and more powerful way of developing mindfulness of your actions than is becoming obsessed, as so many Westerners are, with the cultivation of single-pointed concentration (*samadhi*) and insight meditation (*vipassana*).

. . . Guarding your karma day in and day out is also meditation and can be a powerful way to develop insight. In this way your entire life can be used to bring you closer to the wisdom of egolessness. When you understand the nature of karma, you are constantly aware of everything you do. Thus, wherever you go, you cannot escape from meditation. . . . This makes you conscious all the time.

*Lama Thubten Yeshe Rinpoche*


## THE SWEEPER ARHAT    5.20

In Buddha Shakyamuni's entourage there was a monk who was not very bright and could not even learn the alphabet. But since he had great faith in Buddha and great aspiration for the Dharma, some of his companions went to Buddha to ask for advice on how to help him. Buddha responded, "He can still attain realization. He should do good deeds, abandon any harmful ones, and be the temple sweeper," and gave specific instructions on how he should sweep the temple, mindfully. The monk did this for years and purified his mind of obscurations. His intelligence grew more and more acute. Finally, while Buddha was teaching the Four Noble Truths, the sweeper understood the teaching and reached *arhat* status [one who has become free of all passions and defilements]. He remains known as one of the great *arhat*s [enlightened disciples] of the Buddha's followers.

*Kalu Rinpoche*

## MEDITATION HELPS US LIVE A GOOD LIFE                    5.21
Try as much as possible to generate a good heart, and genuinely do something that is beneficial for others. Genuine dharma practice is to make sure that one's life is led in such a way that you are able to die without any regret, knowing that your life has been helpful to someone. For that, meditation is essential. The practices help you strengthen the ability to generate compassion and to genuinely discover and realize the inherent nature of basic goodness.

*Venerable Khandro Rinpoche*

## BUDDHIST MEDITATION IS NOT JUST FOR
## ONESELF ALONE                    5.22
Buddhist meditation is not just about oneself. It is about being able to develop a ground of familiarity with who you are, so that the genuine, basic goodness inherent in each person is able to get a little bit more breathing space. If that is strengthened, perhaps one will manifest as a good person, with a little bit more command over the actions of one's body, speech, and mind.

*Venerable Khandro Rinpoche*

## THE IMPORTANCE OF LEARNING JUST TO BE                    5.23
From a Buddhist point of view, if you can just be, really just be in your true, natural state, then all good qualities are already there. You don't

Photo by Brian Spielmann.

*Venerable Khandro Rinpoche*

need to try to do something to make yourself joyful, for example—if you can really be yourself, then the joyfulness manifests on its own.

*Ringu Tulku Rinpoche*

## COMMITMENT TO MINDFULNESS AND AWARENESS IS CRITICAL                                                    5.24

You have to commit yourself. In some sense, you have to take a kind of vow that you are willing to be mindful and aware. This is like saying to yourself: "This is my work for today and for the rest of my life. I'm willing to be aware, I'm willing to be mindful." When you have such a strong and real conviction to begin with, there are no further problems at all. Any further problems are just some kind of frivolity, which tries to overrule your memory that you should be mindful. So once you have taken that attitude of commitment, that commitment automatically brings absent-mindedness [awareness], which then results in your being mindful constantly.

*Chögyam Trungpa Rinpoche*

## MEDITATION INVOLVES CONSTANT CHALLENGE          5.25

It's very difficult to make meditation into a habit. Even though you've been doing it for twenty years, still there's constantly a certain sense of struggle involved. This shows that meditation is different from the rest of habitual things. It [involves] some kind of challenge, constantly.

*Chögyam Trungpa Rinpoche*

## IS MEDITATION THERAPEUTIC?                               5.26

Meditation is not regarded as medicine or even as therapeutic. It is just an unconditional way of being in life.

*Chögyam Trungpa Rinpoche*

## THE FIRST, MOST IMPORTANT, AND MOST CONSTANT                                                        5.27

Of the aspects of meditation, *shamatha* [calming the mind] and *vipashyana* [insight], the one that is usually practiced first is *shamatha*. This can be seen in the fact that all the different approaches to Buddhism (all the various vehicles) begin their instruction in meditation with an explanation of methods of resting the mind, which is the practice of *shamatha*. This is the way that meditation has been presented in the Buddhist tradition since its original presentation by the Buddha himself. *Shamatha* is not simply a preliminary practice—something that is done as a beginner and then discarded. It is an essential element of all meditation practice. Therefore, it must be present in the beginning, throughout the path, and in the end as well. It is not simply the first meditation; one could also say it is the last, the most important, and the most constant.

*The Dzogchen Pönlop Rinpoche*

## THE ETYMOLOGY OF *SHAMATHA* 5.28

According to Jamgon Lodro Thaye, the aspects and meaning of the practice of *shamatha* meditation can be found etymologically in both the Tibetan and Sanskrit terms for this practice. The Tibetan term is *shiné* [*shi-ne*], and the Sanskrit is *shamatha*. In the case of the Tibetan, the first syllable, *shi,* and in the case of the Sanskrit, the first two syllables, *shama,* refer to "peace" or "pacification." The meaning of peace or pacification in this context is that normally our mind is like a whirlwind of agitation. The agitation is the agitation of thought. Our thoughts are principally an obsessive concern with past, conceptualization about the present, and especially an obsessive concern with the future. This means that usually our mind is not experiencing the present moment at all. We are usually miles ahead of ourselves. As long as this process continues, our mind never comes to rest, and we can never experience any state of pliability or happiness. As long as this continues, we never really appreciate the present moment because we are always looking forward, constantly imagining future experiences. What we are doing at any given moment, as long as we are under the sway of this process, is preparing for the future. When we get to the future that we are preparing for, we are preparing for another future. We never reap the fruits of our constant, obsessive preparation. So the first syllable, *shi,* or *shama* in Sanskrit, refers to the pacification, or the slowing or cooling down, of this whirlwind of thought. It consists of the mind falling naturally or gliding to rest in an experience of nowness or the present moment.

The second syllable of the Tibetan is *ne*, which means "to abide or remain." This is the equivalent of the final syllable of the Sanskrit, *tha*. When the mind has come to rest in this way, through the pacification of the thoughts of the three times, it then abides in this state of rest unwaveringly. The mind and the *shamatha* of the mind become mixed, inseparable. In fact, the aspects of *shamatha* and the essence of *shamatha* can both be seen from the etymology of the terms that are used to describe it.

*The Dzogchen Pönlop Rinpoche*

## SHAMATHA INSTRUCTIONS                                                    5.29

First, begin with the posture. You need to sit straight. If you have had instructions on how to sit cross-legged, do that. If you sit on a chair, you can rest your back in whatever way is comfortable, but make sure that the spine is straight. Gently cross your legs. Place the palms on your knees. Slowly lower your gaze directly in front of you, following the bridge of your nose, and gaze directly in front of you. If you are using an object as a focus, you can choose any object directly in front of you. Look at that and allow the concentration to just be there. All of the channels of the six senses join one-pointedly on that object. If you are focusing on the breath, at first simply generate an understanding that this silence allows the mindfulness and awareness of body, speech, and mind, which, in turn, enable compassionate actions of body, speech, and mind. With that commitment, allow the eyes to lead, followed by all the senses, to slowly and gently become calm and focused on the breath. Simply sense yourself breathing. There is neither an emphasis on the exhalation nor on the inhalation, but simply bringing the mind back to this activity. It is not stagnant; there is a movement that allows the mind to go in and out with the breath. This is the way to practice *shamatha*.

*Venerable Khandro Rinpoche*

## SHAMATHA HELPS US TO BECOME CALM                                        5.30

In *shamatha* meditation, we use the medium of the breath as a way of relaxing. We use the breath as a yogic practice to work with the physical body, to synchronize our body and mind. So the physical aspect of *shamatha* meditation is simply sitting and breathing. When we practice *shamatha*, we begin by settling our body. We begin to calm down, relax, and, to a degree, let go of distractions and block out the world. Sights, sounds, smells, and so on, are distractions in the sense that they use energy. In *shamatha*, because we are spending less energy on those distractions, we are calm. It's like shutting down an engine; everything comes to a halt.

*Sakyong Mipham Rinpoche*

## THE NEED FOR FOCUS                                    5.31

*Shamatha* has to be approached knowing what we're doing. It's not enough just to hope that someone will inspire us or that we'll read something nice. To settle [the mind], it is necessary to focus. Focusing means being present, but being present doesn't mean being uptight or paranoid. Focusing is similar to concentrating, but it is not the same as concentrating on a math problem and not stopping until we solve it. Focusing doesn't mean balancing a pin on its end and hoping it doesn't fall over. If we are focused, we're not wondering, "Am I good? Am I bad?" Focus is a sense of clarity. We are connected with reality. We are clear about who we are and what we're doing. We're not thinking about what we want to do; we know what it is, whether it's getting a master's degree, working as a cook, or whatever. Needless to say, it takes time to develop that kind of focus. It takes confidence and the willingness to relate to our innate wholesomeness.

*Sakyong Mipham Rinpoche*

## THOUGHTS                                              5.32

When one begins to exert effort in establishing one-pointedness, often various things occur. Thoughts come up while you are trying to focus on the breath. Simply allow thoughts to be recognized, but without defining or judging. Simply see them as thoughts. "Oh, here's a thought"—something like that. Then return to, "I'm breathing." Similarly, if you hear a sound, such as someone coughing or sneezing, or whatever sounds there may be, again, "that's sneezing," and you return to, "I'm breathing." Similarly, if various movements occur, "that's a person," or, "that's a movement." Then back again, "I'm breathing." As you blink, "that's blinking," and then again, back to, "I am breathing." Bring the mind continuously back to breathing and recognizing your own breathing.

*Venerable Khandro Rinpoche*

## OVERWHELMING THOUGHTS: THE FIRST
## EXPERIENCE OF CALMNESS                                    5.33

Our first introduction to our mind, through *shamatha*, is the experience of encountering our own tremendously overwhelming thoughts and the violent nature of these thoughts. It is as if this flow of thoughts never stops, never ceases. Thoughts are bombing in continuously, nonstop for thirty minutes, sixty minutes, or for however long we are sitting in meditation. The continuous nature of this flow of thoughts, this overwhelming experience of distraction, restlessness, irritation, emotions, emotionalism, and whatever, seems far from our idea of meditation. However, such experiences of distraction and the violent nature of erupting thoughts are the very experience of calmness. That is the beginning of experiencing calmness.

In some ways, whether we are talking about sutra, tantra, Madhyamaka, or Mahamudra, there is not much difference. All of these sources tell us that if we are looking for an experience of calmness outside of these thoughts, we will not find it. If we are looking for a certain experience of clarity or emptiness outside of this overwhelming experience of thoughts, concepts, and emotions, we will not find it.

*Shamatha* only becomes more and more irritating. It becomes so irritating because our thoughts, confusion, and emotions are so kind. These intense experiences come up because they *really* want us to experience calmness. They *really* want us to experience clarity. That is why they arise so intensely. They know that we are struggling to experience calmness, to experience peace, to experience emptiness, and that is why they are coming up. They come up because we are looking for that. It is that simple. We want to experience peace, calmness, clarity, and emptiness, and that is why thoughts, confusion, and emotions are manifesting so intensely.

*The Dzogchen Pönlop Rinpoche*

## As We Continue to Practice

Over time, as we continue to practice, the mind will remain calm. It's like a sack of potatoes: we put it down, and it stays. This stability is the peace of *shamatha*. That peace exists intrinsically, but we have to train ourselves to be with it. We are not trying to attain an everlasting state, but a relative level of synchronicity of body and mind. And as we become more familiar with the peace of *shamatha*, we can remain in it longer. We're no longer trying to figure out every little problem. It's not that everything is hunky dory and there are no problems. We know there's plenty to worry about, but we don't need to do the worrying. Not worrying takes strength and the willingness to remain in the present moment: that is peace. In coming back to that place, we begin to let go of frivolity and become decent meditators.

*Sakyong Mipham Rinpoche*

## Simply Keep the Mind from Wandering Outside

If you conquer the primordial nature by distinguishing mind
    from awareness,
The view of the absolute will gradually become clear.
Even if inwardly awareness is not yet clear right now,
Simply keep the mind from wandering outside;
This will do, for awareness lies in the very depth of the mind.

*Dilgo Khyentse Rinpoche*

## Awareness Is Totality

In the Buddhist tradition, awareness has been described as the first experience of egolessness. . . . This is the first introduction to the understanding of egolessness. Awareness in this case is totality rather than one-sidedness. A person who has achieved awareness or who is working on the discipline of awareness has no direction, no bias in one direction or another. He is just simply aware, totally and completely.

*Chögyam Trungpa Rinpoche*

THE HIGHER SEEING OF VIPASHYANA                          5.37
Through the steadiness of *shamatha*, we progress to the level of *vipashy-ana*, or insight meditation. In Tibetan, *vipashyana* is *lhagthong*. *Lhag* means "higher," "superior," or "greater"; *thong* is "view" or "to see." So *lhagthong* is a higher view, a higher seeing. It is not that we are literally above, but that *lhagthong* brings a distance that allows us to pen-etrate into the nature of experience.

*Sakyong Mipham Rinpoche*


WHAT IS VIPASHYANA?                                      5.38
Meditation does not consist only of *shamatha*. The other aspect is *vipa-shyana*, or insight, which in Tibetan is called *lhagthong*. The term *lhag-thong* literally means "superior seeing." This can be interpreted as a *superior manner of seeing*, and also as *seeing that which is the essential nature*. Its nature is a lucidity, a clarity of mind, based on the foregoing *shama-tha*, that enables one to determine the characteristics and ultimate nature of all things unmistakenly, without confusion or mix-up of any kind. Fundamentally, it consists of a recognition of the abiding or basic nature of everything, in an unmistaken manner. For this reason, *vipashyana* meditation is referred to as superior seeing or superior vision, *lhagthong*.

*The Dzogchen Pönlop Rinpoche*


VIPASHYANA IN OUR EXPERIENCE                             5.39
We are not talking about hypothetical possibilities. You can actually experience this in your life, in your being. And in fact, potentialities of *vipashyana* are already prominent in our experience; they take place all the time. But we have not actually acknowledged them or perhaps even seen them.

*Chögyam Trungpa Rinpoche*


MINDFULNESS AND AWARENESS                               5.40
Mindfulness is very detailed and very direct, but awareness is something panoramic, [an] open . . . awareness of the atmosphere or environment.
. . . Once you are aware of the atmosphere, you begin to realize that

thoughts are no big deal. Thoughts can just be allowed to diffuse into the atmosphere. . . .

But sometimes we feel we are so wrapped up in our little game, our little manipulation, that we miss the totality. That is why it is necessary for students to begin with *shamatha*—so that they can see the details of such an eruption, such a manipulation, the details of the game that goes on. Then beyond that, having established some kind of relationship with that already, they begin to see the basic totality. Thus *vipashyana* is understanding the whole thing.

*Chögyam Trungpa Rinpoche*

## AWARENESS AND MINDFULNESS                                    5.41

Awareness is a state of absent-mindedness [in a positive sense]. The point here is that when there is no mind to be absent, energy comes in, and so you are accurate, you are precise, you are mindful—but absent-minded at the same time. . . . Absent-mindedness in this case acts as the instigator or evoker of the background, and mindfulness is the occupant of that background. So you are there, but at the same time, you are not there. And at the same time you can fulfill your daily duties, relate to your living situation, your relationships, carry on conversations, and so forth. All that can be handled mindfully as long as there is absent-mindedness as the background. . . .

Approached in this way, mindfulness is no longer a problem . . . it is not energy-consuming at all.

*Chögyam Trungpa Rinpoche*

## FROM SHAMATHA TO VIPASHYANA                                  5.42

Based on the development of *shamatha*, we can be here, undistracted, with some openness. Within that, we become curious because a whole new range of experiences comes into focus. These things were always there, but we never quite noticed them. It's like walking outdoors. As we walk along, at first we're engaged by the mountains and trees and boulders. After a while, we are not so impressed by them; they no longer dominate our mind. Then we begin to notice the greenery, grass, and flowers, the butterflies and insects flying around. What's happened is that we've settled down. We have relaxed and can see what's going on; we can see the display of phenomena. In *lhagthong*, we begin to see the qualities of our experiences. If *lhagthong* were simply an intellectual understanding, it could go only so far, because intellect is conditioned. The insight of *lhagthong* is unconditioned, natural, a part of our being.

*Sakyong Mipham Rinpoche*

UNIFYING SHAMATHA AND VIPASHYANA                    5.43

The way these two aspects of meditation are practiced is that one begins with the practice of *shamatha*; on the basis of that, it becomes possible to practice *vipashyana* or *lhagthong*. Through one's practice of *vipashyana* being based on and carried on in the midst of *shamatha*, one eventually ends up practicing a unification of *shamatha* and *vipashyana*. The unification leads to a very clear and direct experience of the nature of all things. This brings one very close to what is called the absolute truth.

*The Dzogchen Pönlop Rinpoche*

SHAMATHA, VIPASHYANA, AND THEIR UNION             5.44

Insight, or *vipashyana* (*lhagthong*), is extremely important because it can eradicate the mental afflictions, whereas tranquility [*shamatha*] alone cannot. That is why we want to be able to practice tranquility and insight in a unified manner. This unified practice has three steps: first, we practice tranquility; then we practice insight; and then we bring the two together. Doing this will eradicate the cause of samsara (which is mental afflictions), thereby eradicating the result of samsara (which is suffering). For this reason, it is improper to become too attached to the delight or pleasure of tranquility, because tranquility alone is not enough.

As was said by Lord Milarepa in a song:

"Not being attached to the pool of tranquility
May I generate the flower of insight."

In these two lines, tranquility is compared to a pool of water, and insight to a lotus flower which grows up out of that pool and beautifies the pool. If one is content just with the pool of water, which exists in order that the flower can grow, and one does not actually grow the flower, the pool is not beautified. If, however, one attempts to grow the flower without the pool, it cannot arise (lotuses can only grow out of a body of water); and even if it could arise, it would dry up.

*The Dzogchen Pönlop Rinpoche*

## THE ANALYTICAL METHOD    5.45

[The] ultimate nature transcends the intellectual or conceptual mind. However, it is necessary to begin with a conceptual examination of it. In the midst of a conceptual examination, one can view or acquire a glimpse of the wisdom that itself transcends concept. In fact, one has to proceed in that way. One cannot say at the very beginning, "This wisdom and this nature are totally transcending conceptual mind, and so there is no point in attempting to reach it gradually." One has to make use of conceptual mind; conceptual investigation will lead to a realization that transcends concepts.

*The Dzogchen Pönlop Rinpoche*

## VIPASHYANA AT THE HINAYANA LEVEL REVEALS THE SELFLESSNESS OF PERSONS    5.46

One begins by looking for what we call "I," looking for our "self," looking for this thing to which we constantly exhibit clinging. According to buddhadharma, when you analyze this "I," to which we have so much clinging, you find that it consists of what are called the five aggregates. Aside from these five aggregates, there is no self that can be found. Finding that it must be, if it exists, one or more of the five aggregates, then one tries to determine which one of the five it is. Is it form? Is it sensation? Is it perception? Is it mental formation? Is it consciousness? Each of these is, as the name "aggregate" implies, an agglomeration of many things. One determines that even if it is one of the five, it must not be that entire one; if it is a unitary thing, it must be one part of one of the five. One analyzes each of the five, and each of their components, to try to determine which part of which of the five this "self" actually is. One asks, "Can I actually find it?" and one attempts to look for it.

What we are looking for is this self that we normally take to be present and a unitary thing. We analyze the ego-clinging self and try to determine whether it has any accuracy. This imputation or this clinging is the root of mental affliction. When we analyze this imputed self, we cannot find it. We determine through the analysis that it cannot exist or be present in the manner in which we conceive of it. This experience that we sometimes have through the practice of analysis, of not being able to put one's finger on the self, is a glimpse of the wisdom that transcends concept.

*The Dzogchen Pönlop Rinpoche*

## THE "SELF"    5.47
The self is simply a vague and convenient concept that we project now here and now there onto a stream of experiences, and is nothing in or of itself.

*Khenpo Tsultrim Gyamtso*

## LETTING AWARENESS COME TO US    5.48
We are referring to a kind of openness that is related with letting self-existing awareness come to us. And awareness is not something that needs to be manufactured: when there is a gap, awareness enters into us. So awareness does not require a certain particular effort. Such an effort is unnecessary. . . . Awareness is like a wind. If you open your doors and windows, it is bound to come in.

*Chögyam Trungpa Rinpoche*

## BOREDOM IN VIPASHYANA    5.49
At the introductory level, when you first have such [*vipashyana*] experiences, obviously you feel excited. You feel that this is something new you've gotten. But as you use such experiences as part of your practice, you wear out the novelty of them very quickly—particularly in this case—and it all turns into a very powerful boredom. . . . The boredom

*Khenpo Tsultrim Gyamtso Rinpoche*

that develops from irritation still has a reference point of *this*, whereas the boredom of boredom that develops in *vipashyana* is more all-pervasive, like having the flu.

*Chögyam Trungpa Rinpoche*


## THE CHALLENGE OF BOREDOM                                    5.50

There are different types of boredom that we usually experience. Insecurity, lack of excitement, being idle, nothing happening. . . . In *vipashyana*, the boredom we are talking about is a sense of being idle, and this is unconditional boredom. The experience of *vipashyana* awareness has a quality of all-pervasive, thick cream. It has body, at the same time it is fluid, and it is somewhat challenging.

*Chögyam Trungpa Rinpoche*


## VIPASHYANA AWARENESS IS JUST BEING                          5.51

[Awareness] is a state of not manufacturing anything else; it is just being. And there is a misunderstanding, particularly in connection with *vipashyana*, which regards attaining awareness as an enormous effort. . . . That is the wrong attitude. One doesn't try to hold oneself in the state of meditation, the state of awareness.

*Chögyam Trungpa Rinpoche*


## THE ALL-PERVASIVENESS OF VIPASHYANA                         5.52

Sometimes this is spoken of in terms of light, luminosity. . . . It refers to the sense of clarity that exists in this experience. Once you feel that basic, all-pervasive experience, then there is nothing else but *that* (the other), and *this* (oneself) is long forgotten. Maybe at the beginning, *this* tried to struggle, to fight with *that*, the all-pervasiveness. But though *this* might struggle, at some point the all-pervasiveness is all over the place, and a sense of suffocation begins to develop. And that subtle suffocation turns into boredom. That is the vital point when you are actually getting into the all-pervasiveness of the *vipashyana* experience.

*Chögyam Trungpa Rinpoche*

THE FOUR TYPES OF VIPASHYANA                                5.53

There are four main forms of *vipashyana*.

The first kind of *vipashyana* is the *vipashyana* of the Tirthika (non-Buddhist) traditions and is found mainly in India. These non-Buddhist traditions practice *shamatha* to pacify and eliminate most of the obvious *kleshas* [obscurations].

The second kind of *vipashyana* is the *vipashyana* teachings the Buddha gave to the *shravakas* [disciples] and *pratyekabuddhas* [solitary realized meditators] who could not understand the very profound or vast meaning. In the *vipashyana* of the *shravakas* and *pratyekabuddhas,* the actual nature of [the] four [noble] truths is understood. . . .

The third kind of *vipashyana* is the *vipashyana* of the bodhisattvas who follow the six *paramitas* [virtues perfected by the bodhisattva]. The *vipashyana* meditation of the Mahayana is on the realization of emptiness. This means that all phenomena that arise have a dependence upon other phenomena and therefore no true existence of their own. . . . These teachings are very profound and vast.

The fourth kind of *vipashyana* is that which uses bliss as a special method for attaining realization, or the *vipashyana* of the Mantrayana.

*Thrangu Rinpoche*

*Part Three*
# MAHAYANA

# → 6

# *The Great Vehicle*

THE PASSAGES IN THIS CHAPTER revolve around three themes: first, the notion of the Mahayana as the "great vehicle"; second, the ideal of the bodhisattva, the person who follows the Mahayana path; and third, bodhichitta, the awakened (*bodhi*) heart or mind (*citta*), that aspect of our experience that is not ego bound and that forms the basis of the Mahayana path.

The Mahayana, the basic Buddhist orientation of Tibet, is divided into two major stages, Hinayana, the lesser vehicle, and Mahayana, the great vehicle. In Tibet, Hinayana and Mahayana do not refer to historical traditions but rather to the attitudes with which one carries out spiritual practice. The Hinayana involves a focus on one's own spiritual development, something entirely appropriate in the early phases of one's path, but clearly limited. Mahayana refers to an attitude, an aspiration, and a commitment that focus on the ultimate aim of benefiting all sentient beings. In the Mahayana, one aspires to attain enlightenment in order to be able to help others and lead them to liberation (6.1).

The Mahayana phase of the path is understood to be composed of two aspects, the Sutrayana and the Mantrayana, "the way of mantras," or Vajrayana (6.2). The Sutrayana involves study of the conventional Mahayana sutras and commentaries, and practice of the six *paramitas*, the virtues perfected by the bodhisattva. The Mantrayana, or Vajrayana, involves intensive meditation in which one visualizes oneself as an enlightened being (buddha), practices various forms of esoteric yoga, and trains in the nature of the buddha-mind itself. Hinayana, conventional Mahayana, and Vajrayana were usually practiced in order.

The "great vehicle" is great because we include all other beings in our aspiration and our practice. Nothing is excluded from our practice, whether aspects of our selves or our world—everything is included and used (6.3). This is why renunciation in the Mahayana does not mean leaving the world and abandoning social connections and responsibilities. Rather, it involves a more inner renunciation in which we give up our designs and preconceptions regarding others and aspire to work with them as and where they are (6.4).

The person who practices the Mahayana is the bodhisattva and the next set of passages concern this figure. Within each Mahayana practitioner, each aspiring bodhisattva, there is, as a potentiality, the vast and powerful motivation to benefit and free others. This motivation is the key to the Mahayana path and needs to be awakened in each one of us (6.5). The Mahayana cultivates completely unbiased love and compassion in the bodhisattva so that he or she really comes to care equally and unconditionally for each and every being (6.6). The bodhisattva's insight that all beings suffer and yet desire happiness fuels his or her desire to relieve suffering wherever it occurs (6.7). It is especially the bodhisattva's developing sense of the nonexistence of the self that frees him or her to assist others in whatever situation of distress and sorrow they may be found (6.8).

Tibetan tradition speaks of two different kinds of bodhisattvas—on the one hand, practitioners such as ourselves who are in the process of developing the bodhisattva qualities and, on the other, the high-level, celestial bodhisattvas such as Avalokiteshvara, Manjushri, and Vajrapani, to whom we might pray for assistance along our path (6.9). The two kinds are connected, though, for the high-level bodhisattvas represent our path as it will come to be at a certain, advanced stage.

The next several teachings spell out further aspects of the bodhisattva ideal. An etymology is given of the term *bodhisattva* (6.10). In our own practice, we are encouraged to work with our tendency to retreat from the demands of our bodhisattva commitment (6.11), and emphasis is placed on the importance of the commitment to our own realization

(6.12). Even if we meet people who think and act differently, we still need to help those beings in any way we can (6.13). We are enjoined to fulfill our commitments patiently, not being in a hurry (6.14). And a list of the kinds of prayers we need to say on behalf of others gives us a clear, if daunting, portrait of how selfless the bodhisattva's life needs to be (6.15).

The last set of teachings in this chapter concern bodhichitta, the awakened heart or mind (6.16). Bodhichitta is, precisely, the motivation to become enlightened for the benefit of all (6.17) and it is this that makes a person a bodhisattva (6.18). It is the basic quality that must permeate whatever practice we may do (6.19). Bodhichitta is compassion that has reached its highest level (6.20). It is the one true antidote to our self-importance and self-cherishing and the fount of love and compassion for others (6.21). How does one become a bodhisattva? Simply by generating bodhichitta (6.22).

There are two aspects of bodhichitta, ultimate bodhichitta and relative bodhichitta. Ultimate bodhichitta is related to the mind itself, the wisdom of enlightenment, insight into ultimate reality, the utter emptiness of all things. Relative bodhichitta is the generation and cultivation of compassion, and its expression in words and deeds that help other beings (6.23). In order to reach enlightenment, we need to cultivate both types of bodhichitta (6.24).

Absolute or ultimate bodhichitta is an experience of the ultimate nature of mind itself (6.25). Relative bodhichitta has two aspects, aspiring (wishing) and entering (acting or applying) (6.26). Aspiration means wanting to achieve enlightenment; entering is making the journey (6.27). In the practice, one begins with meditation on relative bodhichitta as it is most accessible (6.28). The practice of relative bodhichitta, which even a beginner can perform, leads naturally to the arising of absolute bodhichitta (6.29).

How are ultimate and relative bodhichitta related to the two central themes of the Mahayana, wisdom and compassion? Ultimate bodhichitta is correlated with wisdom and relative bodhichitta with compassion. Meditation develops our wisdom or ultimate bodhichitta, while engagement with others develops our compassion or relative bodhichitta (6.30). In the Mahayana, wisdom and compassion, meditation and engagement, must work together, like the wings of a bird (6.31). By glimpsing the ultimate nature of mind (absolute bodhichitta, wisdom), the foundation for relative bodhichitta is laid. Practicing relative bodhichitta deepens our understanding of absolute bodhichitta (6.32). Again, only by cultivating wisdom will our compassion be accurate and unbiased (6.33). Bodhichitta has a natural radiance with great positive impact on all who feel it (6.34) and great benefits to everything that we do (6.35, 6.36).

## HINAYANA AND MAHAYANA                                    6.1

Mahayana is usually distinguished from . . . Hinayana, which literally means "small vehicle." Mahayana is the "large vehicle." The basic point here is that a follower of the Hinayana path has embarked upon a path with a very narrow vision or goal, insofar as that particular person wants to achieve enlightenment for himself or herself alone. . . . A Mahayana follower . . . wants to expand his or her vision of spiritual growth . . . [Mahayana followers] perceive their goal not simply as ridding themselves of suffering, but rather as ridding other beings of suffering. . . . We see, then, that Hinayana and Mahayana are not determined by doctrines, schools, or belief systems, but by the internal attitude held by practitioners in regard to their spiritual practice.

*Traleg Kyabgon Rinpoche*

## THE TWO ASPECTS OF MAHAYANA                              6.2

The Mahayana tradition has two aspects: the Sutra tradition of Mahayana and the Tantra tradition of Mahayana.

*Traleg Kyabgon Rinpoche*

## MAHAYANA                                                 6.3

In Sanskrit, *maha* means "great," and *yana* means "way" or "vehicle." The Mahayana is the great vehicle. The Mahayana teaches us how to take the next step of working with others. This is a big undertaking, so we need a great path, a great practice.

The ground of the Mahayana is great; the path is great; and the result is great. Its basis is great because the Mahayana encompasses everything. Nothing is excluded; everything is included. The path—the way we engage in our activity—is great, because we can use everything we've got: our mind, our body, our speech. The fruition is great because as a result of our practice, we can see the depth and profundity of everything.

*Sakyong Mipham Rinpoche*

## In Mahayana, the Attitude Is Most Important 6.4

It is not the world that we have to renounce; it is not that we have to shun all social responsibilities in order to develop spiritually. It is our attitude that is the most important thing. . . . Practitioners of Mahayana mainly emphasize the mind and the attitude that we have toward the world, toward other people, and toward ourselves. If we can have a proper attitude, then whatever we do will become wholesome.

*Traleg Kyabgon Rinpoche*

## The Motivation of the Bodhisattva 6.5

The bodhisattva's motivation . . . is vast, far-reaching, and extremely powerful. Of all the things that one tries to awaken in the mahayana, this motivation is really the key. From the very beginning one tries to develop this very vast and powerful attitude, in which one develops love and compassion along with wisdom that is unbiased and a genuine desire to free everyone from suffering. This approach is the very core of bodhicitta, the driving force of motivation.

*Thrangu Rinpoche*

## The Bodhisattva's Unbiased Love 6.6

The attitude of the bodhisattva, the mahayana practitioner, is not being concerned just for oneself, but feeling the same concern for everyone. The reason a bodhisattva has unbiased love and compassion is that when we identify with a certain group and concentrate on its benefit, there is the danger we might harm others outside the group. Therefore, the mahayana path cultivates a completely unbiased love and compassion, caring equally for every being, including nonhuman beings such as animals.

*Thrangu Rinpoche*

## THE BODHISATTVA'S CONCERN FOR ALL BEINGS    6.7

The attitude of the bodhisattva is to want to help all beings find happiness and to relieve them of all their suffering. The bodhisattva doesn't believe there are some beings who want happiness and others who don't. The bodhisattva doesn't think that there are some who need to be freed from suffering and others who don't need to be freed from suffering. He or she realizes that absolutely all beings need to be helped to attain happiness and all beings need to be liberated from suffering. So the concern is for each and every being.

*Thrangu Rinpoche*

## THE BODHISATTVA'S OUTLOOK    6.8

We are usually so obsessed with ourselves that we hardly ever even think about the welfare of others—in fact, we are not more interested in others than a tiger is interested in eating grass. This is completely the opposite of the outlook of the Bodhisattva. The ego is really just a fabrication of thought, and when you realize that both the object grasped and the mind that grasps are void, it is easy to see that others are not different from yourself. All the energy we normally put into looking after ourselves, Bodhisattvas put into looking after others. If a Bodhisattva sees that by plunging into the fires of hell he can help even a single being, he does it without an instant of hesitation, like a swan entering a cool lake.

*Dilgo Khyentse Rinpoche*

## TWO KINDS OF BODHISATTVAS    6.9

There are two different kinds of Bodhisattvas: the ideal Bodhisattva and the Bodhisattva who aspires to achieve enlightenment. "Ideal Bodhisattvas" are part of the Buddhist pantheon. In Mahayana, unlike in early Buddhism, we have many different images of realized beings, both mythological and real. The mythological Bodhisattvas in particular are seen as models who embody certain qualities of the Bodhisattva. So we talk about Bodhisattvas such as Avalokiteshvara (called Chenrezik in Tibetan), Manjushri, and Vajrapani. . . . The other type of Bodhisattva corresponds to the idea that everyone has the ability to become enlightened, to become a Bodhisattva. . . . The Bodhisattvas who are ideal images already embody all the qualities of the Bodhisattva, or at least some of them. But those who belong to the second type of Bodhisattva need to cultivate the qualities they do not have.

*Traleg Kyabgon Rinpoche*

## THE ETYMOLOGY OF *BODHISATTVA* IN TIBETAN    6.10

In Tibetan, *bodhisattva* is *changchub sempa*. *Changchub* means enlightenment, or buddhahood, because *chang*, the first syllable, means "totally free from all obscurations," totally free from all our emotional disturbances or garbage. The second syllable, *chub*, means "attainment," attaining all the qualities of wisdom; it also means "realization," realizing the wisdom aspect and the compassion quality of our mind. Therefore, *changchub* means enlightenment, which has the quality of being completely free from all the obscurations as well as having attained all the wisdoms. In the second word, *sempa*, *sem* means "heart," or "attitude," referring to the enlightened attitude, enlightened heart, or enlightened aspiration. The last syllable, *pa*, comes from *pawo*, meaning "warrior." *Sempa*, therefore, means "warrior," "heroic," or "the courageous one." We might translate *changchub sempa* as a person who has a brave mind that has been purified and expanded.

*The Dzogchen Pönlop Rinpoche*

## THE BODHISATTVA'S ASPIRATION TO LEAVE
## THE COCOON BEHIND    6.11

What is the point of our life if we are only living comfortably, only just staying in our cocoon? We are born with this thing wrapped around us, and somehow, if it is ripped off us, we create another one, and then we stay in it forever. It is very limited; it's almost like we were never born. We were born from our mother's womb, and for survival reasons, the placenta was ripped away so we could breathe. But then, through self-importance, caring for and protecting the self only, again we wrap it all around ourselves, and then we just stay in this cocoon.

It's almost like we [resist] being in this world. Even just to be in this world seems to be so much of a hassle, so much of a pain, so much of a burden. We sigh every other minute about how hard it is to be in the world, how hard it is just to live this stage of our life. There's isn't a sense of courage; there isn't a sense of embodying anything beyond just the survival level of maintaining our cocoon and trying to be comfortable in that cocoon. This is really what we are mostly used to.

But if one is to embark on the path of enlightenment, the path of bodhisattvas, one very much needs to reconsider how one lives and how one actually dwells in the mind. We *must* challenge ourselves to come out of our cocoon. We *must* be thankful for whatever challenges our cocoon. We *must* begin to develop the greatness and the depth of the bodhisattva's aspiration to leave our cocoon behind.

*Dzigar Kongtrul Rinpoche*

## THE BODHISATTVA'S COMMITMENT                    6.12

One must dedicate one's own life to attaining enlightenment. Only by attaining enlightenment will we be able to guide others, to protect them, to care for them and cherish them. A baby cannot take responsibility for caring for a baby; a child cannot take responsibility for caring for a child. Instead, a baby is brought into adulthood by parents who are adults. In the same way, one must oneself attain enlightenment in order to bring babylike sentient beings to enlightenment.

*Dzigar Kongtrul Rinpoche*

## WHEN THE BODHISATTVA MEETS PEOPLE WHO THINK DIFFERENTLY                    6.13

According to Mahayana Buddhism, when a Bodhisattva meets people who do not share his or her ideas, people who think differently or do things differently, he or she would still try to have an open-minded approach and to communicate in the best way possible to help those beings who may even be hostile.

*Traleg Kyabgon Rinpoche*

## THE BODHISATTVA SHOULD NOT BE IN A HURRY          6.14

The Bodhisattva should not be in a hurry to attain enlightenment. We have the ability to actually postpone our own enlightenment as long as necessary because, as Bodhisattvas, we feel that it is better for others to achieve enlightenment before we do ourselves. We have no sense of urgency and can say, "I will work for the benefit of others; I want others to attain enlightenment before I do."

*Traleg Kyabgon Rinpoche*

## THE BODHISATTVA'S PRAYERS FOR OTHERS 6.15

At all times, again and again, we should make vast prayers for the sake of all beings. When falling asleep we should think, "May all beings achieve the absolute state"; when waking up, "May all beings awake into the enlightened state"; when getting up, "May all beings obtain the body of a Buddha"; when putting on clothes, "May all beings have modesty and a sense of shame"; when lighting a fire, "May all beings burn the wood of disturbing emotions"; when eating, "May all beings eat the food of concentration"; when opening a door, "May all beings open the door to the city of liberation"; when closing a door, "May all beings close the door to the lower realms"; when going outside, "May I set out on the path to free all beings"; when walking uphill, "May I take all beings to the higher realms"; when walking downhill, "May I go to free beings from the lower realms"; when seeing happiness, "May all beings achieve the happiness of Buddhahood"; when seeing suffering, "May the suffering of all beings be pacified."

*Dilgo Khyentse Rinpoche*

## A DEFINITION 6.16

The Sanskrit term *bodhichitta* means "mind of enlightenment," "seed of enlightenment," "awakened heart," or "open heart."

*Sakyong Mipham Rinpoche*

## BODHICHITTA 6.17

Bodhicitta [is] the motivation to become enlightened for the benefit of all living beings.

*Lama Thubten Yeshe Rinpoche and Zopa Rinpoche*

*Lama Zopa Rinpoche*

## BODHICHITTA IS THE GATEWAY 6.18

[Bodhichitta] is the gateway to the Mahayana path, and whoever develops it is worthy of being called the son or daughter of the victorious Buddha.

*Lama Thubten Yeshe Rinpoche and Zopa Rinpoche*


## BODHICHITTA IS FOUNDATIONAL 6.19

With bodhicitta . . . we aim at the target of enlightenment for the benefit of others every moment. . . . Bodhicitta is foundational to all we do, like the root of a medicinal tree whose branches, leaves, and flowers all produce life-enhancing medicine. The quality and purity of our practice depend on its permeating every method we use. With it, everything is assured. Without it, nothing will work.

*Chagdud Tulku Rinpoche*


## WHAT IS THE ESSENCE OF BODHICHITTA? 6.20

What is the essence of bodhichitta? It is actually compassion, but it is compassion that has been developed so much that it has come to the essence of bodhichitta. . . .

When our compassion reaches its highest level, it is called bodhichitta. This is the desire to achieve enlightenment for the sake of all beings. It is the understanding that all beings will end all their suffering when they achieve enlightenment. So once compassion has become complete, it automatically turns into bodhichitta.

*Thrangu Rinpoche*


## BODHICHITTA IS THE ESSENCE OF BUDDHISM 6.21

Bodhichitta is the heart of Buddhism. It is the cure for all ills. Our self-importance and self-cherishing are so deep in all of our hearts. In order to get to the root of that, in order to get to all the deep layers of self-importance and self-cherishing, we need to cultivate bodhichitta. The essence of bodhichitta is to completely replace all of that with a sense of care, a sense of love, a sense of kindness, a sense of compassion toward all mother sentient beings.

*Dzigar Kongtrul Rinpoche*

## HOW DOES ONE BECOME A BODHISATTVA?                    6.22

How does one become a Bodhisattva? There is just one necessary and sufficient condition, which is to generate bodhichitta, or the "heart of enlightenment." *Bodhi* means "enlightenment," and *chitta* means "heart."

*Traleg Kyabgon Rinpoche*

## THE TWO ASPECTS OF BODHICHITTA                       6.23

Bodhichitta also has two aspects, one being the relative aspect and the other being the ultimate aspect. *Ultimate* bodhichitta refers to the nature of the mind itself, or what we call Buddha-nature. *Relative* bodhichitta is the cultivation and generation of compassion.

*Traleg Kyabgon Rinpoche*

## THE TWO TYPES OF BODHICHITTA                          6.24

The two types of bodhicitta are relative bodhicitta, compassion, and ultimate bodhicitta, the insight into emptiness. Unless we connect with the two types of precious bodhicitta, we will not approach enlightenment even in the slightest; this is certain. . . . Dharma practice devoid of these two kinds of bodhicitta will not bring the practitioner even one step toward enlightenment—I will swear to that.

*Tulku Urgyen Rinpoche*

## ULTIMATE BODHICHITTA                                  6.25

Ultimate bodhicitta is a state of mind that dwells unceasingly in being away from all conceptual extremes. It is the realization that the ultimate nature of mind is, and always has been, the source of all the phenomena of samsara and nirvana. Thus ultimate bodhicitta is the state of realization of the ultimate nature of mind. . . . On the ultimate level, bodhicitta is merely a recognition of that ultimate state of mind, not anything more active than that.

*Deshung Rinpoche*

*Deshung Rinpoche*

## THE TWO ASPECTS OF RELATIVE BODHICHITTA     6.26

Relative, or conventional, bodhichitta has two aspects: *mönpa*, aspiring [or wishing], and *jukpa*, entering [or action].

*Sakyong Mipham Rinpoche*

## RELATIVE BODHICHITTA: ASPIRING AND ENTERING (OR ACTION)     6.27

The aspiration aspect of relative Bodhicitta means that there is a wish to achieve enlightenment, just as one might wish to journey to a particular place. The action aspect is like the actual journey to the place desired.

*Khenpo Könchog Gyaltsen*

## ONE BEGINS WITH RELATIVE BODHICHITTA     6.28

There are two aspects of Bodhicitta, the relative and the absolute. One begins with meditating on the relative as it is easily accessible. Within the relative aspect, there are two stages: the aspiration Bodhicitta aspires to Buddhahood while the applied Bodhicitta focuses on the methods of attaining Buddhahood, the six transcendent actions.

*Dilgo Khyentse Rinpoche*

## RELATIVE AND ABSOLUTE BODHICHITTA     6.29

Relative Bodhicitta is practiced on the basis of the ordinary, conceptual mind, and is perfectly possible to accomplish, even for a beginning [student], provided he looks within himself and practices properly. When this relative Bodhicitta has been perfected, moreover, absolute Bodhicitta, the wisdom of Vipashyana, the realization of no-self, arises by itself. This is what the Kagyüpas call Mahamudra and the Nyingmapas call Dzogchen.

*Dilgo Khyentse Rinpoche*

## WISDOM AND COMPASSION     6.30

If one wants to achieve enlightenment, one needs to do it with a two-pronged approach. The two prongs are wisdom and compassion. One can develop wisdom through the practice of meditation, but one cannot develop compassion by simply meditating on compassion. . . . We have to engage ourselves with the world.

*Traleg Kyabgon Rinpoche*

### COMPASSION AND WISDOM GO HAND IN HAND 6.31

Compassion and wisdom go hand in hand. The Mahayana teachings say that compassion and wisdom should be used like the two wings of a bird. If a bird has only one wing, it cannot fly. In a similar way, if we want to stay aloft, we need wisdom and compassion in the spiritual realm. . . . Formal meditation is a solitary journey in which we grapple with our own inner demons and attempt to come to terms with and develop understanding of our own varied psychic forces and states, and this may then lead to the development of wisdom. In order for a spiritual practice to be complete, it must be complemented by compassionate activities in interpersonal situations. In Mahayana Buddhism meditation and activity go hand in hand.

*Traleg Kyabgon Rinpoche*

### HOW ABSOLUTE BODHICHITTA AND RELATIVE BODHICHITTA SUPPORT EACH OTHER 6.32

The absolute bodhicitta is the inseparability of voidness and uncontrived compassion. It is the simplicity of the nature state which spontaneously benefits sentient beings. Having glimpsed one's mind as such provides the proper perspective for beginning to practice the relative bodhicitta and, in turn, the relative bodhicitta deepens and matures one's understanding of the absolute bodhicitta.

*Dilgo Khyentse Rinpoche*

### WHY DOES COMPASSION NEED TO BE COMPLEMENTED BY WISDOM? 6.33

It is only through developing proper wisdom that we will be able to have compassion and do things for others in a way that is not partial. It does not take very much for us to be compassionate in a partial way.

For instance, we can easily feel compassion toward people whom we like or animals that we cherish. But ideally, from the Mahayana Buddhist point of view, we should aim higher; our compassion should extend even beyond our own dear ones, and that can only be done through wisdom. If wisdom is not present in compassion, compassion can become degenerated and polluted, owing to our selfishness, sentimentality, or need.

*Traleg Kyabgon Rinpoche*

## THE NATURAL RADIANCE OF BODHICHITTA                   6.34

Bodhicitta is very beneficial for oneself and for all others. So, when someone has bodhicitta, whatever he or she does is like medicine or healing nectar which brings calmness, peace, and coolness. . . . Take the supreme example of bodhicitta: when the Buddha taught, he led a very simple life and everything happened spontaneously around him. . . . There is the natural radiance of bodhicitta and the activity of the Buddha, which through his very pure mind allow the dharma and its meaning to spread from one person to another in a very spontaneous and natural way.

*Thrangu Rinpoche*

## THE GREAT BENEFITS OF BODHICHITTA                      6.35

The greatest benefits of bodhicitta appear in terms of our actual dharma practice. Every spiritual action we perform becomes more powerful and effective when done with an enlightened motive—if we dedicate it toward our attainment of enlightenment for the sake of others. . . . For example, it is said that giving a handful of food to a dog, if done with bodhicitta, brings us more benefit than giving a universe of jewels to every living being without such a motivation. Thus it is not the material of our offerings, or the status of the recipient, or even the specific practice we follow that determines how far or fast we progress along our path. Rather, as with everything else, it is our state of mind that is of primary importance. As bodhicitta is the highest possible motivation, it empowers our actions to a far greater extent than our ordinary selfish impulses.

*Lama Thubten Yeshe Rinpoche and Zopa Rinpoche*

## Bodhichitta Generates the Qualities of Buddhahood

6.36

The Buddha in one of his teachings said, "Noble sons and daughters, the seed that gives birth to all the qualities of the Buddhas is bodhicitta." Bodhicitta can give birth to those qualities both in oneself and in others. It is not just a tiny seed that will give birth to one fruit, but it is an extraordinary seed that will bear billions and billions of fruits. Bodhicitta will generate the qualities of Buddhahood for oneself and others. These are the great benefits of bodhicitta, and becoming aware of them, we will try to develop this noble state of mind.

*Thrangu Rinpoche*

# → 7

# The View of Mahayana

LIKE THE HINAYANA, the Mahayana phase of the path rests upon a particular philosophical perspective or "view." Just as the view of Hinayana is defined by the first turning of the wheel of dharma, the view of Mahayana is defined by the second and third turnings. In the second turning of the wheel, at Rajagriha, the Buddha preached the Prajnaparamita Sutras, or sutras on the perfection of wisdom. These sutras articulate his teachings on emptiness, or *shunyata,* as the ultimate nature of all things. In the third turning of the wheel, the Buddha taught various sutras on buddha-nature, the pristine wisdom of an awakened one that resides at the heart of all beings. Our passages on the Mahayana view are accordingly divided into two sections expressing, first, the Mahayana teachings on emptiness and, second, those on buddha-nature.

## EMPTINESS

The Buddha's teachings on emptiness, given in the second turning of the wheel of dharma in the Prajnaparamita Sutras, articulate the ultimate nature of reality. Originally not understood by most of his followers, they were later propagated by the master Nagarjuna (7.1). Out of Nagarjuna's teachings, the Madhyamaka, the doctrine of the middle way, developed as the most important Mahayana philosophical school in India, Tibet, and elsewhere. Within Tibetan Buddhism, emptiness is regarded as the ultimate and final nature of reality, and an understanding of it is considered indispensable both for a correct understanding of the Mahayana and for the practice of Vajrayana.

The core teaching of Nagarjuna is that all things are ultimately devoid of any fixed or substantial self. Anything that we may experience is lacking in any definitive quality or characteristic that makes it one thing and not another. In the classical terminology, it lacks a *svabhava*, a self-nature or inherent essence. All things are empty in the specific sense that they lack this inherent character or essence.

This teaching seems to fly in the face of our normal experience. It certainly *seems* that everything we experience has some kind of inherent characteristic, identity, or objectifiable essence that enables us to recognize it, label it, think about it, and relate with it. Nagarjuna would agree that this is certainly the way things *appear* to be. This level of apparent reality is called "relative truth" in his thought. On a relative level, it certainly is either day or night and, if someone tells us during the day that it is night, we would quite rightly say that he is mistaken. But, Nagarjuna would argue, this is not in fact how things ultimately are, in and of themselves. In other words, the identity or essence that we seem to find in the objects of our experience does not exist inherently within the object, in and of itself. Rather, it represents something that we project—in the form of a mental projection—onto the object (7.2).

The attribution of "self nature" to our experiences is a problem because we don't realize that we are doing it. When we see something as being a certain thing and we experience it in our preconception, we think we are experiencing the thing itself. We think we are in touch with reality and this makes us feel confident and secure in our view. But it is just our own version of things. Sometimes we find out how self-serving and one-sided our view can be when we suddenly find it challenged by something that happens and we discover ourselves stubbornly hanging on to our own version—even in the face of evidence contradicting our view. It is an interesting question why we are so resistant to realizing emptiness. Mahayana thought identifies two kinds of obstacles that hinder us from seeing emptiness: acquired cultural habits of thinking and the innate human tendency to attribute a fixed essence to experience (7.3).

Nagarjuna did not just state that phenomena are empty of essence. He also employed a variety of ways to show us how and why this is so. One of the most clear and compelling is his teaching on interdependent origination (7.4). This is the teaching that all phenomena arise based on causes and conditions, and it is, of course, a fundamental doctrine in earliest Buddhism. In Nagarjuna's hands, however, it became a potent vehicle for illustrating the principle of emptiness.

We tend to assume that things are independent in the sense of standing on their own and having a fixed identity. However, no phenomenon can exist on its own. If we consider carefully, we can see that everything depends for its existence on many causes and conditions (7.5). When we see the play of causes and conditions, we see that nothing is solid, as it seems, but is, rather, empty (7.6, 7.7).

The equation of interdependent origination with emptiness reveals an important point: the teaching on emptiness is not nihilistic; emptiness is not a mere void, blank, or black hole. Instead, the emptiness of things means that phenomena do appear, but they do so as relational appearances, a fruition of causes and conditions, rather than the expression of a substantial self (7.8, 7.9). Seen in this light, emptiness is the essence and final reality of the colorful, myriad phenomena of the relative world. More than this, we are led to an understanding of emptiness, ultimate truth, not by ignoring or abandoning the relative truth of our everyday world, but rather by deeply contemplating it. This brings us to the heart of Nagarjuna's argument, that ultimate truth and relative truth do not inhabit two different planes or spheres of existence. Rather, emptiness is the ultimate truth of the apparently solid, objective world of our everyday experience (7.10).

A correct understanding of emptiness, then, does not imply nihilism. However, it is quite possible to misunderstand the teachings and in this case we will experience serious problems (7.11). In addition, if we do not understand emptiness properly, we can remain in a conceptualized version of compassion, and then our attempt to help others will backfire (7.12).

A conviction in emptiness can be arrived at through intellectual analysis, as we have just seen. But one can also come to an understanding of emptiness through direct experience. Of course, within the Mahayana tradition, it is said that an unmediated experience of emptiness does not occur until the bodhisattva is well advanced and, in fact, until he or she has reached the lofty attainment of the first *bhumi,* or stage of awakening. Nevertheless, it is possible for us to have glimpses of emptiness and, in fact, the experience of emptiness underlies everything we go through (7.13) and manifests itself in the sense of groundlessness that we often feel in our lives (7.14).

Although emptiness is not "something," nevertheless, it has definite impacts and fruitions. Most important, a realization of emptiness is itself wisdom (7.15). Beyond this, understanding emptiness, far from leading to a rejection of the world, makes the bodhisattva's full engagement with the world possible (7.16). And the wisdom of emptiness can be most useful in a practical way. For example—as we shall see further below—the way to overcome defiling emotions is by realizing their emptiness (7.17). More of this practical implication is revealed in a helpful anecdote told by Dzongsar Khyentse Rinpoche of an interaction with his grandfather, Khyentse Rinpoche, the gist of which is that both praise and blame are ultimately empty (7.18). At the upper limits of the path, emptiness takes on the aspect of fruition, as complete identification with the phenomenal world (7.19) and as the mind of the buddhas (7.20).

## NAGARJUNA'S CONTRIBUTION                                    7.1
The Buddha gave the profound teachings on the Perfection of Wisdom (Prajnaparamita in Sanskrit) [the teachings on emptiness], but most of his followers did not understand these teachings at the time. About 500 years later, these teachings were thoroughly understood by the great master Nagarjuna. He understood the Prajnaparamita remarkably clearly, not just from the level of intellectual understanding but from actual experience. Nagarjuna was able to present these teachings thoroughly and completely through logical arguments.

*Thrangu Rinpoche*

## ALL PHENOMENA ARE EMPTY                                     7.2
When we say "all," that means everything, including the Buddha, enlightenment, and the path. Buddhists define a phenomenon as something

with characteristics, and as an object that is conceived by a subject. To hold that an object is something external is ignorance, and it is this that prevents us from seeing the truth of that object.

The truth of a phenomenon is called *shunyata*, emptiness, which implies that the phenomenon does not possess a truly existent essence or nature. When a deluded person or subject sees something, the object seen is interpreted as something really existent. However, as you can see, the existence imputed by the subject is a mistaken assumption. Such an assumption is based on the different conditions that make an object appear to be true; this, however, is not how the object really is. It's like when we see a mirage: there is no truly existing object there, even though it appears that way. With emptiness, the Buddha meant that things do not truly exist as we mistakenly believe they do, and that they are really empty of that falsely imputed existence.

*Dzongsar Khytense Rinpoche*

## WHAT BLOCKS US FROM UNDERSTANDING EMPTINESS?                                                    7.3

There are two things blocking or hindering us from appreciating [emptiness]; the first obstacle is acquired and the other is innate. The acquired obstacle is that of education and cultural or religious accretions. I don't want to use the word "brainwashing," although that immediately comes to mind. We have been inculcated in a particular way so that we do not stop to evaluate the truth of what we have absorbed through education and through certain familiar concepts. We fail to examine; we just accept things as fact whether they are true or not. . . . The other obstacle is innate, which means within the human condition there is an instinctive belief that things do have an enduring essence.

*Traleg Kyabgon Rinpoche*

## INTERDEPENDENT ORIGINATION IS EMPTINESS                            7.4

Nagarjuna said that emptiness is interdependent origination and interdependent origination is emptiness. So when we say that things are interdependently produced, or that things come into being through the interdependence of causes and conditions, it is the same as saying things are empty by nature.

*Traleg Kyabgon Rinpoche*

## How Nagarjuna Shows Emptiness 7.5

[Nagarjuna] shows that all phenomena we experience—each and every phenomenon—only exist through dependence upon other things and that no phenomenon has an essential existence of its own. Through demonstrating that things merely exist relatively, he showed that they are devoid of an ultimate nature. This is one of the . . . main ways in which Nagarjuna presented emptiness, in reliance on an understanding of interdependent origination.

*Thrangu Rinpoche*

## How an Understanding of Interdependence Leads to Realizing Emptiness 7.6

Understanding that all things that manifest to our mind are interdependent means that we can begin to understand the ultimate truth. This happens because, by studying the way things appear through the play of interdependence, we begin to realize that nothing is as solid, as real, as concrete, as it seems to be. In fact, things manifest as what they really are, which is empty.

*Thrangu Rinpoche*

## The Interdependence of Phenomena Reveals Their Emptiness 7.7

The Tibetan word for "conventional reality" is *kunzop*, meaning literally "totally artificial or fake." Everything is a fabrication and its very nature depends upon the components out of which it is fabricated. No phenomenon can exist on its own. All things depend upon other things for the nature they take on at a particular time. By understanding interdependence we can also come to understand that all things are empty, in that they are devoid of any lasting reality.

*Thrangu Rinpoche*

## EMPTINESS IS INTERDEPENDENT ORIGINATION                    7.8

All phenomena are empty. This emptiness, however, does not mean that phenomena are completely nonexistent. It is not a blankness of everything. What it means is that all things depend upon one another for their manifestation because they are interrelated. . . . All the various outer things are related and rest upon one another. Yet, when one looks for the "things" properly and thoroughly, one finds an emptiness; they simply don't exist in those terms.

For instance, if I take a two-inch and a four-inch stick of incense, the four-inch stick is the longer one and the two-inch stick is the shorter one. If I show this to a hundred persons and ask, "Which one is the longer one?" they would all say that the four-inch stick was definitely the longer one. Then when I add a six-inch stick and remove the two-inch stick, the four-inch stick becomes the shorter one. . . . So I can't really say "this is long"or "this is short" without seeing the interrelationship of the two. There is the relative definition of things and that definition depends upon other factors to which the thing is related. Things depend upon one another; they are interdependent; and this is the way all phenomena manifest to us. They don't have a meaning and significance by themselves; their significance emerges because of their relationship to other things. . . .

It is not that there is an absolute quality permanently engraved into the object. . . . Because of interdependence in the relative world, there is this manifestation of these various relative qualities. Yet, when we examine them closely, there is nothing of an absolute value to be found in them. If we look for the absolute quality of beauty, edibility, or, as we saw with the sticks, the absolute quality of longness or shortness, bigness or smallness, etc., these qualities cannot be found.

In the relative world, things continue to manifest to us, even though there is absolute emptiness. This means that suffering and all things happen on a relative level. Yet, when we really search, we can never find the suffering, only the emptiness of suffering.

*Thrangu Rinpoche*


## SOME EXAMPLES OF EMPTINESS                    7.9

Take, for example, good and bad: some things are good compared to others, and vice versa. The same is true for beautiful and ugly, here and there, self and other. In all cases, the value assigned to something is only a relative value that depends upon other things for its meaning. So something is "only" beautiful because in one set of relative values it is "more" beautiful than some other things, but when compared to something else it may be ugly. The point is that nothing is beautiful, nothing is long, nothing is bad in itself; they are beautiful, long, or bad in a relative sense.

On a conventional level, things have a particular value. But, from an ultimate point of view, we cannot say that this "thing" is once and forever ugly or long, or that once and forever [it is] over there and not over here. By examining such logical arguments, we can examine things in a gross way to get some understanding of the relative interplay and the ultimate emptiness of phenomena. Therefore, in the sutra method of teaching, emptiness is presented by way of this logical reasoning.

*Thrangu Rinpoche*


## Ultimate Truth Is Reached by Understanding the Relative
7.10

In Madhyamaka philosophy, ultimate reality is not seen as something that exists outside of or above the empirical reality with which we are confronted every day. Rather, emptiness is the nature of the very world that we live in. . . . Nagarjuna makes the point that it is through an understanding of relative truth that we can come to have some understanding of absolute truth. . . . In fact, the ultimate is understood only through an understanding of the relative, because ultimate truth is, in fact, the nature of the relative.

*Traleg Kyabgon Rinpoche*


## A Correct Understanding of Emptiness Does Not Lead to Nihilism
7.11

There is another kind of a problem that arises from not understanding emptiness. It occurs with rather superficial and even jaded Buddhists. Somehow, within Buddhist circles, if you don't accept emptiness, you are not cool. So we pretend that we appreciate emptiness and pretend to meditate on it. But if we don't understand it properly, a bad side

*Traleg Kyabgon Rinpoche*

effect can occur. We might say, "Oh, everything's emptiness. I can do whatever I like." So we ignore and violate the details of karma, the responsibility for our action. We become "inelegant," and we discourage others in the bargain. His Holiness the Dalai Lama often speaks of this downfall of not understanding emptiness. A correct understanding of emptiness leads us to see how things are related, and how we are responsible for our world.

*Dzongsar Khytense Rinpoche*

## WITHOUT AN UNDERSTANDING OF EMPTINESS, OUR COMPASSION CAN BACKFIRE                                    7.12

As Buddhists we practice compassion, but if we lack an understanding of this third seal—that all phenomena are empty—our compassion can backfire. If you are attached to the goal of compassion when trying to solve a problem, you might not notice that your idea of the solution is entirely based on your own personal interpretation. And you might end up as a victim of hope and fear, and consequently of disappointment. You start by becoming a "good mahayana practitioner," and, once or twice, you try to help sentient beings. But if you have no understanding of this third seal, you'll get tired and give up helping sentient beings.

*Dzongsar Khytense Rinpoche*

## SENSING EMPTINESS                                          7.13

Emptiness is the sense of moving through life looking for something that, through our wisdom—*yeshe*—we know is somehow not there. We experience it as a feeling that something's always missing. We want to find something that feels good and makes sense, a real and solid reference point, and we keep looking, even though we know that we're never going to be quite satisfied.

To understand the profound teachings on emptiness, we have to relate to them not only in our meditation practice, but also in our everyday experience. If we eat an apple, though our stomach might feel full, we still feel like something is missing. Our experience of emptiness doesn't always have to be negative. Even when we have great happiness, there's a quality of intangibility, as if we're trying to hold on to a slippery watermelon seed.

*Sakyong Mipham Rinpoche*

## A TERRIFYING PROSPECT 7.14

It is obviously a terrifying prospect that . . . you cannot have ground to struggle with, that all the ground is being taken away from you. The carpet is pulled out from under your feet. You are suspended nowhere—which generally happens anywhere, whether we acknowledge it as it actually happens or not. . . . You are suspended in nowhere. That's the *shunyata* experience. No ground to walk on, no ground to work with. You have no function. . . . As far as the ground of *shunyata* is concerned, there is no warmth. It is an unkind world, uncompassionate, ruthless. I think you have to give up hope; it's a hopeless situation.

*Chögyam Trungpa Rinpoche*

## WISDOM 7.15

Wisdom . . . comes from understanding that the self and others are not separate, because everything is interdependent: mind, matter, organic, inorganic—everything that exists in the world is interdependent, and therefore nothing has substantiality. . . . Everything is interdependent, nothing has self-existence or autonomous status; this is what is meant by emptiness (*shunyata*). Wisdom comes from this realization.

*Traleg Kyabgon Rinpoche*

## UNDERSTANDING EMPTINESS MAKES THE BODHISATTVA'S WORK POSSIBLE 7.16

Through understanding emptiness one is able to overcome attachment, clinging, and grasping. The Bodhisattva seeks to overcome attachment, not so as to become detached or indifferent to the world, but in order to get even more involved with the world. There is no longer that duality existing between the Bodhisattva and others—between the self and the world—because the self and the world both have the same nature, which is emptiness. Therefore, Bodhisattvas are able to execute their compassionate activities in a much more beneficial and far-ranging manner.

*Traleg Kyabgon Rinpoche*

## HATRED ITSELF IS THE ONLY ENEMY                    7.17

Instead of allowing wild thoughts to enslave you, realize their essential emptiness. If you subdue the hatred within, you will discover that there is not a single enemy left outside. Otherwise, even if you could over-power everyone in the whole world, your hatred would only grow stronger. Indulging it will never make it subside. The only truly intoler-able enemy is hatred itself. Examine the nature of hatred. You will find that it is no more than a thought. When you see it as it is, it will dissolve like a cloud in the sky.

*Dilgo Khyentse Rinpoche*

## BEYOND PRAISE AND BLAME                    7.18

I remember something His Holiness Dilgo Khyentse once told me. I used to be very wild, and sometimes people would report my actions to him in hope that he would scold me and discipline me. But instead, he would tell me who it was who told on me and would make a game of it. He used to say, "Don't worry. You must remember that whenever there is one person out there who doesn't like you or who thinks you are crazy, there will be a hundred people who are going to like you. And similarly, whenever there is one person who likes you, you shouldn't get too excited about it, because there will be a hundred people who can't stand you." So liking and disliking are completely irrelevant.

*Dzongsar Khytense Rinpoche*

## THE REAL DEFINITION OF SHUNYATA                    7.19

The real definition of *shunyata* is awareness without choice, or aware-ness that contains no experience. That is why *shunyata* is described as full and empty at the same time. Emptiness here does not mean seeing everything as just energy, so that you could walk through tables and chairs. Rather you begin to see yourself as tables and chairs or rocks and sky and water. You begin to identify with the phenomenal world completely. Your existence is one of those phenomena, so everything is transparent and fluid. There is a sense of uniformity, sameness. At the same time there is a sense of difference.

*Chögyam Trungpa Rinpoche*

## EMPTINESS IS THE MIND OF THE BUDDHA                7.20

When sunlight falls on a crystal, lights of all colors of the rainbow appear; yet they have no substance that you can grasp. Likewise, all thoughts in their infinite variety—devotion, compassion, harmfulness, desire—are utterly without substance. This is the mind of the Buddha. There is no thought that is something other than voidness; if you recognize the void nature of thoughts at the very moment they arise, they will dissolve. Attachment and hatred will never be able to disturb the mind. Deluded emotions will collapse by themselves. No negative actions will be accumulated, so no suffering will follow.

*Dilgo Khyentse Rinpoche*

## BUDDHA-NATURE

The Buddha gave two major cycles of Mahayana teaching. In the second turning of the wheel of dharma he taught emptiness, and in the third turning he explained the buddha-nature, the idea that all sentient beings possess within them the potentiality of enlightenment. While both second and third turnings concern the "view" of Mahayana, they do so in slightly different ways. The second turning addresses how we should think (or rather how we should not think) about ultimate reality. By contrast, the third turning is immediately applicable to the path: it shows us that because all possess buddha-nature, buddhahood is within the reach of everyone (7.21, 7.22). Moreover, everyone's buddha-nature is the very same, without distinction (7.23).

Buddha-nature is the foundation of our being. In fact, this same foundation nature exists in all beings. However, it is covered over and obscured by defilements. Because it is our essence and foundation, we can remove these obscurations through practice (7.24). This buddha-nature is the essence of enlightenment. Therefore we can say that the enlightenment of the buddhas is not something new, but has been in us from the very beginning, just waiting to be discovered (7.25).

Within the buddha-nature are the enlightened body, speech, and mind of a buddha, which are the buddha's three bodies, *nirmanakaya* (*vajra* body), *samghogakaya* (*vajra* speech), and *dharmakaya* (*vajra* mind). This somewhat technical way of speaking is telling us that the complete enlightenment of a fully awakened buddha is not somewhere else in another sphere or at the end of some interminable journey, but rather is dwelling within us right now, at this very moment, in its complete form (7.26). In addition, our ordinary human qualities arise in a temporary way as manifestations of our enlightened nature (7.27). But we don't realize this. Instead, we stubbornly see ourselves as impure beings, and we think of ourselves and pity ourselves as defiled. However, realizing our buddha-nature is a way to cut off such negative, self-deprecating thinking (7.28).

It is precisely because we don't realize our buddha-nature that we invest our "self" and the objective world with solid, substantial reality and then cling to our creations. It is this entire process that needs purification (7.29). The buddha-nature is like the clear sky and our habitual thinking is like clouds that obscure the sky (7.30). The buddha-nature is beyond words and concepts (7.31). In this sense, it is utterly empty, signless, and wishless (7.32). It is beyond one or many (7.33). It is voidness and clarity inseparable (7.34). And it is not something purely internal, for all phenomena appear within it (7.35).

Within Tibetan tradition, the buddha-nature has been the subject of much philosophical thinking and analysis. Given next are the three traditional proofs of buddha-nature (7.36), the three different levels of defilement among beings (7.37), its inherent qualities (7.38), and the four qualities of its fruition (7.39). This chapter concludes with a reminder that it is not enough just to have the buddha-nature; we must cultivate it through practice (7.40).

The teachings on buddha nature are of special importance in Tibet and particularly within those lineages that emphasize practice. The reason is that the third turning of the wheel of dharma, expounding buddha-nature, has an especially close connection with the third *yana*, the

Vajrayana. In fact, doctrine of buddha-nature provides the necessary foundation for tantric practice. As we shall see, in the Vajrayana, the teacher introduces the student to a direct experience of his or her own buddha-nature. Then, through the various tantric practices, the student's obscurations are purified and that initial experience is deepened and expanded. The entire Vajrayana path is, then, nothing other than making the acquaintance with the buddha-nature and working to develop one's relationship with it.

## THE THIRD TURNING OF THE WHEEL OF DHARMA          7.21
In the third turning, the Buddha revealed the ultimate nature of phenomena by showing that this voidness [taught in the second turning] was not a total absence, a total emptiness of everything, but has qualities of the ultimate nature of phenomena. These teachings also show that all beings possess the essence of the Buddha. If they work on the path, they will be able to develop the perfect knowledge of a Buddha.

*Thrangu Rinpoche*

## YOUR NATURE IS GOOD          7.22
According to Buddhism, the nature of the mind [the buddha-nature] is enlightened. So your nature is good. The big problem is the negative habits of the mind, how you look at everything. These mental patterns [the defilements] can get quite built up and rigid, and they color and influence your perspective.

*Tulku Thondup Rinpoche*

## BUDDHA-NATURE IS PRESENT IN ALL WITHOUT
## ANY DISTINCTION          7.23
This essence of Buddhahood is present in all beings without any distinction, which means that whoever practices can realize and reach Buddhahood. There is no difference between a man and a woman, or [between] races or social classes, or anything else, because everyone has this essence of enlightenment.

*Thrangu Rinpoche*

Photo by Nancy Dyer Mitton.

*Tulku Thondup Rinpoche*

## THE FOUNDATION OF OUR BEING                    7.24

The foundational nature of the mind is already gold; we simply don't recognize it as such. The goal of the spiritual path is complete realization of the gold; the path is how we accomplish that goal, making obvious what already exists.

*Chagdud Tulku Rinpoche*


## BUDDHA-NATURE AND ENLIGHTENMENT                7.25

Enlightenment is not anything new or something we create or bring into existence. It is simply discovering within us what is already there. It is the full realization of our intrinsic nature. In Tibetan, *buddha* is *sang gyay*. *Sang* means that all of the faults have been cleared away, while *gyay* means "full realization"; just as from darkness, the moon waxes, likewise from ignorance, the qualities of the mind's intrinsic nature emerge.

Like water, which is fluid in its natural state but turns to ice when frozen, the true nature of mind . . . seems different when obscured by confusion and delusion. But that nature hasn't gone anywhere, just as the water hasn't gone anywhere. When the ice melts, the water regains its natural qualities. When mind's obscurations are removed, our nature becomes apparent.

*Chagdud Tulku Rinpoche*


## THE THREE KAYAS ARE PRESENT IN OUR
## BUDDHA-NATURE                                  7.26

Intrinsic to our buddha nature are qualities called the three *kayas,* or the innate body, speech, and mind, also known as the three *vajras*. The *vajra* body is the unchanging quality of the buddha nature; the *vajra* speech is its inexpressible, unceasing quality; and the *vajra* mind is its unmistaken quality. In this way the *vajra* body, *vajra* speech, and *vajra* mind are inherently present as our buddha nature . . . the three *kayas* are inherently present, indivisibly, in our buddha nature.

*Tulku Urgyen Rinpoche*

ENLIGHTENED QUALITIES ARE OUR BASIS                7.27

The ordinary body, speech, and mind of sentient beings temporarily rose from the expression of the qualities of enlightened body, speech, and mind.

*Tulku Urgyen Rinpoche*

WE SEE OURSELVES AS IMPURE                7.28

We project impurity upon the pure. "I was born with impurities, I am impure now, I will die impure and end up in hell." Even if we don't consciously think this, it is there inside us. We believe we are fundamentally impure. "How can I be pure?" our self-pity mind thinks. We must rid ourselves of this idea, which is the cause of all our diseases of body and mind. . . . The nondual nature of our mind has always been pure, is pure now, and will always be pure. What we call impurities are the superficial clouds of ego that come and go. . . . They can be removed. . . . Realizing this cuts off the self-pity ego.

*Lama Thubten Yeshe Rinpoche*

BECAUSE WE DON'T RECOGNIZE THE
BUDDHA-NATURE                7.29

Because we don't recognize our essential nature—we don't realize that although appearances arise unceasingly, nothing is really there—we invest with solidity and reality the seeming truth of self, other, and actions between self and others. This intellectual obscuration gives rise to attachment and aversion, followed by actions and reactions that create karma, solidify into habit, and perpetuate the cycles of suffering. This entire process needs to be purified.

*Chagdud Tulku Rinpoche*

THE BUDDHA-NATURE AND THAT WHICH
OBSCURES IT                7.30

The qualities of buddhahood pervade all beings just as oil pervades a sesame seed. These qualities have always been there, complete and never-changing, as the naturally radiant expression of the absolute nature. In that sense, it can be said that all the qualities of nirvana are completely present throughout samsara, the realm of suffering and delusion, as well.

What is the relationship between the phenomena of delusion and those of enlightenment? Consider the clouds in the sky. When clouds form, they do so thanks to the sky. Yet the sky never changes; clouds manifest within it, and then, when they are dispersed by the wind, the sky reappears just as it has always been. In the same way, no phenomena, even those of samsara, are ever relinquished by the enlightened nature of nirvana. They manifest within that enlightened nature but do not modify it in any way.

Are the phenomena of enlightenment, therefore, also permeated by the phenomena of delusion? No, they are not, because the absolute nature never changes. It cannot be affected by any amount of delusion. So, we can say that the phenomena of delusion are never other than the absolute nature, yet the absolute nature does not contain the phenomena of delusion. The buddha nature is present in delusion, but delusion is not present in the buddha nature.

*Dilgo Khyentse Rinpoche*

## THE BUDDHA-NATURE IS BEYOND WORDS
## AND CONCEPTS                                              7.31

It doesn't help much to talk about it. It's better just to drop our hope and fear, let the mind rest, and allow the experience of that which is beyond concepts to arise. It's not a dull or sleepy state, not like being in a coma. The Buddha said that our true nature simply is; there are no words for it. If you have words to explain it, you're relying on concepts and you've lost it. The truth is so close, yet we don't recognize it.

Like the horse that never left the stable, our true nature is not somewhere else; it's just that our concepts and the mind's poisons prevent us from recognizing it. As these are purified, we can realize our nature directly, just as it is.

A person who has never tasted sugar might ask someone else what it's like. The reply will probably be, "It's very sweet." But what is "sweet"? There really is no way to explain it—you have to taste it for yourself. In the same way, the direct experience of our true nature can't be explained in words.

*Chagdud Tulku Rinpoche*

## THE BUDDHA-NATURE IS COMPLETELY EMPTY 7.32
This essence, from beginningless time, is completely substanceless, empty. Although we might try to find characteristics by which to define and understand emptiness, it can't be conceived by ordinary concepts. It is thus without sign or character. We need nothing more than to maintain recognition of our essential nature in order for the fruit—the full qualities, the complete realization—to be revealed. What we reveal is not beyond this nature, and in that sense is beyond wishing. There is nothing outside, nothing elsewhere to aspire to in order for this to happen, so it is beyond wishing or aspiration.

*Chagdud Tulku Rinpoche*

## IS BUDDHA-NATURE ONE OR MANY? 7.33
I'll say "many" because it's closer to the truth. If there were only one horse and only one person had it, the implication would be that others didn't have it. Yet all beings have buddha nature. However, if one person gains complete realization of his or her true nature, this doesn't mean that everyone becomes enlightened. Similarly, one being might have a hellish existence, but not all beings do. So we can't really say it's just one.

But if we think there are many horses, we start seeing differences such as big horses or small, horses so many hands high, and so on. Yet there is no way to measure our nature, for emptiness has no boundaries. In this sense you could say we're speaking of one horse. But ultimately you can't say that there is just one horse or that there are many. . . . The truth is really beyond "one" or "many."

*Chagdud Tulku Rinpoche*

## THE BUDDHA-NATURE: VOIDNESS AND CLARITY
## INSEPARABLE 7.34
The absence of a "self" is voidness (*shunyata*), but this voidness is not to be misunderstood as blankness, a complete emptiness. It is not like

empty space because empty space is frozen and no change can manifest from it. *Shunyata* has a different quality. This voidness is by nature clarity (Tib. *salwa*). Having the nature of clarity means that when beings are still impure, all the various appearances of phenomena can manifest with this clarity. When individuals have eliminated their impurities Buddhahood is manifested in clarity. Within this clarity the forms (Skt. *kayas*) of the Buddha and the activity of the Buddha can manifest. So this voidness is full of all these possibilities. . . . So clarity and emptiness are completely united, and the union of these two is the essence of all Buddhas and is present within the mind of all beings. If one can realize the unity of clarity and voidness, one can reach Buddhahood.

*Thrangu Rinpoche*

## THE WHOLE WORLD APPEARS WITHIN THE
## BUDDHA-NATURE                                      7.35
Just as the whole world, with its mountains, continents, and everything else, exists within infinite space, so too do all phenomena appear within the buddha nature.

*Dilgo Khyentse Rinpoche*

## THREE TRADITIONAL "PROOFS" FOR
## BUDDHA-NATURE                                      7.36
There are three reasons for buddha nature being present in all beings. First, the *dharmakaya* of the Buddha pervades all phenomena and can give rise to any phenomena, so it is present everywhere. Second, the suchness or the actual nature of nirvana and samsaric phenomena is undifferentiated, so there's no "good suchness" which relates to nirvana and no "bad suchness" which relates to samsara. There is only one suchness of all phenomena. Third, all beings possess the foundation for buddha nature and when purified it can develop into full Buddhahood.

*Thrangu Rinpoche*

## THE THREE STAGES OF DEFILEMENT              7.37
The reason one does not realize the essence of enlightenment [the buddha-nature] is that it is obscured by defilements. One can distinguish

three stages of defilements. In the impure phase, the stage of ordinary beings, buddha nature is totally obscured by defilements. In the second phase, of the bodhisattvas, the impurities are slightly purified with the obscurations partly removed. Finally, in the phase of total purity, one is a Buddha.

*Thrangu Rinpoche*

## THE QUALITIES POSSESSED BY THE
## BUDDHA-NATURE                                               7.38

Buddha nature can be compared to the ocean because the ocean contains many precious things. In the same way, buddha nature has the potential for achieving Buddhahood because it already has all the various qualities of Buddhahood. These qualities are the qualities of the body of the Buddha and the qualities required on the path to Buddhahood such as faith, courage, *prajna*, and so on.

*Thrangu Rinpoche*

## THE FOUR QUALITIES OF THE FRUITION OF
## BUDDHA-NATURE                                               7.39

Fruition . . . occurs when buddha nature has completely manifested. . . .

The fruition of buddha nature has the transcendental qualities of purity, identity, happiness, and permanence. Complete purity is achieved when Buddhahood is achieved. When one is beyond self and non-self, one achieves the transcendent quality of identity. There is also the quality of transcendental happiness and permanence at the time of fruition. . . .

The quality of transcendental purity is beyond pure and impure. . . . The purity of buddha nature is . . . extremely pure and complete; it is masked just by impurities. It is transcendental purity because when these fleeting impurities have been removed, the purity is complete. . . . The second quality is the transcendental quality of identity. . . . Transcendental identity corresponds to the complete pacification and disappearance of all illusory fabrications of the idea of a self or non-self. . . . The third quality is the transcendental quality of happiness. . . . The ultimate nature is beyond both the idea of suffering and the idea of happiness, and this is transcendental happiness. . . . The fourth quality is transcendental permanence. . . . The actual nature of things is beyond the ideas of permanence and impermanence; it is transcendental permanence because the whole of samsara and nirvana is identical and the qualities inherent in nirvana are already present in samsara. This permanence should be understood in terms of no change because everything is identical.

*Thrangu Rinpoche*

## IT IS NOT ENOUGH JUST TO HAVE THE
## BUDDHA-NATURE                                                    7.40
It is not enough to have the seed of enlightenment; we must cultivate it so it develops fully into Buddhahood. We must exert ourself to remove all the impurities for the goal to be achieved.

*Thrangu Rinpoche*

# → 8

# *The Practice of Mahayana*

## Relative Bodhichitta

T HE PREVIOUS CHAPTER explored the character of wisdom. This chapter particularly concerns the second of the two qualities needed by the bodhisattva, namely, compassion. How does the bodhisattva develop compassion? Just as wisdom is the essence of ultimate bodhichitta, so compassion is the essence of relative bodhichitta. It is through the array of practices known as relative bodhichitta that the great compassion of the buddhas is fostered and brought to fruition.

It is important to remember, however, that wisdom and compassion are ultimately not separate things. In a similar way, the methods of cultivating wisdom and compassion are not as separate as they might at first appear. Wisdom is not only cultivated through the three *prajna*s as applied to the "view," it is also developed through the relative bodhichitta practices: the more we engage with others, the more we come to understand how empty everything is—ourselves, others, and the ways we engage. Far from leading to a withdrawal from the situation, this recognition frees us for even deeper and fuller engagement. Likewise, compassion is not only ripened through the relative bodhichitta practices: through deeper understanding of the view of emptiness, our compassion becomes less self-referential and increasingly unfettered and applicable.

Relative bodhichitta has three components: first, the development of compassion for suffering beings; second, the rousing of "aspiration" or "wishing" bodhichitta, the strong aspiration to attain enlightenment for the benefit of all beings; and third, "entering" or "engaging" bodhichitta, which involves actually entering the path and carrying out the various Mahayana practices (8.1). These three components unfold in a logical, progressive order. First, one develops awareness, empathy, and identification with the suffering of beings (compassion). Second, out of this, one gives birth to the intense aspiration to benefit them through developing one's wisdom and compassion and, ultimately, attaining enlightenment (aspiration bodhichitta). And, third, based on this strong aspiration, one enters and pursues the Mahayana path (entering bodhichitta). Our passages on the Mahayana path follow this threefold logic of compassion, aspiration bodhichitta, and entering bodhichitta.

Compassion emerges out of *shunyata,* or emptiness. Real compassion is able to arise precisely because we understand the groundlessness of our own nonexistence and the insubstantiality of the world. Because of this radical groundlessness, we can afford to give to others unconditionally (8.2). The starting point of compassion is realizing the open space of nonexistence and providing the accommodation that simply lets things be (8.3). This kind of pure, fearless, nondualistic compassion is quite different from the "little game" of a more conventional approach in which we might try to be "kind" and impose our own version of compassion on others (8.4). Genuine compassion emerges from an attitude of wealth: precisely because of our own nonexistence, our complete lack of preconceptions, we can realize the fundamental richness that our own lives already possess. Therefore, it is natural to give to others (8.5). One can trace the evolution of this sense of richness in the process of meditation: meditation leads to the experience of nonexistence or basic openness; and openness gives birth to clarity, which contains appreciation, warmth, the feeling of abundance, and the desire to share this with others (8.6). When wisdom and compassion are united, this union is known as *skillful* (the wisdom aspect*) means* (the compassion aspect) (8.7). Two concluding passages describe the bodhisattva warrior and contrast this approach with that of "idiot compassion" (8.8), and explain genuine "peace on earth" as transcending concepts of peace and war (8.9).

Compassion arises unfailingly from a meditative state that is vast and free (8.10). Compassion, in the manifestation of the celestial bodhisattva, Avalokiteshvara, is supreme sovereign of the world (8.11). Sometimes we fail to realize how critically important compassion is to all Buddhist practice (8.12). In essence, compassion is making room within our hearts for all beings (8.13) even to the point of caring for them as we do for the limbs of our own bodies (8.14). And the practice of compassion contains a paradox: only by leaving our self-concern aside and developing compassion for others does our own realization draw closer (8.15).

The next set of passages concern the second and third aspects of relative bodhichitta, namely, those of aspiring and entering. These two are sequential, for the aspiration must precede the actual entering (8.16) and the aspiration must find its fulfillment in entering (8.17). The process of aspiring to help others emerges out of stillness and involves contemplation of the intention to be kind to others (8.18). Aspiration bodhichitta must begin with our own lives and our personal experience of suffering. We must touch the depths of our own experience of pain in order for our aspiration to help others to be grounded and real (8.19). Aspiration bodhichitta must rest in a pure vision of the suffering in our lives, a vision that is developed through daring and courage in exploring, penetrating, and fathoming the full extent of the pain of our human existence (8.20). In this sense, our own sadness can become a tremendous resource for rousing understanding of the suffering that others experience and also the aspiration to be of benefit to them (8.21).

Entering bodhichitta involves the actual practices that expose and activate our compassion (8.22). It includes four main types of practice: the bodhisattva vow; the six *paramitas*; the four immeasurables; and *tonglen*, sending and taking. The bodhisattva vow, marking the beginning of the bodhisattva path, involves a public, ritual declaration that makes our commitment definitive (8.23). The vow itself commits us to put others before ourselves (8.24). It is based on our recognition of suffering in ourselves and others (8.25). The vow has tremendous power because it is not made for ego's sake (8.26).

The second major area of relative bodhichitta practice, the six *paramita*s, includes generosity, discipline, patience, exertion, meditation, and wisdom. The term *paramita,* or transcendent action, refers to actions that transcend ego (8.27). In attempting to carry out the *paramita*s, it is important not to try to be perfect, but to practice them in a realistic way, at our own level, working with our own resistance. In this, we are not failing. This *is paramita* practice (8.28). The next selections provide descriptions of each *paramita* by Thrangu Rinpoche and Chagdud Tulku. Each lama points to particular facets of the practice, Thrangu Rinpoche providing more of an overview and Chagdud Tulku speaking about the kinds of activities that make it up (8.29–8.38). There is a difference between the first five *paramita*s, which are considered relational or relative practices (being subject–object oriented), and the sixth *paramita* of wisdom, in which we touch a state of mind that is nondual. The sixth *paramita* must undergird and permeate the other five in order for their practices to be truly transcendent, that is, not ego based (8.39, 8.40). When we are working from the ground of the sixth *paramita*, wisdom, our compassion will be pure and effective (8.41).

As the six *paramita*s suggest, the Mahayana practices are sometimes more meditative and sometimes more outward and active. Among the practices that are more meditative in nature, of particular importance are the four immeasurables: loving-kindness (*maitri*), compassion (*karuna*), sympathetic joy (*mudita*), and equanimity (*upeksha*). These are four contemplative practices that help us get in deeper touch with our own inner wellsprings of compassion and further awaken our desire to relieve others' suffering (8.42). Within the four immeasurables, equanimity plays a unique role and, in some interpretations, it is placed first (8.43). The four immeasurables are customarily summarized in a famous quatrain: "May all sentient beings enjoy happiness and the root of happiness; may they be free from suffering and the root of suffering; may they not be separated from the great happiness devoid of suffering; may they dwell in the great equanimity free from passion, aggression, and prejudice." Each of the four is described in the next four passages (8.44–8.47). This chapter concludes with a description of another extremely important practice, namely, that of *tonglen*, sending and taking (8.48).

## THE THREE COMPONENTS OF RELATIVE
## BODHICHITTA                                                    8.1

[Relative] bodhicitta has three components: arousing compassion for the suffering of all beings; aspiring to attain enlightenment in order to benefit all beings, called *wishing* [or aspiring] *bodhicitta*; and actively engaging in the path of liberation in order to accomplish that goal, called *engaging* [or entering] *bodhicitta*.

*Chagdud Tulku Rinpoche*

## EMPTINESS AND COMPASSION 8.2

Whenever there is the absolute *shunyata* principle, we have to have a basic understanding of absolute compassion at the same time. *Shunyata* literally means "openness" or "emptiness." *Shunyata* is basically understanding nonexistence. When you begin realizing nonexistence, then you can afford to be more compassionate, more giving. . . . Understanding *shunyata* means that we begin to realize that there is no ground to get, that we are ultimately free, nonaggressive, open. We realize that we are actually nonexistent ourselves. . . . Then we can give. . . .

Compassion develops from *shunyata*, or nonground, because you have nothing to hold on to, nothing to work with, no project, no personal gain, no ulterior motives. Therefore, whatever you do is a clean job, so to speak. So compassion and *shunyata* work together. It is like sunning yourself at the beach: for one thing, you have a beautiful view of the sea and ocean and sky and everything, and there is also sunlight and heat and the ocean coming toward you.

*Chögyam Trungpa Rinpoche*

## COMPASSION IS OPEN SPACE 8.3

Just not dwelling on a point of reference provides a lot of space to be. Compassion is open space in which things can be accommodated. It contrasts strongly with our repulsing situations because we are not willing to accommodate anything. So compassion is creating open space, accepting things happening. . . .

In order to develop compassion you have to be willing to be alone or lonely. You are completely and totally in a desolate situation, which is also open space at the same time. The development of compassion is not a matter of acquiring a partnership with things, but rather of letting everything be open. So the sense of loneliness or aloneness is the real starting point for compassion.

*Chögyam Trungpa Rinpoche*

## THE FUNDAMENTAL CHARACTERISTIC    8.4

The fundamental characteristic of true compassion is pure and fearless openness without territorial limitations. There is no need to be loving and kind to one's neighbors, no need to speak pleasantly to people and put on a pretty smile. This little game does not apply. . . . Real openness exists on a much larger scale, a revolutionarily large and open scale, a universal scale. . . . The point is not to want to benefit anyone or make them happy. There is no audience involved, no "me" and "them." It is a matter of an open gift, complete generosity without the relative notions of giving and receiving. That is the basic openness of compassion: opening without demand. . . . If you will just "be," then life flows around and through you.

*Chögyam Trungpa Rinpoche*

## COMPASSION IS AN ATTITUDE OF WEALTH    8.5

Compassion is the ultimate attitude of wealth: an anti-poverty attitude, a war on want. It contains all sorts of heroic, juicy, positive, visionary, expansive qualities. And it implies larger-scale thinking, a freer and more expansive way of relating to yourself and the world. . . . It is the attitude that one has been born fundamentally rich rather than that one must become rich.

*Chögyam Trungpa Rinpoche*

## HOW COMPASSION EVOLVES NATURALLY
## FROM MEDITATION    8.6

The best and most correct way of presenting the idea of compassion is in terms of clarity, clarity which contains fundamental warmth. At this stage your meditation practice is the act of trusting yourself. . . . As much space and clarity as there is, there is that much warmth as well, some delightful feeling of positive things happening in yourself constantly. . . . Meditation is a delightful and spontaneous thing to do. It is the continual act of making friends with yourself.

Then, having made friends with yourself, you cannot just contain that friendship within you; you must have some outlet, which is your relationship with the world. So compassion becomes a bridge to the world outside. Trust and compassion for oneself bring inspiration to dance with life, to communicate with the energies of the world. . . .

When a person develops real compassion, he is uncertain whether he is being generous to others or to himself because compassion is environmental generosity, without direction, without "for me" and without "for them." It is filled with joy, spontaneously existing joy, constant joy in the sense of trust, in the sense that joy contains tremendous wealth, richness.

*Chögyam Trungpa Rinpoche*

## SKILLFUL MEANS                                              8.7

When a person is both wise and compassionate, his actions are very skillful and radiate enormous energy. This skillful action is referred to as *upaya*, "skillful means." There "skillful" does not mean devious or diplomatic. *Upaya* just happens in response to a situation. If a person is totally open, his response to life will be very direct, perhaps even outrageous from a conventional point of view, because "skillful means" does not allow any nonsense. It reveals and deals with situations as they are: it is extremely skillful and precise energy.

If the coverings and masks we wear were suddenly to be torn away by this energy, it would be extremely painful. It would be embarrassing because we would find ourselves with nothing on, naked. At such a moment this kind of openness and directness, the outrageously blunt nature of *prajna* and compassion, might seem extremely cold and impersonal.

*Chögyam Trungpa Rinpoche*

## GENUINE COMPASSION AND THE WARRIOR              8.8

There are two ideas of compassion. . . . One ["idiot compassion"] is that you would like to see somebody happy; the other [genuine compassion] is that you help somebody because they need you, which is a different idea altogether. The first type of compassion is based on overpowering, undermining the colorful and beautiful aspect of situations, and trying to mold them into your shape, your pattern; whereas

*Chögyam Trungpa Rinpoche*

the other is just purely relating with the situation as it is and working along with it, which is the warrior quality.

The warrior has to make every move of his or her practice of fighting in accordance with that without failing. If he reflects back on himself for one moment, one flash of a second; if he reflects back on his territory, his ego, his survival, then he's going to get killed, because he wasn't quick enough to relate purely with things as they are.

*Chögyam Trungpa Rinpoche*

## PEACE ON EARTH　8.9

The ultimate implication of the words "peace on earth" is to remove altogether the ideas of peace and war and to open yourself equally and completely to the positive and the negative aspects of the world. It is like seeing the world from an aerial point of view: there is light, there is dark. Both are accepted. You are not trying to defend the light against the dark.

*Chögyam Trungpa Rinpoche*

## MEDITATION: RELAX INTO THE VASTNESS　8.10
The source of all phenomena of samsara and nirvana
Is the nature of mind—void, luminous,
All-encompassing, vast as the sky.

When in that state of skylike vastness,
Relax into its openness; stay in that very openness,
Merge with that skylike state:
Naturally it will become more and more relaxed—
Wonderful!

If you become accomplished
In this method of integrating mind with view,
Your realization will naturally become vast.
And just as the sun shines freely throughout space,
Your compassion cannot fail to shine on all unrealized beings.

*Dilgo Khyentse Rinpoche*

## WHO IS AVALOKITESHVARA?                    8.11

[Avalokiteshvara] is the Supreme Sovereign of the World. As the embodiment of universal compassion and the essence of all the Buddhas, he manifests as the great Bodhisattva for the sake of sentient beings. His compassion extends to all beings, from kings and queens to the common people, from the Sravakas and Pratyekabuddhas to all the Bodhisattvas of the Ten Bhumis. He is the great compassion, inseparable from the vast expanse of the Buddha's Mind. . . . In his relative aspect Avalokiteshvara is the great Bodhisattva who attained the Tenth Bhumi and is the heart-son of all the Buddhas of the infinite Buddha-fields. In his absolute aspect, he is the ground from which all the Buddhas and all their celestial Buddha-fields arise.

*Dilgo Khyentse Rinpoche*

## ONE OF THE GREATEST TEACHINGS                    8.12

Sometimes people feel disappointed when they hear about practicing compassion: "You mean I have to be nice?" It's a kind of letdown. We often overlook compassion, seeing it as merely a pit stop on the way to more advanced practices. We want something more; we don't even know what. But that's just a trick of our mind. One of the greatest teachings is the practice of compassion.

My hope is that as people progress in the buddha-dharma, they'll take the time to meditate on compassion with the same emphasis that they place on *shamatha*. We shouldn't think of practicing the Mahayana as being only halfway there, at a midpoint on the path. If we can actually understand the Mahayana, we've understood the essence of the teachings. If we can begin to generate unconditioned compassion, we've done most of the work.

*Sakyong Mipham Rinpoche*

## WE HAVE TO CULTIVATE THE SENSE OF BIG HEART                    8.13

We have to cultivate the sense of big heart. The big heart has to really have room for all sentient beings; it has to have room to love all sentient beings as it loves itself, as it makes room for itself. This very heart has to be stretched to have room for *all* sentient beings. It is a big stretch to not just have room for one person or a few persons who are related to us but to have room for *all* sentient beings—all who are actually in need of happiness, all who are in need of freedom from suffering. For that reason, we must find room for all sentient beings in our heart.

*Dzigar Kongtrul Rinpoche*

## WE MUST CARE FOR OTHERS AS WE CARE FOR THE PARTS OF OUR OWN BODIES                                     8.14

As Shantideva said, we have hands, legs, a head, and many other body parts, and we hold onto and care for them all as part of ourselves. We automatically care for all the different parts of our body, and there are many. We don't see this as being particularly complicated; it's quite automatic. In the same way, if one gets used to the training of the *bodhi* heart, it won't be complicated to care for all beings; it won't be so very different from caring for the many different parts of one's body. One must care for all the many beings. One must have the feeling of deep care that covers the vast numbers of beings that exist.

*Dzigar Kongtrul Rinpoche*

## COMPASSION BRINGS ENLIGHTENMENT CLOSER               8.15

By developing the infinite compassion that a Bodhisattva is able to develop, one brings enlightenment closer, whereas without that kind of compassion, enlightenment is far off. [Without compassion], even if one desperately wants to become enlightened, one is unable to do so.

*Traleg Kyabgon Rinpoche*

## THE TWO ASPECTS OF RELATIVE BODHICHITTA               8.16

[Bodhichitta] has two aspects. One aspect is the wish and the other aspect is the action. When we begin, we cannot actually put bodhicitta into practice. It remains a wish, with us thinking, "May I be able one day to help all beings be free from their suffering forever. May I be able to help them find happiness forever." So it is a desire that the day will come when we can actually do this. This wish is completely impartial and unbiased, applying to all beings without exception. Once the wish is fully developed, it turns into the action of actually working toward enlightenment. The way this is done is thinking in terms of "I must achieve Buddhahood so I can really be able to help beings. I must increase this power in order to help beings." When both the wish and the practice toward enlightenment are found together, then this is the seed of the power to remove the suffering of others and achieve Buddhahood for oneself.

*Traleg Kyabgon Rinpoche*

## ASPIRING AND ENTERING                                              8.17
Aspiring to attain enlightenment for ourselves and all beings is called *wishing* [or *aspiring*] *bodhicitta*. . . .

Although essential to our practice, [wishing bodhicitta] alone will not accomplish our goal. Wishing bodhicitta is like looking at the vast ocean of samsara and wanting to get ourselves and others to the opposite shore. If we don't have a boat and a means to propel that boat, no amount of wishing will get us across. We must also become actively involved—we have to actually enter the path of practice. Fully utilizing the methods that reduce and purify negative thoughts and actions, and enhance positive qualities, while simultaneously recognizing the true nature of mind, so that we can liberate ourselves and others is called engaging bodhicitta.

*Chagdud Tulku Rinpoche*

## BEING ABOUT TO GO                                                   8.18
Aspiration is a sense of going, or being about to go. Before we do something, we contemplate it, think about it; there is a thought-process involved. Aspiration is our desire, our intention, our deepest wish, as if we were a child at Christmas, really wishing for some present. In aspiration, we contemplate all sentient beings having been our mothers and we vow to repay their kindness, and so on. That thought, that aspiration, is the heart of contemplative meditation. We begin by sitting until we experience some stillness, some peace. Out of that we conjure up a thought, an intention, an aspiration: "My intention today is to try to be kind to others."

*Sakyong Mipham Rinpoche*

## ASPIRATION BODHICHITTA BEGINS WITH OUR
## ORDINARY LIVES                                      8.19

The basic vision of enlightenment for a bodhisattva begins right here within our own ordinary life, within our ordinary experience of suffering, within our ordinary experience of *kleshas*. This is called *aspiration bodhichitta*.

Aspiration bodhichitta should not be too conceptual or too impersonal or too theoretical. It sounds very good to say, "Oh, I'm going to liberate all sentient beings from suffering and the causes of suffering," or, "I'm going to help all sentient beings achieve enlightenment and the causes of enlightenment." It sounds like a very good aspiration to recite in our rituals, but if there is no heart in it, then it is just absolute rubbish from the Mahayana point of view.

Aspiration bodhichitta is not having just an abstract idea about sentient beings and their suffering. It is not a theory of enlightenment. Aspiration bodhichitta is not a path somewhere far away, somewhere outside our own experiences of dharma, experiences of life, and experiences of the path. In fact, aspiration bodhichitta should start with our own experience of pain. It should start from our own experience of suffering and our own heart, with daring to inquire further about this experience of suffering. It arises from our sense of fearlessness and courage in going further, without any reservations, into the depths of such pain and suffering. Then we will have a good possibility of generating and cultivating aspiration bodhichitta and connecting with the path of bodhisattvas. Therefore, the aspiration bodhichitta is very much present in our basic heart of suffering, our basic heart of compassion, love, and kindness.

*The Dzogchen Pönlop Rinpoche*

## THE ASPIRATION ASPECT OF BODHICHITTA              8.20

The aspiration aspect of bodhichitta is working with *pure vision*. Pure vision arises from experiencing pain and suffering. Pure vision arises from our basic heart of daring, which is the courage to penetrate further into the experience of suffering. This is the heart that is not afraid to explore, in depth, the nature of pain and suffering. It is the heart that has a full sense of curiosity or inquisitiveness to find out the ultimate intensity of pain and suffering, of agony. That heart is the aspiration bodhichitta.

Without acceptance of such pain, without acknowledgment of such suffering and agony, and without the willingness to really find out what this experience is, what this agony is all about, there is no arising of the heart of *bodhi*. Therefore, aspiration bodhichitta is working with the basic heart of suffering, the basic heart of pain. It is working with courage and a certain sense of curiosity about our experience of pain and furthering our experience of agony. We are all afraid of this experience, and because of our fear, we have difficulty developing this aspiration bodhichitta, the basic vision of enlightenment.

*The Dzogchen Pönlop Rinpoche*

## How Can We Use Our Own Sadness to Benefit Others?

8.21

When you are hit by an event in life that creates a lot of sadness in you, treasure that sadness and let it lead you to an understanding of what suffering means. Until we are stricken by sadness, we have no understanding of it and we cannot even imagine how sadness affects others. We move around in our world with an oblivious attitude. However, when a loved one dies and we are hit by our own sadness, then we realize, "This is how it is," and perhaps we begin to look and open up to consider that others have the same feeling. This allows us to go beyond our own experiences of what we think is suffering.

Treasure that sadness and that grief, and, in some way, make it grow into something healthy. That is the second step. Do something really beneficial through that grief. There are spiritual methods, such as *tonglen* meditation, which is a very effective way of transforming grief into something positive. But even more than that, do something good. Resolve to refrain from harmful actions. Dedicate any merit that may arise from that to another grieving person, so that he or she may find the way to a good life. Aspire that any sentient being that may encounter you may benefit from this action. In this way, dedicate your life to doing something that really benefits others.

*Venerable Khandro Rinpoche*

## PRACTICE ACTIVATES OUR LIMITLESS COMPASSION    8.22

Compassion, the first aspect of bodhichitta, is also inherent within us. Although we naturally have a good heart, it is usually rather limited. Through practice, we can expose and awaken our own perfect, boundless compassion.

*Chagdud Tulku Rinpoche*

## WHY IS THE BODHISATTVA VOW NECESSARY?    8.23

It is not sufficient just to think, "From now on, I will try to do my best to generate compassion and overcome my egocentricity, because it is not only beneficial for others but is also beneficial for myself." We have to make a formal commitment, which is called the taking of the Bodhisattva vow. As we know, living with somebody for many years in a de facto relationship is different from signing on the dotted line. Somehow that makes a difference.

*Traleg Kyabgon Rinpoche*

## WHAT IS IMPLIED BY THE BODHISATTVA VOW?    8.24

The bodhisattva vow is the commitment to put others before oneself. It is a statement of willingness to give up one's own well-being, even one's own enlightenment, for the sake of others. . . . Taking the bodhisattva vow implies that instead of holding onto our individual territory and defending it tooth and nail, we become open to the world that we are living in. It means we are willing to take on greater responsibility, immense responsibility. In fact, it means taking a big chance. But taking such a chance is not false heroism or personal eccentricity. It is a chance that has been taken in the past by millions of bodhisattvas, enlightened ones, and great teachers. So a tradition of responsibility and openness has been handed down from generation to generation; and now we too are participating in the sanity and dignity of this tradition.

*Chögyam Trungpa Rinpoche*

## WHAT IS THE BODHISATTVA VOW BASED ON?    8.25

Taking the bodhisattva vow is a real commitment based on the realization of the suffering and confusion of oneself and others. The only way to break the chain reaction of confusion and pain and to work our way outward into the awakened state of mind is to take responsibility ourselves. If we do not deal with this situation of confusion, if we do not do something about it ourselves, nothing will ever happen. We cannot count on others to do it for us. It is our responsibility, and we have the tremendous power to change the course of the world's karma. So in taking the bodhisattva vow, we are acknowledging that we are not going to be instigators of further chaos and misery in the world, but we are going to be liberators, bodhisattvas, inspired to work on ourselves as well as with other people.

*Chögyam Trungpa Rinpoche*

## THE POWER OF THE BODHISATTVA VOW                    8.26
Taking the bodhisattva vow has tremendous power for the very reason that it is not something we do just for the pleasure of ego. It is beyond oneself. Taking the vow is like planting the seed of a fast-growing tree, whereas something done for the benefit of ego is like sowing a grain of sand. Planting such a seed as the bodhisattva vow undermines ego and leads to a tremendous expansion of perspective. Such heroism, or bigness of mind, fills all of space completely, utterly, absolutely.

*Chögyam Trungpa Rinpoche*

## WHAT DOES *PARAMITA* MEAN?                    8.27
When we say that *paramita* means "transcendent action," we mean it in the sense that actions or attitude are performed in a non-egocentric manner. "Transcendental" does not refer to some external reality, but rather to the way in which we conduct our lives and perceive the world—either in an egocentric or a non-egocentric way. The six *paramitas* are concerned with the effort to step out of the egocentric mentality.

*Traleg Kyabgon Rinpoche*

## PARAMITA PRACTICE FOR ORDINARY BEINGS LIKE OURSELVES                    8.28
We should not expect our [*paramita* practice] to be completely pure, completely perfect, completely transcendental right from the beginning.

Shantideva said that, as an ordinary person, you will have many thoughts. First you will have a thought of giving, and then you will have a second thought, "No, no. I don't want to give that; I may need it. Even though I have a spare copy of my book, as a backup, I may need it." Shantideva said that such a thought is very ordinary, very natural, and very normal for people, for ordinary bodhisattvas.

However, he also said we must work with such thoughts. We must try to transcend them, and try to process them by maintaining a certain vision of *paramita* practice. For example: once we have a thought of giving, no matter what second thought we may have, we should try to give.

It is clear that we can have many thoughts and many ideas; we can struggle and have a certain sense of impurity in our practice, but that does not mean we are not practicing the *paramita*s. That does not mean that we are not practicing the Mahayana path, or that we are not being successful on the path. This is very important for us to know.

*The Dzogchen Pönlop Rinpoche*

## THE FIRST PARAMITA IS GENEROSITY    8.29

The first [*paramita, dana,*] is generosity, which means giving. There is giving to those who are worse off than oneself, such as the poor, needy, and hungry. Then there is giving to those who are better off than oneself, which means offering to the three jewels. These are the two main areas of generosity of the bodhisattva. When giving to those who are worse off, what is important is compassion, and when giving to those who are better off, what is important is faith, devotion, and confidence. So when one gives to the poor, one relieves their poverty and hunger temporarily because of compassion. When one makes offerings to the three jewels, one makes an expression of devotion. If one never gives to those worse off, then compassion isn't there and it is not complete. In the same way, if one doesn't make offerings to the three jewels, then one's faith, confidence, and appreciation in the meaning of the three jewels isn't quite right either. So offerings are a very important sign of what is going on in terms of compassion or devotion. Besides cultivating love, compassion, and devotion, the bodhisattva has to actually practice the *paramita* of generosity.

*Thrangu Rinpoche*

## WHAT KINDS OF ACTIONS DOES GENEROSITY INCLUDE?                                                    8.30

There is the material generosity of sharing food, clothing, and other things of substance; the spiritual generosity of imparting spiritual teachings, of providing freedom from fear and protection to those who are afraid; and the generosity of effort, giving freely of our time and energy as well as our words in sharing, teaching, counseling, and expressing loving kindness to benefit others. Whatever fortune we presently enjoy is the fruit of our past generosity, which we can now rejoice in sharing.

*Chagdud Tulku Rinpoche*

## THE SECOND PARAMITA IS VIRTUOUS CONDUCT                                      8.31

The second *paramita* is moral or virtuous conduct [*shila*]. The very essence of virtuous conduct is that through love and compassion one does not directly harm other beings. If one has love and compassion and yet harms other beings, it is a sign that one's love and compassion isn't really there. So, if one is loving and compassionate, one just really never harms other beings. . . . Therefore virtuous conduct is mainly concerned with the discipline of practicing right conduct with one's body and speech so that one doesn't hurt others directly or indirectly.

*Thrangu Rinpoche*

## THE PRACTICE OF SHILA                                                              8.32

In the practice of moral discipline, we continually check our motivation to ensure that we use our body, speech, and mind skillfully, that we are not only truly harmless but helpful. In addition, we strive to create conditions that will enable us to produce the greatest benefit—learning what we need to learn, pulling together the necessary resources, and so on. Finally, we remain tireless in our discipline.

*Chagdud Tulku Rinpoche*

## THE THIRD PARAMITA, PATIENCE                                                       8.33

The third *paramita* [*kshanti*] deals with something more difficult. It deals with how we react to situations arising from others, particularly what we do in the face of physical and verbal aggression from others. This is the *paramita* of forbearance, often called patience, which is remaining loving and compassionate in the face of aggression. The training of patience is the training of keeping one's love and compassion in the face of those difficulties which come from other people. So if our love and compassion is incredibly stable, when others hit us, no matter how much they hurt us physically, we never reply in a like manner. Our only response is one of love, compassion, and understanding.

*Thrangu Rinpoche*

## HOW WE PRACTICE PATIENCE                                      8.34

There are three basic kinds of patience: forbearance in the face of threats or harm from others, accepting and dealing with the hardships of spiritual practice, and accepting and relating without fear to the profound implication of the true nature of reality. We practice patience by relentlessly pursuing our efforts to benefit others no matter what their reaction or attitude toward us. We also develop patience as an antidote to aggression, anger, and hatred. A Buddhist proverb says, "For an evil such as anger, there is no practice like patience." It contributes to our peace of mind and ultimately to the attainment of enlightenment.

*Chagdud Tulku Rinpoche*

## THE FOURTH PARAMITA, DILIGENCE                               8.35

In order to practice generosity, virtuous conduct, and patience in the face of difficulties, one needs the fourth *paramita* of diligence [*virya*] to implement the first three *paramita*s and make them increase and become even more powerful factors in our life. Diligence doesn't mean some terrible drudge or difficult effort. Rather it is very joyful, meaningful, and vital. If one really thinks something has benefit, one values it, and one will do it very joyfully, and out of this there is an automatic flow of diligence and industry. If one thinks something is not very important, then one will think it is a drag and a bore, and one will do a little bit and then become lazy and stop. . . . Diligence means practicing without falling under the influence of laziness and practicing because one realizes the tremendous value of that practice. One has gained an insight into its value, effortlessly there will be joy and keenness to get on with it. Then automatically one will put lots and lots of effort into it to make it a very productive thing.

*Thrangu Rinpoche*

## STEP BY STEP, EVEN A DONKEY CAN MAKE ITS WAY AROUND THE WORLD                    8.36

Diligence involves preparing for and beginning a task, donning armor-like perseverance to see that task through, and, finally, never turning back. We develop not only positive qualities, but also the means to benefit others. Someone may have abundant loving kindness and the intention to help the sick, but he must first spend years studying and training.

We practice diligence to achieve our goal: the temporary and ultimate happiness of all beings. If it's difficult to move one step forward, at least we shouldn't back up. Slowly, step by step, even a donkey can make its way around the world.

*Chagdud Tulku Rinpoche*

## THE FIFTH PARAMITA, MENTAL STABILITY                    8.37

The fifth *paramita* is mental stability [*dhyana,* or meditation]. . . . To meditate means to commit and to accustom oneself to meditation. It really means to train to settle. Even though we say "my mind," the mind which belongs to us is not under our control. Because we have not worked on it very much, our mind tends to be very distracted; it switches from one thing to another all the time. For instance, we may decide, "I am not going to get angry anymore." Even though we decide that in one moment, we don't have control over our mind and so we fall under the influence of anger a little later. . . . The word "meditation" has this implication of training or habituating our mind so that it does what we want. We habituate our mind by meditating again and again. This is the nature of meditation and the main point of the fifth *paramita*, mental stability.

*Thrangu Rinpoche*

*Thrangu Rinpoche*

## PRACTICES OF THE FIFTH PARAMITA                          8.38

We develop concentration or mental stability by training the mind. The
Tibetan term for this perfection is *samten*, *sam* meaning "to think," to
use the rational mind in contemplation, and *ten* meaning "stable" or
"firm." The mind comes to rest one-pointedly, either upon an idea or
in the natural state of awareness. One type of meditative stability involves thinking about or focusing on a single idea without distraction
so that the mind doesn't wander to other—even parallel—ideas. Concepts and the words that convey them point us to a deeper meaning.
Another kind involves letting the mind fall naturally into its fundamental state, unobscured by thoughts of the three times—past, present, and
future. Yet another, more profound form of meditation stability is imbued with the sixth perfection of wisdom, which acts as a seal applied
to the state of calm abiding.

*Chagdud Tulku Rinpoche*

## THE SIXTH PARAMITA, WISDOM                               8.39

The sixth *paramita* is wisdom, or *prajna* in Sanskrit. How much happiness we get out of worldly things depends on how much understanding
and wisdom we have. So wisdom is the very root of happiness and joy
and determines the values of all other things. In the ultimate sense the
benefit that we can get depends very much on our wisdom and understanding. Also the ability to help others depends on the degree of our
wisdom. Developing ourselves also depends on the degree to which we
have cultivated wisdom. For all these reasons wisdom and understanding are the very root of happiness and out of them joy emerges. How
then does one cultivate this wisdom? For a Buddhist it is cultivated by
the three main approaches of studying, contemplating, and meditating.

*Thrangu Rinpoche*

## THE SIXTH PARAMITA IS BEYOND SUBJECT
## AND OBJECT                                               8.40

The first five of the six perfections function within dualistic framework.
In the case of generosity, we speak of the subject, oneself, who gives;
the object, the person to whom something is given; and the act of

giving. The subject, object, and the action between them are called *the three spheres*. Belief in the solidity of the three spheres is the domain of relative truth. Reality has two aspects: ultimate reality, or absolute truth—things as they are in and of themselves—and relative reality, or relative truth—things as they appear to be on a conventional level. The Tibetan term for relative truth consists of *kun*, meaning "all" or "many," and *dzob*, "that which is not true." So *kundzop* implies the display of myriad phenomena that appear to be something they are not. . . . Ultimate reality remains free of and beyond all conceptual elaborations—one cannot say that things exist, nor that they do not exist, that they are or are not. As we hear teachings, contemplate, and meditate, our intellectual understanding gradually becomes a deeper knowing, of our ultimate nature. . . .

When we apply [this] view to our practice of the first five perfections, we go beyond their ordinary meaning. . . . When our generosity is imbued with wisdom—recognition of the true nature of the three spheres—it becomes the perfection of generosity. Knowing that our actions undertaken to benefit others are empty of inherent existence, yet acting nonetheless, is the essence of the practice of the six perfections and of the path of the bodhisattva.

*Chagdud Tulku Rinpoche*

## WISDOM ENABLES OUR COMPASSION 8.41

It is the attitude that really is the most important thing. If we have the right attitude, arising from wisdom, whatever action we initiate out of compassion will be effective and will be in keeping with the situation. But if we lack such an open and wide vision, even if we are very concerned with social welfare and justice, our attitudes may still be tinged or polluted with our own delusions or obscurations of mind.

*Traleg Kyabgon Rinpoche*

## THE FOUR IMMEASURABLES 8.42

We meditate first to cultivate impartiality, then we go on to meditate on great love, then on great compassion, and finally on bodhicitta. The first immeasurable, impartiality, means not being influenced by attachment or aggression. Great love means wanting everyone to attain happiness. Great compassion means wanting to free everyone from suffering. Bodhicitta, however, is more subtle, as it is the wish to attain Buddhahood to help all beings. Its very nature is a loving and compassionate mind. What makes it subtle is that bodhicitta implies the development of wisdom. Without that wisdom, the love and compassion of the bodhisattva become incomplete love and incomplete compassion.

*Thrangu Rinpoche*

### WHY IMPARTIALITY IS FIRST                                   8.43
Patrul Rinpoche stressed the need for meditating on impartiality from the beginning of Buddhist practice. Normally, we meditate on the four immeasurables as they appear in the prayers, which is in order of limitless love, limitless compassion, limitless joy, and limitless impartiality. Patrul Rinpoche stressed the need for meditating on impartiality first because this removes the danger of having partial or biased love, partial or biased compassion. When we begin on the path, there is a strong tendency to have stronger love toward those we like and lesser love toward those we don't like. Once we have developed wisdom with this meditation, it becomes true love, which cares for each and every person without any bias. This is the purest compassion because it cares for everyone.

*Thrangu Rinpoche*

### (1) LOVING-KINDNESS: "MAY ALL SENTIENT BEINGS
### ENJOY HAPPINESS AND THE ROOT OF HAPPINESS."         8.44
The first immeasurable is loving-kindness. We might wonder where all this loving-kindness is going to come from. Even if we can create some, we'll definitely run out of it before our practice session ends. This practice isn't a matter of creating loving-kindness, but of letting go of *kleshas*, emotions, and thoughts. It takes a lot of letting go. Usually, what come up are thoughts about people we don't like or thoughts about painful things that have happened. At that point, it's not so much that we have to overpower our anger, for instance, and smother it with love. Something deeper tells us that it's okay, we can let it go; that there

exists immeasurable loving-kindness. Loving-kindness is intrinsic. It's part of our being.

In the absolute sense, it's easy to think, "I would like everyone to have the root of happiness, enlightenment." On the relative level, we wish for others to have mundane happiness, to enjoy their lives and feel fulfilled. It's important to include this level of detail in the practice. Struggling with someone and trying to visualize them enjoying themselves may bring up jealousy, agitation, and other emotions. This isn't especially the point of the practice. If it becomes overwhelming, let it go for a little bit and focus more generally. All the same, we can specifically wish happiness for someone we don't like; it could actually make them easier to deal with. If we had a list of ten people with whom we were angry, as we worked our way through the list, we would find it becoming easier to forgive. Because we've practiced some, because we've been through a process, we can let go. Suddenly, we feel a sense of height. That comes from having created a platform of loving-kindness. We see the transparent quality of our grudges and our thoughts, not with negativity, but with a positive outlook.

*Sakyong Mipham Rinpoche*


## (2) COMPASSION: "MAY THEY BE FREE FROM SUFFERING AND THE ROOT OF SUFFERING."    8.45

The second of the four immeasurables is compassion, or *nyingje*, meaning "noble heart." At its root, compassion is based on seeing suffering, relating with it, and letting it go. We think about the whole world and all the beings caught in tremendous suffering, and we rouse the aspiration to develop the power to ease their pain. We wish that every being were liberated, enlightened, and that therefore they would not suffer. To do this, we have to relate directly to suffering. We have to understand its cyclical, samsaric aspect. If we fear suffering, we think, "I don't want to think about the horrendous pain that people bring on themselves through their own actions." However, having understood what suffering is, we are no longer fearful of it. Fear comes from not knowing what's going to happen; the situation is unpredictable. But by now, we have understood the predictability of the whole situation.

The experience of pain brings a sense of feeling trapped, of having no way out. Contemplating that aspect of pain develops compassion. That compassion doesn't come from thinking that we're better and are going to have compassion for others because they don't know what's going on. Genuine compassion comes from egolessness, which is the basis of wishing that all beings be free from suffering. We see that all beings are trapped in the cycle of samsara, and we want to help alleviate their suffering. As we generate compassion, it becomes stronger and begins to melt our aggression. The more we do the practice, the more we develop faith and trust.

If we want to meditate on compassion but don't feel a relationship to it, a pragmatic way to start is simply to sit down and conjure up the aspiration. We say, "May all beings be free from suffering and the root of suffering." On a basic level, as soon as we think of the suffering of others, we're automatically practicing. It's more than just thinking—if we see someone in excruciating pain, we're immediately sucked into the situation. For a moment, we're not thinking of ourselves. We're right there with the pain because we know what the experience is. We may not have experienced exactly the same pain, but it's close enough for us to understand. We can't underestimate that.

In the beginning, compassion may seem somewhat comforting. But penetrating the practice takes exertion and energy. Sometimes we find it difficult to do these practices because we lose focus or inspiration. We think, "It's too difficult to practice. I have other things on my mind." Although those things may not be enjoyable or interesting, it's somehow easier for us to dwell on them than it is to practice. Working with that is part of the practice.

*Sakyong Mipham Rinpoche*

(3) JOY: "MAY THEY NOT BE SEPARATED FROM THE
GREAT HAPPINESS DEVOID OF SUFFERING."                    8.46
The next one is joy, or *gawa*. Joy is knowing that all sentient beings have buddha-nature—in Sanskrit, *tathagata-garbha*. The essence of buddha-nature is the potential to achieve awakening, enlightenment. We have a fully enlightened buddha inside us, which we can discover through the path of meditation. Because of buddha-nature, all beings have the ways and means of achieving enlightenment. Our joy in this is endless,

because in every situation we encounter, we know that every being could achieve enlightenment. The bodhisattva, the practitioner of compassion and loving-kindness, isn't in a bad mood, feeling like she is taking on the weight of the world. The bodhisattva takes delight in practicing because she sees the possibility that everyone has to discover buddha-nature, *tathagata-garbha*.

*Sakyong Mipham Rinpoche*

## (4) EQUANIMITY: "MAY THEY DWELL IN THE GREAT EQUANIMITY FREE FROM PASSION, AGGRESSION, AND PREJUDICE."

8.47

Equanimity is an evenness by which we gauge things. It doesn't mean doing the minimal, not rocking the boat. It has more to do with higher understanding, *prajna*, knowing. If we practice the four immeasurables without equanimity, what we develop is conventional loving-kindness, because we haven't let go of our conceptual split between self and other. If we practiced all the immeasurables except equanimity, eventually we would develop compassion and loving-kindness, but it would be only for those whom we care about or for whom we easily have compassion. This actually leads to aggression because we don't want anyone to harm those we care about. The purpose of developing equanimity is to liberate those negative emotions.

*Sakyong Mipham Rinpoche*

## TONGLEN: SENDING AND TAKING

8.48

A crucial element of the Mahayana is the bodhichitta practice of *tonglen*, or sending and taking. In Tibetan, *tong* means "to send," and *len* means "to retrieve." Having a basic understanding of the practice of sending and taking, we meditate and begin to draw in the pain of others and send out goodness. We can practice this exchange in many ways. We can do it specifically for someone who is ill. We can do it by visualizing the inbreath and outbreath as dark and light, respectively, drawing in negative energy and sending out goodness.

We can do *tonglen* practice at any stage, but to practice properly, we need to develop equanimity and an understanding of the four immeasurables. Otherwise, we will inevitably feel that our supply of compassion is limited. Or, if we are practicing *tonglen* for someone who is sick, we might think we're going to get his or her sickness. Sometimes at first people are paranoid about doing a practice that seems ridiculous or even stupid: sitting and thinking of someone and taking in their sickness and giving them goodness. But after a while, they're afraid that it might actually work!

*Tonglen* is a potent practice. It helps us develop confidence in kindness and compassion. It brings sanity to us and to others because it provides a way of working with our mind in a practical way. If we are practicing *tonglen* for someone who is close to us, we're not spinning out of control, thinking about what could happen. We're meditating and we're calm. The meditation actually brings some sanity to us and to the other person.

Inevitably, sending and taking brings us closer to others. In fact, the ultimate purpose of *tonglen* is complete union with other, meaning not only other people, but also the world at large. What does that union mean? It means to see the world as it is, to see its true nature, which is selflessness and emptiness. Realizing that people are suffering because they don't see the true nature of things, we practice *tonglen*.

*Sakyong Mipham Rinpoche*

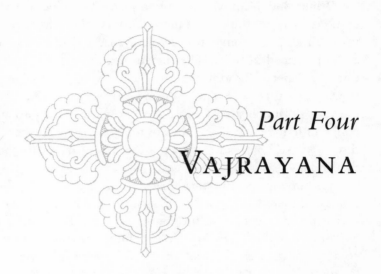

*Part Four*

# VAJRAYANA

THE THIRD OF THE THREE *yanas*, the Vajrayana, or "Diamond Vehicle," is considered the epitome of Buddhist practice in Tibet. The Vajrayana (or Tantrayana, "Tantric Vehicle," as it is also known) owes its unique stature to the richness and potency of its meditative traditions. In contrast to the Hinayana and conventional Mahayana, which take a more gradual approach, it is said that through the tantric methods one can achieve enlightenment in one lifetime.

Indian Buddhism held that the tantric *yana* was preached by the Buddha during his lifetime and thereafter kept secret for many centuries. Be this as it may, it seems to have gathered momentum sometime during the first number of centuries of the common era and to have come into historical (that is, visible) prominence on the Indian subcontinent from the seventh century onward. Those who practiced the tantra in its early days were not monastic people but rather men and women meditators living in retreat, in jungles, mountains, and other out-of-the-way places and also, often anonymously, as lay people.

When Buddhism was being transplanted to Tibet between the seventh century and the end of the twelfth century, the early non-Mahayana schools, the conventional Mahayana, and the Vajrayana were all being practiced in India. The Indian gurus from whom the major lineages of Tibetan Buddhism were derived were tantric practitioners. It appears that they were already using a three-*yana* concept to integrate the various Buddhist traditions then known in India into an organized, coherent framework. The Tibetans followed these teachers in using the three-*yana* scheme and in viewing the Vajrayana as the pinnacle of all the Buddha's teachings.

Within Tibetan Buddhism, as we have already seen, the Vajrayana is not considered a separate turning of the wheel of dharma. The reason is that the concept of a "turning of the wheel" applies to distinctive expositions of the "view" or philosophical dimension of the dharma. In contrast to what is presented in the three turnings, when the Buddha taught the Vajrayana, he did not introduce a new "view" or philosophical standpoint. Instead, he presented a body of highly efficacious meditative practices.

As we saw above, the Vajrayana is considered a Mahayana tradition. In Tibetan Buddhism, after taking the bodhisattva vow and practicing the conventional Mahayana, the next and final step is to become a tantric practitioner and seek to fulfill one's Mahayana vow to attain enlightenment for the benefit of others in that way. The Mahayana character of the Vajrayana is also seen in the fact that the second and third turnings of the wheel of dharma provide the view or philosophical standpoint of the Vajrayana, and the purpose of the tantric view is to bring the Mahayana view to fulfillment.

Within Tibetan Buddhism, the three *yana*s are not considered separate and distinct traditions of practice. The Hinayana is considered the foundation of Mahayana, and both Hinayana and Mahayana are considered the basis of Vajrayana practice. Put another way, what is taught, practiced, and realized in the Hinayana is accepted in the Mahayana, and the Mahayana is understood as a further refinement of the Hinayana. In a similar way, the Hinayana and Mahayana provide the substance of the tantric practitioner's Buddhism, and the Vajrayana is seen as bringing the earlier traditions to a new level of subtlety and efficacy.

Thus the selections in this part all presuppose the Hinayana and Mahayana foundation. For this reason, nearly all of our teachings focus on what is distinctive about the tantric vehicle, assuming that the four noble truths and the bodhisattva path have already been fully integrated into the practitioner's state of being. In this part, then, the intense practice orientation of the Vajrayana is evident throughout. What may be of particular interest in reading these is the specifically tantric, practice-oriented flavor that permeates the topics, whether suffering, karma, compassion, meditation, or anything else. This part is divided into four chapters: the tantric orientation, the *vajra* master, the tantric path, and making the journey.

The Vajrayana emerged historically as the collection of dozens and even hundreds of separate lineages, each with its distinctive way of practicing tantra. Much of this abundance and variety was taken into Tibetan Buddhism. For this reason, the Vajrayana can be an extremely complex tradition, difficult to follow in all of its details. In this part, I have avoided going too far into this complexity and, rather, have sought passages that reflect the major themes of the Vajrayana as it is practiced in Tibetan Buddhism.

# ⇢ 9

# Tantric Perspectives

THE SELECTIONS IN this chapter highlight some of the more important themes of the tantric perspective. Vajrayana as the epitome of
Buddhism in Tibet is the subject of our first selections (9.1, 9.2). At the
same time, we should realize that it is precisely its ability to bring about
the full realization of the unsurpassable "view" of Mahayana that makes
the Vajrayana so extraordinary (9.3, 9.4). Next, the etymology of *tantra*
as continuity is explained as the relentless manifestation of ego's nonexistence in our lives (9.5). It is nothing other than this that is the changeless face of enlightenment, the *vajra,* or "indestructibility," that
underlies our experience (9.6). This wakefulness is not only inner but
in the external world, present in the experience of "pure perception"
or "sacred outlook" toward all phenomena (9.7).

The next several passages illustrate tantric perspectives on the path.
The Vajrayana goes beyond *shunyata* because a mere notion of emptiness provides no guidance or direction in terms of our lives. It is implied
here that the tantric way shows us how to take our lead from the magic
and wisdom in appearances (9.8). The following passages caution those
interested in the Vajrayana. Reading about the tantra and attempting to
take it on a purely intellectual level, without studying under a teacher
or practicing, "is like a person doctoring himself with the same methods
that made him ill in the first place." (9.9) Even if our conception of

spirituality is merely too sensible and logical, we won't be able to proceed (9.10). Colorful though it may seem, the Vajrayana does not involve daydreaming, fantasizing, and concocting exotic experiences. (9.11) The Vajrayana, in fact, requires sacrifices. We need to give up our concern with appearances and reputation (9.12). In fact, the only way to go forward is even to give up hope of attainment itself (9.13). In particular, we need to remember that in tantric practice, motivation is everything. If we practice Vajrayana in order to benefit ourselves alone, this will be no basis for the path. Only if we have fully assimilated the perspective of bodhichitta, that our practice is for the welfare of all beings, can we really enter tantra (9.14). And, finally, the Vajrayana practices are incredibly, uniquely powerful (9.15). Part of their distinctiveness is that rather than rejecting desire, as the lower *yana*s do, they use desire on the path (9.16).

### VAJRAYANA AS THE FINAL STAGE                    9.1
Tantra, or vajrayana, is the most fundamental and final stage of the development of wisdom in Buddhism. It is the final development of the enlightenment experience.

*Chögyam Trungpa Rinpoche*

### SUTRAYANA AND VAJRAYANA PATHS COMPARED        9.2
In the Sutra system, one gathers the accumulations and purifies obscurations, slowly proceeding towards buddhahood, which is achieved after three incalculable aeons. "Incalculable" is a name for the enormous number expressed by ten followed by fifty-two zeros, and refers to not just days, but aeons. That is an incredibly long time. Through Vajrayana it is possible to attain complete enlightenment within this very body and lifetime.

*Tulku Urgyen Rinpoche*

### THE RELATION OF VAJRAYANA TO MAHAYANA          9.3
Because we talk about three vehicles—the Hinayana, the "narrow or small vehicle"; the Mahayana, the "great vehicle"; and the Vajrayana, the "indestructible vehicle"—we assume that each one is better than

the last and that there is a progression through the three *yana*s. However, it's important to understand that, within the context of the three-*yana* approach, the enlightenment of the Vajrayana is the same as that of the Mahayana: the complete and full experience of bodhichitta, starting with relative and progressing to absolute. For complete realization, for utter enlightenment—meaning the profound and deep understanding of our being—there is no more vast or profound realization than that of the Mahayana. The skillful means of the Vajrayana are a more efficient process and way of progressing in the Mahayana journey.

*Sakyong Mipham Rinpoche*

## THE SKILLFUL MEANS OF THE VAJRAYANA                9.4
On the whole, the buddha-dharma, and the Vajrayana in particular, is an expression of skillful means. It uses the most appropriate way—meditation, imagery, study, discussion, and so on—to point out the enlightened aspect of our being. There are times in our life when we're willing and capable of doing and taking on more. That is what the Vajrayana is about. The Vajrayana is the diamond vehicle, the indestructible vehicle, not because it is better than the Mahayana, but because the methods used in the Vajrayana are perfect, and therefore they produce realization.

*Sakyong Mipham Rinpoche*

## *TANTRA* MEANS "CONTINUITY"                9.5
[The continuity of tantra] cannot be challenged because this kind of continuity never depends on superficial continuity or discontinuity. It is unconditional continuity. Obviously, the enlightenment experience involves the discontinuity of ego with its fixation, but there is also the element of all-pervasiveness—enlightenment is right now but later as well. . . . There is a thread of enlightenment that goes on all the time. The sense of the nonexistence of ego is the greatest continuity.

*Chögyam Trungpa Rinpoche*

## THE VAJRAYANA WORKS WITH THE CHANGELESS                9.6
The word *vajra* means "immutability" or "indestructibility." On the relative level there are all the samsaric phenomena which are imperma-

nent and change from one thing into another. On the absolute level the essence is always there and never changes and is not affected by one's relative viewpoint. The main concern of the tantric teachings, then, is working on this changeless, immutable essence. That is why it is called the vajrayana, or "the vehicle of the changeless."

*Thrangu Rinpoche*

## PURE PERCEPTION OR SACRED OUTLOOK                    9.7

The profound attitude of Vajrayana is pure perception or sacred outlook, viewing all things as pure. The practice of Vajrayana entails imagining that the world is a buddhafield, our dwelling place is a celestial palace, all male and female beings are *daka*s and *dakini*s, all sounds are mantra, and that the thoughts and emotions of all sentient beings are the continuity of immense, innate wakefulness. In this way, sights, sounds, and thoughts are perceived as the exalted *mandala* of the deity, mantra, and wisdom. This is called training in seeing things as they really are, not superimposing something artificial.

*Tulku Urgyen Rinpoche*

## BEYOND SHUNYATA                                     9.8

*Shunyata* alone does not provide any guidance, even with skillful means. You still need a certain trust toward and respect for magic, the magical aspect of the phenomenal world. . . . That magical or miraculous quality of phenomenal display is always there.

*Chögyam Trungpa Rinpoche*

## A WORD OF CAUTION TO THE INTELLECTUAL               9.9

A word of caution to the intellectual: Reading tantric teachings on your own, without the power of the appropriate initiation, is just an intellectual pastime. Only by practicing correctly, under the guidance of a fully qualified and experienced teacher, can you evolve beyond the intellect, beyond conceptual thought, into the true wisdom of pure, spontaneous being. I am not trying to be mysterious or exclusive here but simply saying that if you think that you can understand, let alone experience, the methods of tantric yoga merely by reading books, you are deceiving yourself—like a terminally ill person doctoring himself with the same methods that made him ill in the first place.

*Lama Thubten Yeshe Rinpoche*

## NAROPA'S "SANITY" IS NOT ADEQUATE
## TO VAJRAYANA                                         9.10

Because Naropa was born a prince and was educated and became a professor at Nalanda University, he regarded himself as . . . an educated, sensible person, someone highly respected. But this sensible quality, this sanity of his, turned out to be a very clumsy way of relating with the teachings of Tilopa—the teachings of the Kagyü lineage. Because he was not enough of a freak, because he was not insane enough, he couldn't relate with them at all. Insanity in this case is giving up logical arguments, giving up concept. Things as they are conceptualized are not things as they are.

*Chögyam Trungpa Rinpoche*

## BEFORE WE GO INTO VAJRAYANA                         9.11

Before we go into Vajrayana, a proper warning should be given. If we're really going to do this, if we're going to spend all our time and money and energy on these things, it's important that we understand what we're doing. If we resort to just daydreaming or fantasizing about exotic experiences, then we're really misleading ourselves. Having understood Mahayana and actually practicing it and integrating it, then Vajrayana practices become wonderful. They become very good.

*Sakyong Mipham Rinpoche*

## IF WE WANT TO ENGAGE IN TANTRIC PRACTICE            9.12

If we want to engage tantric practice, we should follow Naropa's example and give up our concern with our appearance and reputation, with the way we look and what people think of us. Perhaps we should take off our clothes and sit on a tiger with ashes on our body like an Indian *sadhu* [wandering mendicant].

*Lama Thubten Yeshe Rinpoche*

*Lama Thubten Yeshe Rinpoche*

GIVING UP HOPE                                              9.13

Naropa's experience of discovering Tilopa is connected with finally giving up hope, giving up hope of getting what he wanted to get. For Naropa, finally that search for an ultimate answer had to be given up.

*Chögyam Trungpa Rinpoche*

BODHICHITTA IS ESSENTIAL TO VAJRAYANA
PRACTICE                                                    9.14

If we approach Vajrayana practice thinking, "I need to work on myself, and I'm going to apply the techniques of Vajrayana to do that," the result will be the fruition of the Hinayana, not of the Vajrayana. Or, if we think, "Once I get to the Vajrayana, such and such is going to happen," unless we understand the Mahayana, nothing much is going to happen. A crucial element is missing, which is the Mahayana practice of bodhichitta.

In many ways, the Vajrayana is an extension, a further glorification, of the Mahayana. In fact, the essence of the Vajrayana path is the Mahayana practice of bodhichitta. Vajrayana texts and liturgies such as *sadhana*s always begin with taking refuge, taking the bodhisattva vow, and rousing bodhichitta. Vajrayana deities are often depicted standing on a moon disc, which represents bodhichitta. In fact, the Vajrayana imagery and visualizations in general are all expressions of compassion. In the same way, the first part of an empowerment, or *abhisheka*, usually establishes bodhichitta as the basis. If we don't take the essential step of establishing bodhichitta, the Vajrayana becomes dangerous. We are beginning to deal with very potent material and ways of meditating. Thinking only, "What can I get out of this? I'm going to use the Vajrayana to achieve enlightenment for me," is very dangerous. That is not the basis of the path.

*Sakyong Mipham Rinpoche*

THE POWER OF VAJRAYANA                                     9.15

I have really been thinking about this, and the more I reflect on the practices of Vajrayana, of deity, mantra, and *samadhi*, the more amazed I am. Really, these practices are incredible in purifying the latent tend-

encies in our minds which we have accumulated from countless lifetimes. It's only because these practices are so profound that all our
misdeeds can totally be cleared away.

*Tulku Urgyen Rinpoche*


## DESIRE IN SUTRAYANA AND TANTRAYANA                    9.16

According to Lord Buddha's general teachings, known as Sutrayana,
desire is the cause of human beings' problems, so it must be avoided.
According to Tantrayana, however, this very desire can be used in the
path to enlightenment.

*Lama Thubten Yeshe Rinpoche*

# ✣ 10

# *The Vajra Master*

THE TEACHER (Skt. *guru*, Tib. *lama*) occupies a central position within all the sects, schools, and traditions of Tibetan Buddhism. Your learning may be impeccable, your "view" sophisticated, your behavior above reproach, and your practice solid. But if you don't have a qualified teacher, you will be like a blind person stumbling through a dangerous jungle. In a very real sense, the teacher is our eyes and helps us at critical points when we have lost our way.

Within the Vajrayana, the teacher—the *vajra* master—plays an extraordinarily important role. We can gain some perspective on this by looking at the evolution of the teacher-student relationship from the Hinayana through the Mahayana to the Vajrayana. In the traditional analogy, at first, on the Hinayana level, the teacher is like a doctor. He or she has knowledge and remedies that we, as beginning practitioners, lack and desperately need. At the Hinayana stage, the relationship of teacher and student is strictly hierarchical, with the teacher being all-knowing and all-powerful, and the student mired down in his or her own ignorance. The student enters the Mahayana when he or she has attained some level of practice experience and maturity. At the Mahayana level, the teacher is now a "spiritual friend" with whom one can share the ups and downs of the meditative journey, encouraging us when we are doing fine and being a sounding board and a foil when we need to think things through to a deeper level.

When one enters the Vajrayana, the relationship between teacher and student undergoes a dramatic alteration. The teacher is still the Hinayana physician, as need dictates, and is still the spiritual friend with whom one shares the journey. But superceding and overriding these kinds of relationship, on the Vajrayana level, the teacher is now defined primarily by the liturgical and symbolic roles that he or she performs. It is not so much that the teacher him/herself has changed. Rather, the teacher is seen to take on a certain majestic, implacable, even terrifying demeanor by virtue of now being primarily a ritual figure. It is not so much the human teacher that is frightening, but rather the power of reality that he or she points out to us and the power that comes through. Through his or her own empowerment, the teacher now performs the function of connecting us with the underlying wisdom, potency, and magic of the universe.

This chapter begins with selections that express various facets of the role of the *vajra* master in the tantric *yana*. We read, first, that "without the lama there would be no buddhas" (10.1). To make any connection with a spiritual teacher will lead us closer to liberation (10.2) Those with whom we associate have an enormous impact on us. If we spend our time with spiritual mentors, we will find our mind gradually imbued with their auspicious qualities. The teacher is kinder than the buddhas in the sense that he or she brings the dharma to us in a human form that we can meet and learn from (10.3). A teacher can be a source of great blessings (10.4). Before we rely on a teacher, we need to ascertain his or her qualities (10.5–10.7). For us, the guru is buddha, dharma, and sangha (10.8), and the guru embodies the three bodies of a buddha (10.9). We are to think of his or her wisdom as no different from that of the Buddha (10.10). In spite of his or her sometimes august demeanor, it is also important that we realize that the teacher is a traveler too, a person continuing on their own spiritual journey (10.11). In summation, the role of the *vajra* master can be clarified through various analogies: a ship that carries us across the perilous ocean of samsara, a rain of nectar putting out the flames of our own insanity, a treasury of vast and deep instructions, and so on (10.12).

The next set of selections concern what is involved in relating and studying with a Vajrayana guru. One needs to examine the teacher and ascertain his or her qualifications and suitability. But then one should not worship or adore the teacher, rather, one should be willing to have some trust in him or her and be open to what he or she has to teach (10.13). In order to do so, one needs to follow the teacher's instructions diligently and purposefully (10.14). In this, it will not do merely to imitate one's mentor. Ultimately, one has to rely on oneself and make one's own journey or else the journey will be artificial and fake (10.15). Our aim, ultimately, should not be to appreciate someone else's realization, but to attain realization ourselves (10.16).

In any case, the universal panacea in the relation to the teacher is devotion (10.17). If one has complete devotion to one's teacher, then gradually all of his or her spiritual qualities will develop in oneself (10.18). Devotion is so important because it is an act of great openness. If we are open in the manner of devotion, then we are able to receive the compassion and the blessings of our teacher (10.19). The development of devotion begins with fabrication and leads to the unfabricated. That is, in the beginning, one needs to make an effort to rouse feelings of love and devotion. But, after a period of time, they will arise naturally, without effort (10.20). In fact, devotion is a mark of our practice. When we see our teacher as a buddha, that is a mark of the evolution of our Vajrayana practice (10.21).

The next selections address the various ways in which the guru appears. Beyond the human teacher, as such, the sangha—the community of the teacher's students—carries the atmosphere of the teacher, the teaching, and the lineage (10.22). As our practice evolves, as mentioned, we will come to see our own teacher as a real buddha, "even if he or she is in hell" (10.23). Again, we need to visualize our *vajra* master (or root guru) as the supreme, celestial buddha, Vajradhara (10.24). As our understanding deepens, we begin to realize that the guru is ultimately not an external figure, but the unconditioned, boundless wisdom aspect of our own inner nature that has presented itself in the form of the external teacher (10.25). We need to realize that when the tantric texts say that all realization comes from the guru, they are speaking ultimately of the final, inner guru (10.26), the inner voice that we usually don't heed or even hear (10.27). Ultimately, we find the guru within our own heart, in the unending, inherent mind. We can identify with him simply and directly, and receive the full measure of his blessings, by resting in the natural state (10.28). In this sense, the ultimate teacher is never separate from us and we begin to see all phenomena as the face of the absolute guru (10.29). All this being said, however, the relative guru is still vitally important (10.30). But with the human guru, we should not expect to have a normal, conventional relationship (10.31). Finally, while the human teacher is important, if we spend our whole life trying to follow spiritual teachers, something is wrong (10.32).

## WITHOUT THE LAMA, THERE WOULD BE
## NO BUDDHAS                                                    10.1
The Buddha said, "Without the lama, there would be no buddhas." Many of the Buddhist scriptures and commentaries state that before the advent of the teacher in one's life, not even the concept of enlightenment exists, let alone the determined search for it. All spiritual methods, starting with the initial steps of taking refuge and bodhisattva vows, come from the lama.

*Chagdud Tulku Rinpoche*

## IN PRAISE OF THE TEACHER                                     10.2
To make any connection with the [spiritual teacher], whether seeing him, hearing his voice, remembering him, or being touched by his hand, will lead us toward liberation. To have full confidence in him is the surest way to progress toward enlightenment. The warmth of his wisdom and compassion will melt the ore of our being to release the gold of the Buddha-nature within.

*Dilgo Khyentse Rinpoche*

## WHY IS A SPIRITUAL TEACHER SO IMPORTANT?                     10.3
A crystal takes on the color of the cloth upon which it is placed, whether white, yellow, red, or black. Likewise, the people you spend your time with, whether their influence is good or bad, will make a huge difference to the direction your life and practice take.

Spending your time with spiritual friends will fill you with love for all beings and help you to see how negative attachment and hatred are.

Being with such friends, and following their example, will naturally imbue you with their good qualities, just as all the birds flying around a golden mountain are bathed in golden radiance.

To free yourself from samsara, the vicious circle of suffering existence, and attain the omniscience of enlightenment, you have to rely on an authentic teacher. . . . He shows you what to do to make progress on the path, and what obstacles to avoid. An authentic spiritual teacher is like the sail that enables a boat to cross the ocean safely. . . .

Although the teacher appears to us in ordinary human form, and seems to behave in an ordinary human way, in reality his mind is no different from the Buddha's. The only difference between the teacher and the Buddha lies in his kindness to you, which in fact exceeds that of all the Buddhas of the past—for though they were perfectly enlightened, you can neither meet them in person nor hear their teachings. Your spiritual teacher, on the other hand, has come into this world in your time. You can meet him and receive from him the instructions that will lead you out of the mire of samsara to enlightenment.

*Dilgo Khyentse Rinpoche*

## BLESSINGS ARE CONTAGIOUS 10.4
Blessings are contagious, so to speak, and are transmitted in a fashion that is rather like catching a cold. If somebody has a cold and you are too close, you catch a cold too. Likewise, if you get close to a master who has blessings, they can be transmitted to you. Blessings here mean the sense of some power of realization or power of *samadhi*, some kind of atmosphere of realization that is naturally present. You move close to him, in the sense of opening yourself up through devotion and making sincere, heartfelt supplications. In other words, you lower your defenses, whatever doubts and suspicions that prevent you from being "infected" with blessings. The moment you do that, you catch a cold as well.

*Drubwang Tsoknyi Rinpoche*

## BE SKILLFUL IN CHECKING THE LAMA 10.5
All great masters and teachings repeatedly advise that one should always be skillful in checking the lama before one takes him as one's master.

We have that option, and we should take advantage of it. It is vital to study the teachings extensively in order to be prepared to take on a teacher. In fact, some of the vajrayana scriptures mention that one should check a potential teacher for twelve years before becoming his student.

*Dzongsar Khytense Rinpoche*

## THE QUALIFICATIONS OF A TEACHER                    10.6
Before we come to rely on a lama, it is essential that we carefully examine his qualities, just as we would investigate a doctor's qualifications before placing our life in her hands. . . . A spiritual teacher must fulfill two requirements: first, that she has listened to, contemplated, and understood the teachings and, second, has meditated upon them and gained realization of their essential meaning.

*Chagdud Tulku Rinpoche*

## THE ONE WE CHOOSE AS OUR GUIDE                    10.7
The one we choose as our guide on the spiritual path should at least have certain qualities. The teacher should not only thoroughly understand the teachings but have attained some direct realization of them, enjoying the inner warmth of meditative insight, and energy that penetrates to the heart of the Buddha's words. The teacher's practice should have reached a state where an indwelling confidence in the deeper meaning of the teachings and the dynamic energy of realization has been attained. Such a teacher's mindstream is filled with spontaneous, unfabricated love and compassion for all beings.

*Chagdud Tulku Rinpoche*

## THE GURU IS THE BUDDHA, THE DHARMA, AND THE SANGHA                    10.8
The lama embodies the Three Jewels of Buddha, Dharma, and Sangha. . . . The mind of the lama, the lama's realization of absolute truth, is identified with the buddha principle of the Three Jewels. The speech of the lama embodies the dharma principle, the transmission of the

teachings that benefits all who hear. The body of the lama is the principle of the sangha and the enactment of virtuous activity that leads beings to liberation.

*Chagdud Tulku Rinpoche*

## THE GURU EMBODIES THE THREE KAYAS                    10.9

The mind of the lama is *dharmakaya*, original purity beyond confusion and delusion. The lama's realization of the formless, substanceless nature beyond words is transmitted nonverbally from mind to mind. The speech of the lama is *sambhogakaya*, that which is halfway apparent or intangible. The physical body of the lama is the *nirmanakaya* display of enlightened mind appearing in tangible form to show us the path, to guide and lead us to liberation.

*Chagdud Tulku Rinpoche*

## OUR PERCEPTION OF THE GURU                    10.10

In vajrayana, in order to enable the guru to help us and work on our dualistic ego-centered preoccupations, we are supposed to think that the guru is no different in wisdom than the Buddha. This is the highest form of mind training. We are literally making a hero out of someone who, because he sees our potential, has no qualms about challenging and even abusing our narrow-minded and habitual patterns. This is a very radical, difficult, and revolutionary method. From a conventional point of view, or from the point of view of ego-cherishing, the whole notion of the guru-disciple relationship is something almost criminal. Yet the point to remember is that the only purpose of the existence of the guru is to function as a skillful means to combat habits of dualistic conceptualizations, and to combat the tricks and tenacity of ego-clinging. In this way the guru is a living manifestation of the teachings.

It needs to be emphasized that it is our perception of the guru which enables the guru to function as a manifestation of the dharma. At first we see the guru as an ordinary person, and then as our practice develops we start to see the guru as more of an enlightened being, until finally we learn to recognize the guru as being nothing but an external manifestation of our own awakeness or buddhamind. In a subtle way, then, it is almost irrelevant whether or not the teacher is enlightened. The guru-disciple relationship is not about worshipping a guru, but providing the opportunity to liberate our confused perceptions of reality.

*Dzongsar Khyentse Rinpoche*

## THE TEACHER SHOULD BE A TRAVELER TOO                    10.11
The teacher should be a traveler too, someone who is traveling with you. That's very important. Rather than being stuck with enlightenment and unable to go beyond it.

*Chögyam Trungpa Rinpoche*

## METAPHORS OF THE GURU                    10.12
The teacher is like
>    a great ship carrying us across the perilous ocean of existence
>    an unerring navigator guiding us to the dry land of liberation
>    a rain of nectar extinguishing the inferno of negative emotions and
>        actions
>    a bright sun and moon dispelling the darkness of ignorance
>    the firm earth patiently bearing the weight of both good and bad
>    a wish-granting tree bestowing both present and ultimate
>        happiness
>    a treasury of vast and deep instructions
>    a wish-granting gem providing whatever beings need on their path
>    a father and mother loving all beings equally
>    a great river of wide and swift compassion
>    a great mountain of joy rising above worldly concerns and
>        unshaken by the winds of emotions
>    a great cloud raining down its benefits impartially everywhere,
>        uninfluenced by like or dislike.

*Dilgo Khyentse Rinpoche*

## WHAT IS INVOLVED IN RELATING TO A TEACHER?                    10.13
[Relating to the teacher] does not mean worshipping or adoring the teacher. You just need a sense of basic openness, a feeling that the teach-

er's approach to the teaching is accurate. . . . What the teacher has to say becomes relevant to you. That is what is called the meeting of two minds.

*Chögyam Trungpa Rinpoche*

## THE NEED FOR COMMITMENT AND DILIGENCE   10.14

It is risky to make too hasty a commitment to a lama. But once you have come to a carefully considered decision, you must follow his or her teachings diligently and purposefully. If you are sick but don't take the medicine your physician prescribes, you won't get well. So after looking for a lama skillfully, you must listen and train skillfully. If you carefully apply the instructions you have received, then slowly your negativity will decrease, and love and compassion will increase. In this way, you will learn what the lama has learned. The lama is like a mold that shapes the student's mind. A student won't develop good qualities from a poor teacher, but will benefit infallibly by following a good teacher's instructions.

*Chagdud Tulku Rinpoche*

## IT IS NOT ENOUGH TO IMITATE YOUR GURU   10.15

It is not enough to imitate your master or guru; you are not trying to become a replica of your teacher. The teachings are an individual, personal experience. . . . It is essential to relate to yourself, to your own experience, *really*. If one does not relate to oneself, then the spiritual path becomes dangerous, becomes purely external entertainment, rather than an organic, personal experience.

*Chögyam Trungpa Rinpoche*

## WE HAVE TO REALIZE THE TRUTH OURSELVES   10.16

Relating to a teacher is like plugging into an electrical outlet. If electricity is flowing, it will come directly to us. But if there isn't any electricity coming through, nothing will happen. This may not be the best of examples, but in a way it's a good one because we don't know exactly what electricity is. We only know what it can do. By relating to one

who has a direct experience of the absolute truth, we can connect with
that truth. The purpose of honoring, accepting, having faith in, and
being receptive to the teacher, then, is to realize this truth ourselves,
not simply to appreciate someone else's realization of it.

*Chagdud Tulku Rinpoche*

## DEVOTION IS THE UNIVERSAL PANACEA                    10.17

In the Kagyü and Nyingma traditions it is said that devotion is the
universal panacea, the medicine that can cure all sickness. If one just
focuses on devotion one does not need to spend years studying debate,
philosophy, grammar, art, and so forth. In the past, thousands of practitioners attained accomplishment through the path of devotion combined with the paths of Mahamudra and Dzogchen.

*Tulku Urgyen Rinpoche*

## THE POWER OF DEVOTION                               10.18

If one is completely devoted to a spiritual teacher, gradually all his spiritual qualities will develop in oneself. As an analogy, it is said that even
the ordinary wood in the sandalwood forests of Mount Malaya acquires
a wonderful scent. After years of being impregnated with the drops that
fall from the sandal leaves, the fragrance of the ordinary trees becomes
indistinguishable from that of the sandalwood itself. However, if instead
of finding a true spiritual friend, one just relies on confused friends, one
becomes like kusha grass that has fallen into a sewer—very difficult to
get clean.

*Dilgo Khyentse Rinpoche*

## WHY DEVOTION IS NECESSARY ON THE PATH               10.19

How can we make genuine progress in our personal experience?
Chiefly through devotion to the Three Jewels. The compassionate activity of the buddhas is like a hook that is just waiting to catch sentient
beings who are ready and open and who are attuned to this compassion.
If we have faith and devotion, we are like an iron ring that can be
caught by the hook. But if we are closed and lack faith and devotion,

we are like a solid iron ball. Not even the "hooks" of the buddhas can catch an iron ball. . . .

We need to have faith and devotion in order to connect with the compassionate power of the buddhas. If we do not possess these qualities, we cannot open ourselves to this connection, and there is no way that the buddhas can help us. . . . Imagine that you have positioned a mirror facing the sun: the moment you do so, the sun's rays are instantly reflected. It is the same with the buddhas: the moment we think of them, they "gaze" on us; the rays of their compassion contact us. . . . The very moment you open up in devotion, you receive the blessings of the buddhas.

*Tulku Urgyen Rinpoche*

## DEVOTION AND COMPASSION: FROM FABRICATED
## TO UNFABRICATED                                    10.20

The teachings mention that compassion and devotion should be unfabricated, but this doesn't happen automatically in the beginning. We need to cultivate them, to use some effort to produce these feelings. In other words, in the beginning, we must rely on conceptual thought to make it possible to have compassion and devotion. . . . The main practice of devotion is taking refuge, and the main practice of compassion is to generate bodhicitta. . . .

At first, devotion and compassion are necessary to create. They are important stepping stones to recognizing *rigpa* [nondual awareness]. Unfabricated and natural devotion and compassion are the expression of *rigpa*, but not for a beginning student. In the context of Dzogchen, it is said that compassion and devotion naturally occur, without any effort. But frankly speaking, for a beginner it doesn't happen like that. At first we have to cultivate devotion and compassion, to put some effort into developing them. Later on, as we become more stable in awareness, they become effortless and unfabricated.

*Tulku Urgyen Rinpoche*

## DEVOTION IS A MARK OF OUR PRACTICE              10.21

It's sometimes said in Vajrayana that your progress in the Dharma shows in how much devotion you have for your guru: the more you have progressed in your Dharma practice, the more devotion you will naturally have for your guru, because as your experience deepens, so your confidence in your guru becomes stronger. There's a story about the great Tibetan yogi Milarepa and his student Gampopa. When Gampopa had finished his studies and was going away, Milarepa said to him: "Now you must go away and practice meditation. There will come a time when you will see me, your old father Milarepa, as a real buddha. Then you can start teaching because that will be a sign that you have actually experienced the result of your practice." So when you start seeing your own teacher as somebody really like a buddha, that means that you yourself have gained some experience of the Dharma.

*Ringu Tulku Rinpoche*

## THE SANGHA                                    10.22
The sangha carries the atmosphere of the teacher and the teaching and the lineage.

*Chögyam Trungpa Rinpoche*

## SEEING THE GURU AS BUDDHA                     10.23
As our obscurations are more and more purified, eventually we will see our own spiritual mentor, our own lama, as a supreme Nirmanakaya, in other words, having the full thirty-two major and eighty minor marks, regardless of the attainment from his or her own side. When we have attained that level, then even if he or she is in hell, we will see our lama as a supreme Nirmanakaya.

*Gen Lamrimpa*

## SEEING THE GURU AS VAJRADHARA                 10.24
Seeing the essence of Vajradhara [the supreme celestial buddha] as our own root guru brings a feeling of closeness, of personal kindness; and visualizing the guru in the aspect of Vajradhara brings inspiration and realization quickly.

*Lama Thubten Yeshe Rinpoche*

*Ringu Tulku Rinpoche*

## IS THE GURU AN EXTERNAL PERSON?                    10.25

[This] seems to be the problem that Naropa encountered in his meeting
with Tilopa [his guru]. He regarded himself as a student and thought he
had to do something—ask for Tilopa's teaching. Thus he was still seeing
Tilopa as an external person rather than as a part of his own psychological makeup presenting itself as Tilopa.

*Chögyam Trungpa Rinpoche*

## ALL REALIZATION COMES FROM THE GURU              10.26

The tantric texts often mention that all realization comes from the guru.
This is true, but we have to understand that *guru* has two different levels
of meaning. The relative, objective guru is the teacher who, by com-
municating with us in different ways, shows us how to act so that we
can discover our own totality. But on a deeper, more subjective level,
our guru is none other than our own inner wisdom, our own fundamental clarity of mind.

*Lama Thubten Yeshe Rinpoche*

## ORDINARILY, WE DO NOT LISTEN TO THE VOICE OF
## INNER WISDOM                                       10.27

Ordinarily, even though we do possess this inner voice of wisdom, we
do not listen to it. We do not even hear it! We are too busy listening
to the garbage conversation of our gross, dualistic minds. We are so
accustomed to this that even when wisdom does arise, as an intuitive
insight, we often reject it. By practicing guru-yoga [meditation on the
guru], we are able progressively to cut through our superficial ways of
relating to the world and make contact with the innate wisdom at the
heart of our being. When we have done this, then we can communicate
deeply with the outer guru as well. But as long as we are out of touch
with our inner guru, no matter how profound the teachings of the
outer guru may be, we will never be able to integrate them.

*Lama Thubten Yeshe Rinpoche*

## THE ULTIMATE LAMA                                  10.28

Since pure awareness of nowness is the real buddha,
In openness and contentment I found the Lama in my heart.

When we realize this unending natural mind is the very nature
of the Lama,
Then there is no need for attached, grasping, or weeping prayers or
artificial complaints,
By simply relaxing in this uncontrived, open, and natural state,
We obtain the blessing of aimless self-liberation of whatever arises.

*Dudjom Rinpoche*

## The Ultimate Teacher                                     10.29

The ultimate teacher, the absolute, is never separate from us,
Yet immature beings, not recognizing this, look outside and seek
him far away.
Sole father, with your immense love you have shown me my
own wealth;
I, who was a pauper, constantly feel your presence in the depth
of my heart.

Wisdom-teacher pervading all the world and beings, samsara
and nirvana,
You show how all phenomena can arise as teachings,
Convincing me that everything is the absolute teacher;
I long for ultimate realization, and feel your presence in the depth
of my heart.

*Dilgo Khyentse Rinpoche*

## The Relative Guru Is Vitally Important            10.30

But we should not interpret this to mean that the external, relative guru
is unimportant. This is not true; he or she is vitally important. Although
it is true that the tantric teachings of Shakyamuni buddha have been in
existence for 2500 years, do they exist for us if we have not yet met a
qualified master? Are they real for us or not? . . . Can we say that tantra
is a reality for us before someone has introduced it to us? Of course not.
. . . They only become part of our reality once we have realized them,
and this depends upon having met a guru who can show us their truth
clearly in a way we can understand. If we do not have the living exam-

ple and inspiration of the external guru, our inner wisdom will remain weak and undeveloped.

*Lama Thubten Yeshe Rinpoche*

### DON'T LOOK FOR ROMANTIC FULFILLMENT                  10.31

The notion of sexual equality is quite new in the West, and because of this there is a certain rigid and fanatic adherence to the specific way it should be practiced. In vajrayana Buddhism, on the other hand, there is a tremendous appreciation of the female, as well as a strong emphasis on the equality of all beings. This might not, however, be apparent to someone who cannot see beyond a contemporary Western framework. As a result, when Western women have sexual relationships with Tibetan lamas, some might be frustrated when their culturally conditioned expectations are not met.

If anyone thinks they could have a pleasing and equal lover in a Rinpoche, they couldn't be more incorrect. Certain Rinpoches, those known as great teachers, would by definition be the ultimate bad partner, from ego's point of view. If one approaches such great masters with the intention of being gratified and wishing for a relationship of sharing, mutual enjoyment, etc., then not only from ego's point of view, but even from a mundane point of view, such people would be a bad choice. They probably will not bring you flowers or invite you out for candlelit dinners.

If someone goes to study under a master with the intention to achieve enlightenment, one must presume that such a student is ready to give up his or her ego. You don't go to India and study with a venerable Tibetan master expecting him to behave according to your own standards. It is unfair to ask someone to free you from delusion, and then criticize him or her for going against your ego. I am not writing this out of fear that if one doesn't defend Tibetan lamas or Buddhist teachers, they will lose popularity. Despite a lot of effort to convince the world about the pitfalls of the dharma and the defects of the teachers, there will still be a lot of masochists who have the misfortune to appreciate the dharma and a crazy, abusing teacher who will make sure to mistreat every inch of ego. These poor souls will eventually end up bereft of both ego and confusion.

*Dzongsar Khytense Rinpoche*

*Drubwang Tsoknyi Rinpoche*

## ONE SHOULD NOT BE OVERDEPENDENT ON
## SPIRITUAL TEACHERS                                    10.32

Of course we need to follow a spiritual teacher, and of course we need
to receive instructions. Of course we need to put those instructions into
practice. But if one spends one's whole life trying to follow spiritual
teachers, something is wrong there also. We need to supplicate our root
guru in order to discover the indivisible nature of his mind and our
mind. That is definitely necessary. But it's not good to think, "If I'm
not with my teacher, I won't know how to practice"; "If I'm not with
my teacher, I can't deal with disturbing emotions"; or "If I'm not with
my teacher, I am lost, I do not know what to do."

*Drubwang Tsoknyi Rinpoche*

# The Vajrayana Path

THE VAJRAYANA PHASE of the Tibetan Buddhist path is focused almost entirely on meditation and aims to provide methods for the attainment of realization in one's present lifetime. This third of the three *yana*s contains a wealth of meditative and contemplative practices, and these are organized in a graded series, placed according to the level of stability and maturity they presuppose. The tantric path is both detailed and complex, as befits such an intensely practice-oriented tradition. This chapter is organized according to the main stages in the classical tantric journey, with a few selections illustrating each.

All of the Vajrayana practices rest upon the Hinayana and Mahayana foundation. From the Hinayana, it is assumed that one has attained familiarity in the "view," understands the truths of suffering and karma, and is clear that samsara is inadequate to the human desire for happiness and fulfillment. On the practice level, it is further taken for granted that one is committed to living in a kind and ethical way, and that one is well-grounded in meditation—both experienced in the practice and possessing some degree of mental stability. As a result of the Mahayana, understanding and also some experience of both emptiness and buddha-nature are presumed to be in place, as is one's bodhisattva commitment and basically altruistic motivation for the journey. Once this foundation is established, one is then qualified and prepared to engage in the Vajrayana.

Vajrayana practice typically begins with the *ngöndro,* or "preliminary practices." These include 100,000 each of four (or sometimes five) practices: prostrations and refuge (sometimes refuge is carried out as a fifth *ngöndro*), Vajrasattva mantra, *mandala* offering, and guru yoga (11.1). Each practice opens and softens the practitioner, preparing him or her for the teachings that follow. In these selections, I highlight prostrations and guru yoga as of particular interest. Prostrations, so we read, provide a way for us to identify with the "lowest of the low," our basic raw and rugged quality, the ground that tantra works with (11.2, 11.3). The next selections describe guru yoga as uniquely profound and effective, "the core of all our spiritual practice." This is because by generating devotion to, and identification with, our teacher obstacles are removed and the power of the awakened state mediated by him or her can enter our being (11.4, 11.5). Within guru yoga, there is an ever-deepening practice that occurs through the outer, inner, secret, and most secret methods (11.6).

Usually following the *ngöndro*—though sometimes elsewhere on the path—students are given "pointing-out" instruction or mind transmission. Within the Vajrayana, there are three ways in which the teachings are communicated. First and most obvious is the "word lineage," in which one is instructed verbally. Second and more subtle is the "sign lineage," in which the teachings are transmitted nonverbally, through signs and symbols. Finally, there is the "mind lineage," in which the basic state of fundamental awareness, the buddha-nature itself, is nakedly shown, directly transmitted from the teacher to the mind of the disciple. The instruction of pointing out belongs to this third category. This involves a meeting between *vajra* master and student, most often one on one, but sometimes in groups, in which the nature of the inborn awareness is shown (11.7). What is pointed out is our own present wakefulness as it exists in this moment (11.8). The pointing out plays a critical role within the context of the overall Vajrayana journey: first, we are introduced to the awakened state within us; second, we train in sustaining that recognition for longer and longer periods; and third, we attain complete stability in it, known as the complete enlightenment of buddhahood (11.9).

Following the pointing-out instruction, the student is initiated into actual tantric practice through a formal ritual known as *abhisheka*, "empowerment." Through the *abhisheka*, the initiate is introduced to a particular *yidam* (a male or female buddha to be meditated on) and led into the *yidam*'s *mandala* (retinue of deities representing enlightened aspects and qualities) (11.10). There are many, many different *abhisheka*s performed in Tibetan Buddhism, depending upon which particular *yidam* one is being given permission to perform. The empowerment is a quite complex ritual and, although the *yidam* upon which one will meditate varies, the *abhisheka* rite has attained a relatively standard structure and procedure throughout Tibetan Buddhism. In its classical form, the *abhisheka* has four sub-empowerments (11.11): the vase empowerment (11.12), the secret empowerment (11.13), the wisdom-knowledge empowerment (11.14), and the "word" empowerment (11.15).

In the *abhisheka* itself, we must first let go of any desire to reject who we are and become someone else. We must accept ourselves, as we are (11.16) And then, as the rite unfolds, we must let go of our own sense of personal identity and identify with the wisdom mind of the deity. Most important, the deity is nothing other than our own enlightened nature, depicted in apparently external form. *Abhisheka* is, ultimately, the meeting of the mind of teacher and student. In the ritual, the initiate is brought face to face with the mind of the *vajra* master, which is nothing other than the ultimate identity of the *yidam*, the embodiment of our own primordial nature. But even though the essence of the *yidam* is our own nature, we can only find our way to that by first visualizing this deity as external to us and using that, in our practice, as a way to awaken to our own awakened mind (11.17).

This critical point is further explained in the next few passages. The deities to whom we are introduced in *abhisheka* may be peaceful, wrathful, or semi-wrathful; and they may be male or female. The peaceful deities, for example, though seemingly external at first, are ultimately not separate from our own awareness. They represent the completely encompassing peace of our basic nature that cannot be challenged, "that has no age, no end, no beginning"; a peace that, in its implacability, could be terrifying (11.18). Similarly, the wrathful deities embody "the ruthless, unyielding quality" of the basic nature that will not allow sidetracks of any kind (11.19).

The *yidam* is not only an expression of our own basic nature, but also an expression of the nature of the apparently external world. The external manifestation of the *yidam* is particularly evident in his or her *mandala*, composed of at least four deities (each representing one direction of the compass) and up to many hundreds of deities. The essence of the deities is the five elements, the living energies that underlie everything in the phenomenal world without exception (11.20).

Within Tibetan Buddhism, many, many deities are known, *yidam*s, their retinues, protective deities, departed men and women teachers, and so on. These are all understood as manifestations of a central structure, defined by the three bodies of a buddha, the *dharmakaya*, the *sambhogakaya*, and the *nirmanakaya*. Within each major tradition, each of these has the buddha considered its most potent representation, an example of which is given in our next passage (11.21). Again, when we look at any single figure, such as the departed master Guru Rinpoche (Padmasambhava), although he himself is a *nirmanakaya* form, we can discern in him all three *kaya*s (11.22). So the three bodies of the buddha provide a kind of overarching framework for locating and understanding the particular character of each deity and his or her way of functioning.

Part of the *abhisheka* ritual involves certain vows and commitments known as *samaya*. *Samaya* includes both a general vow and also a specific set of commitments. The general vow is not to depart from the insight one gains in the *abhisheka*. This is the awareness that one is ultimately not a lost, confused, suffering samsaric being but rather, at the deepest level, an awakened being. And the world is not an evil, terrible place, but is rather the *mandala* of the *yidam*, alive with the play of awakened wisdom. One needs to hold to this and not fall into thinking of oneself or one's world in a degraded way. The specific commitments follow from this: one needs to respect oneself and others, one needs to honor one's teacher, the teachings, the lineage, and so on.

The tantric approach is clearly dangerous. One could use this kind of "sacred outlook" in exactly the wrong way, to justify one's own aggression and egomania. This is why the *samaya* vow is necessary, so that we maintain our view of sacredness of ourselves and others, our basic bodhichitta, and do not fall back into a pattern of trying to manipulate the world for our own benefit. In this sense, the practice of tantra is like a snake in a bamboo tube. We are the snake that has been put in the tube. We can either go up or down. If we go up—which means keeping *samaya*—then we will attain enlightenment. If we go down—breaking our *samaya*—we will go to the lowest of the lower realms (11.23, 11.24). This principle is vividly illustrated by a traditional Tibetan story (11.25).

Following the *abhisheka*, one enters into Vajrayana practice of the *yidam*. This involves regular practice of the *sadhana*, a structured meditation on the *yidam* and his or her *mandala*. Although the *sadhana* is a meditation ritual with many parts, it is important to realize that it is not something artificial imposed on top of the fundamental nature of things. Rather, "it is a way of acknowledging our original state" (11.26). The *sadhana* provides the formal means to enter into a way of being that needs to characterize our lives from this point onward: we need to rely utterly on the *yidam* as our sole refuge (11.27). In one sense, yes, we are taking complete and and utter refuge in something external. But on a deeper level, it is our own awakened nature that we are training to rely completely upon and, in doing so, we open ourselves to the blessings of the awakened state (11.28).

*Sadhana* practice involves two phases: the first is visualizing, *utpattik-rama*, "the stage of generation" (of the deity) and, second, the dissolving of our visualization into emptiness, *sampannakrama*, "the stage of completion." In the visualization stage, we visualize the deity in front of us according to the instructions given in our *sadhana* text, as having a particular gender; being peaceful, wrathful, or semi-wrathful; having one or more heads, and a certain number of arms and legs; being attired and ornamented in a particular way; standing or sitting in a certain pose; and so on. We then visualize the *yidam* in a celestial palace surrounded by his or her retinue. It is important to realize that our visualization is not just a superficial, artificial product of our imagination. "It is how things already are in actuality" (11.29).

Then we follow an itinerary of relating to this externally visualized deity: we may take refuge, rouse bodhichitta, make offerings, confess our wrongdoing, and offer praises. Then we visualize ourselves as the deity, following the instructions of the text. The purpose of this is to enable us to identify ourselves "as a Buddha, a deity, a fully enlightened being" (11.30). Through the practice, we are training to maintain awareness of ourselves as the deity and not fall into degraded ways of thinking about ourselves. We visualize our body as the body of the deity and, likewise, our speech and mind as the speech and mind of the deity (11.31). We visualize the world as the celestial palace of the deity. This kind of practice purifies our habitual tendencies to think of ourselves and others as poor and pitiful and to solidify the world and cling to it, both of which keep us wandering in samsara (11.32). We continue with the process of purification brought about by *sadhana* practice until we are able to rest without effort or wandering, in the inherent nature itself, known as the ultimate development stage (11.33). At the end of each session of our *sadhana* practice, we dissolve the deity, the retinue, and the *mandala* palace into emptiness and rest in that open, clear, and boundless state. At this point, we are resting in the nature of mind itself. This resting is called, in this context, *sampannakrama*, the completion phase (11.34). Finally, at the conclusion of our session, we dedicate the merit of our practice to all beings (11.35).

The journey from the *ngöndro* to pointing out and through *abhisheka* and *sadhana* practice purifies our minds and brings us closer and closer to the ultimate nature itself. In *sampannakrama* we are beginning to train in that nature a little. There are further practices that work more nakedly with the natural state, called either Mahamudra (in the Sakya, Kagyü, and Gelug—the New Translation schools) or Dzogchen (in the Nyingma—the Old Translation school). In Mahamudra and Dzogchen, one works directly and simply with the nature of the mind that was pointed out in transmission. It is as if, in our habitual life, we are always looking at the ground. In transmission, we are shown the sky for the first time. But then our habitual patterns lead us to look down at the ground again and to forget about the existence of the sky. *Sadhana* practice is a little like still looking at the ground, except that a mirror is placed there so that we can see the sky while we are looking down. Gradually, we become used to the idea that the ground isn't all there is and we gradually become familiar with what the sky is like. In Mahamudra and Dzogchen, however, we take a much more direct path: we are shown how to look back at the actual sky again and again, until eventually we never lose sight of it or forget it again. Mahamudra and Dzogchen are called "essence teachings" because they point directly to the essence of our own inborn awareness. They are usually not taught to practitioners until a considerable amount of previous Hinayana, Mahayana, and Vajrayana practice has sufficiently prepared them to be able to receive these teachings and practice them.

The chapter concludes with a few selections that typify first, Mahamudra, and, second, Dzogchen. Within the New Translation schools, Mahamudra is considered the epitome of the Buddha's teaching (11.36). The meaning of the Tibetan term *chak gya chenpo,* is next defined in terms of the inseparability of emptiness and wisdom (11.37). The core meditation of Mahamudra is Mahamudra *shamatha* and *vipashyana,* attaining stillness and then, from within that stillness, inspecting the mind to ascertain its nature (11.38). When one knows the mind, one sees the nature of all things (11.39). The passages on Mahamudra conclude with summaries of the benefits of Mahamudra *shamatha* and *vipashyana* (11.40, 11.41) and a description of the fruition of Mahamudra as realizing the mind, by its very nature, as the three *kaya*s (11.42).

Dzogchen, "the Great Perfection," plays an analogous role in the Nyingma or Ancient Translation school: it is considered the epitome of all the Buddha's myriad teachings. Our first two selections summarize the spirit of Dzogchen (11.43) and briefly characterize it (11.44). The "Dzogchen moment" is the dawning of immaculate awareness (11.45), and this dawning instantly makes our human life meaningful (11.46). How do we practice Dzogchen? It is recognizing the primordial state (11.47). We send our thinking mind on a holiday (11.48). In a manner similar to Mahamudra, Dzogchen meditation is structured according to *shamatha* (tranquility meditation), here defined as resting in emptiness, and *vipashyana* (insight meditation), not deviating from that state (11.49). One of the most important "texts" in Dzogchen is the epigrammatic "Three Statements Concerning the Essential Nature" by Garab Dorje, the human founder of the Great Perfection. The next selection include this text as well as Dudjom Rinpoche's commentary on it (11.50), which provide a succinct overview of the stages of Dzogchen practice. Madhyamaka, Mahamudra, and Dzogchen are next compared and the question is asked, how are they different? (11.51). The fruition of Dzogchen practice in this life is the attainment of the rainbow body (11.52).

## THE FOUR NGÖNDRO PRACTICES                    11.1

First we take refuge and do prostrations, thereby removing karmic misdeeds and obscurations of our body gathered in countless lifetimes. In
order to remove the negative obscurations of speech which we have
accumulated since beginningless time, we practice the meditation and
recitation of Vajrasattva. To remove the obscurations and negative actions of our mind gathered during beginningless lifetimes, we make the
outer, inner, and secret *mandala* offerings. Finally, to remove the negative actions and obscurations which have been gathered through a com-
bination of body, speech, and mind from beginningless time, we
practice the outer, inner, and secret aspects of guru yoga.

*Tulku Urgyen Rinpoche*

## PROSTRATIONS: A GESTURE OF SURRENDER         11.2

[The practice of prostrations] is the act of falling on the ground in a
gesture of surrender. At the same time we open psychologically and
surrender completely by identifying ourselves with the lowest of the
low, acknowledging our raw and rugged quality. There is nothing that
we fear to lose once we identify ourselves with the lowest of the low.
By doing so, we prepare ourselves to be an empty vessel, ready to receive the teachings.

*Chögyam Trungpa Rinpoche*

## PROSTRATIONS: TO THE OBJECT OF OUR STRONGEST
## NATURAL DEVOTION                              11.3

To take refuge, visualize an object of refuge in front of you . . . the one
for whom you have the strongest natural devotion—in the form of the
precious Lotus-Born Guru, Guru Rinpoche. . . . We should take refuge
with the vast attitude of the Mahayana, taking refuge not only for this
lifetime, but until we attain enlightenment—not only for our own sake,
but in order to bring all sentient beings to enlightenment. . . . Recite
the refuge prayer a hundred thousand times, while doing the same
number of prostrations.

*Dilgo Khyentse Rinpoche*

## GURU YOGA                                                  11.4

Guru yoga is an extremely profound practice which is excellent for
removing obscurations and developing realization. Though it is placed
among the preliminary practices, it is said to be more profound than the
main part of practice itself.

*Tulku Urgyen Rinpoche*


## THE IMPORTANCE OF GURU YOGA                               11.5

The essence of reliance on a teacher is unceasing devotion, and the
most effective means of generating and sustaining unwavering devotion
is precisely the practice of guru yoga. Through this practice, devotion
to the teacher takes firm root within us and eventually grows to pervade
our entire being. It protects our practice from obstacles and ensures
progress on the path. Devotion to the teacher is thus the core of all our
spiritual practice, regardless of the particular stages of the path we cultivate. For these reasons, guru yoga is considered the most vital and necessary of all practices and is in itself the surest and fastest way to reach
the goal of enlightenment.

*Dilgo Khyentse Rinpoche*


## OUTER, INNER, SECRET, AND MOST SECRET
## METHODS OF GURU YOGA                                      11.6

The outer method is to visualize the guru dwelling above our head and
to pray to him ardently, with fierce devotion. The inner method is to
realize, through the practice, that our own body, speech, and mind are
inseparable from the wisdom body, speech, and mind of the guru. . . .
The secret method is to meditate upon the guru in his *sambhogakaya*
form, the body of divine enjoyment. . . . The most secret method introduces us to the natural state of awareness.

*Dilgo Khyentse Rinpoche*


## POINTING OUT OUR ESSENCE                                  11.7

In order to enable us to recognize or know our own essence, the
teacher, the *vajra* master, gives what is called the pointing-out instruc-

tion. It is for that single purpose. And yet, what he points out is not something we don't already have. We already possess the buddha nature.

*Tulku Urgyen Rinpoche*


## THE POINTING-OUT INSTRUCTION                    11.8

The pointing-out instruction is the present wakefulness pointed out as it is. It is not something in the future, not something in the past, but present right now. You don't have to accept or reject it. Don't do anything to it: don't adopt, don't avoid, don't entertain any hope or fear, don't try to change, alter, or improve it.

*Tulku Urgyen Rinpoche*


## FROM POINTING OUT TO BUDDHAHOOD: AN ANALOGY                    11.9

First we must recognize our own nature, our essence. Next we must endeavor with great diligence to continuously sustain that recognition, which is called training. Finally, to reach the state where not even an iota of conceptual thinking remains, when conceptual thinking is totally purified, is called the attainment of stability. This stability is also known as the complete enlightenment of buddhahood.

The teachings of both Mahamudra and Dzogchen give a traditional example for this sequence.

- On the first day of the lunar calendar when we look in the sky we don't see anything; the moon is invisible.
- But on the evening of the third day we see a sliver of the moon. At that time it is possible for someone to point at the moon and say, "There is the moon!" We look and we see that the moon is the moon. That is called recognizing.
- Each following day the moon grows larger and larger,
- until on the night of the fifteenth day it is totally full and brilliant, shining in the sky.

That is the example for the *dharmakaya* of self-existing awareness free from constructs.

Again, pointing out the moon is called recognizing. That it grows further and further is training. When it is finally a full, complete moon, that is the attainment of stability, complete enlightenment.

*Tulku Urgyen Rinpoche*


## WHAT IS ABHISHEKA? 11.10

[*Abhisheka,* or tantric initiation] is the beginning of the experience of meditation and concentration, of penetration into the nature of the reality of all phenomena. Initiation leads us into the *mandala* of a deity and into the totality of the experiences of that deity. It is an antidote to the dissatisfied, samsaric, fanatical, dualistic mind. During initiation we should completely let go of our preconceptions and fixed ideas of who we are, of our limited self-image. Instead, we need to identify with the wisdom-mind of the deity, which is our own perfect potential.

*Lama Thubten Yeshe Rinpoche*


## THE FOUR EMPOWERMENTS OF THE ABHISHEKA 11.11

These four empowerments, also called the vase empowerment, secret empowerment, wisdom-knowledge empowerment, and precious word empowerment, are indispensable for Vajrayana practice. The very profound practices connected with each of these four empowerments enable us to attain complete enlightenment within this very lifetime. However, and this cannot be emphasized enough, these practices cannot be taught to just anyone. Unless a person has openness and faith in the Buddha's teachings, the empowerments will not be of much benefit.

*Chökyi Nyima Rinpoche*


## THE FIRST PART OF THE ABHISHEKA: THE VASE EMPOWERMENT 11.12

The vase empowerment is usually given with the master seated on a throne, the shrine beautifully arranged and decorated, and the disciples sitting on lower seats making *mandala* offerings. At that moment they feel great interest and devotion. The master then reveals the *mandala*

*Chökyi Nyima Rinpoche*

and confers the empowerment by placing a vase and other ritual imple-
ments on the top of each person's head. Later he explains the ritual to
them. That is the general procedure in a vase empowerment. . . . The
vase empowerment is the authorization to practice the development
stage, to visualize the deity and to experience its vivid presence and the
purity of the surrounding environment.

*Chökyi Nyima Rinpoche*

## PART TWO OF THE ABHISHEKA: THE SECRET
## EMPOWERMENT
11.13

The secret empowerment refers to understanding the key points of the
energy-winds and the practices connected with them such as *tummo*,
through which one realizes the unity of luminosity and emptiness. By
recognizing this the seed for attaining *sambhogakaya* is planted. This is
called obtaining the secret empowerment.

*Chökyi Nyima Rinpoche*

## PART THREE OF THE ABHISHEKA: THE WISDOM-
## KNOWLEDGE EMPOWERMENT
11.14

Next is the wisdom-knowledge empowerment. Stories are told of great
masters from the past such as Naropa, Tilopa, and Saraha, who attained
high degrees of realization through the practices connected to this empowerment. However, the person who engages in the practices related
to the third empowerment must already possess the correct view; otherwise he or she is no different from an ordinary worldly person. For
example, Saraha was the most disciplined of the five hundred monks
in his monastery, but he later took an arrow maker's daughter as his
consort.

*Chökyi Nyima Rinpoche*

## PART FOUR OF THE ABHISHEKA: THE "WORD"
## EMPOWERMENT
11.15

Through the fourth empowerment, the word empowerment, all of
samsara and nirvana is resolved to be equal in nature. One realizes the
state of unity beyond concepts. . . . This state of innate wakefulness is

the absence of mental fabrication, and is also known as ordinary mind, fresh and unmodified.

*Chökyi Nyima Rinpoche*

## YOU MUST ACCEPT YOURSELF AS YOU ARE                    11.16
Real initiation (*abhisheka*) takes place in terms of "the meeting of two minds." It is a matter of being what you really are and of relating to the spiritual friend as he or she is. This is the true situation in which initiation might occur, because the idea of having an operation and fundamentally changing yourself is completely unrealistic. No one can really change your personality absolutely. No one can turn you completely upside down and inside out. The existing material, that which is already there, must be used. You must accept yourself as you are, instead of as you would like to be, which means giving up self-deception and wishful thinking. Your whole make-up and personality characteristics must be recognized, accepted, and then you might find some inspiration.

*Chögyam Trungpa Rinpoche*

## THE RELATIVE BUDDHA AND THE
## ULTIMATE BUDDHA                                        11.17
All Dharma teachings have two aspects: the relative or superficial and the ultimate or real. Visualizing the Buddha as being outside ourselves is superficial, and is not enough for enlightenment. The basis for awakening to enlightenment is to experience the buddha in ourselves.

But the recognition of the real is nevertheless dependent upon the superficial, because it is by making offerings, purifying obscurations, and gathering the accumulations with the support of a buddha imagined outside that we can remove the obscurations and realize the buddha within.

*Tulku Urgyen Rinpoche*

## THE PEACEFUL DEITIES                                   11.18
[The peace] of the peaceful divinities [is] not peacefulness in the sense of the love and light experience . . . but of completely encompassing peace, immovable, invincible peace, the peaceful state that cannot be

challenged, that has no age, no end, no beginning. The symbol of peace is represented in the shape of a circle; it has no entrance; it is eternal. . . . This state of absolute peacefulness seems to be extremely frightening, and there is often the possibility that one's faith might be shaken by such a sudden glimpse of another dimension.

*Chögyam Trungpa Rinpoche*

## THE WRATHFUL DEITIES                                                      11.19

The wrathful divinities are another expression of peacefulness, the ruthless, unyielding quality, not allowing sidetracks of any kind. . . . They represent the outrageous, exuberant quality of energy which cannot be challenged. . . .

If you approach them and try to re-shape the situation, they throw you back. . . . When you are involved in ego-manufactured, comforting situations of any kind, the actual reality of the nakedness of mind and the colorful aspect of emotions will wake you up, possibly in a very violent way, as a sudden accident or sudden chaos.

*Chögyam Trungpa Rinpoche*

## THE FIVE ELEMENTS                                                        11.20

All limited or limitless spheres of existence which arise, whether gross or subtle, unhappy or happy, ordinary or sublime, depend on the five elements which are the basis of all pure and impure phenomena. . . .

All generally visible measureless phenomena elements are the display of the self-secret, divisionless, unobstructed Wisdom Mind. . . .

Whenever we do not recognize the pure nature of the manifestation of wisdom display, we cling to unobstructed mind's uncatchable self-arising reflection, obscuring its inseparable emptiness and luminosity, and separating the divisionless phenomena elements into subject and object. As soon as there is division, there is impurity and obstruction. . . . We call this [resulting] divided mind dualistic mind, which is the cause of bad and good karma.

Whenever we recognize the pure nature of the manifestation of the self-secret wisdom display, we are aware of the pure, secret essence of the elements. With this recognition, there is no subject and no object

. . . so there is no karma. With this recognition, absolute truth and relative truth become inseparable, nondualistic, clear awareness space. . . .

*Thinley Norbu Rinpoche*

## THE MANY DEITIES IN TIBETAN BUDDHISM AND
## THEIR SOURCE                                    11.21

The equivalent of a "god" or a supreme being in Buddhism is called Samantabhadra, meaning the Ever-Excellent. He is the primordial *dharmakaya* buddha. When Samandabhadra manifests on the *sambhogakaya* level he is called Vajradhara, the Vajra Holder. His *nirmanakaya* form is called Vajrasattva.

There are an incredible amount of gods and deities in Buddhism, but their basic source, where they manifest from, is the *dharmakaya* buddha Samantabhadra, the *sambhogakaya* buddha Vajradhara, and the *nirmanakaya* buddha Vajrasattva.

*Tulku Urgyen Rinpoche*

## WHO IS GURU RINPOCHE?                          11.22

Who, we may ask, is Guru Rinpoche? In the *dharmakaya*, the absolute level, he is Buddha Amitabha. In the *sambhogakaya*, the level of divine enjoyment, he is Avalokiteshvara. In the *nirmanakaya*, the level of manifestation, he is the Lotus-Born Guru Pema Jungne (Skt. Padmakara), who appeared in this degenerate age when sentient beings, obscured by the afflictions of gross negative emotions and erroneous views, were disinclined to practice the sublime dharma. In this dark age, beings are afflicted with the three calamities of sickness, famine, and warfare. It is in such an age that Guru Padmasambhava manifested as the embodiment of all the buddhas.

*Dilgo Khyentse Rinpoche*

## THE CHALLENGE OF VAJRAYANA SAMAYA             11.23

The practice of the Secret Mantra is the short-cut, the swiftest path to reaching the inconceivable common and supreme accomplishments. As you move up through the different vehicles, the "narrow defile" of this path of *samaya* [commitments] grows increasingly confined; there is less and less room to move, so be on guard. . . . The *samayas* of Vajrayana are to never let your body depart from being the deity, your voice from being mantra, and your mind from the state of *samadhi*. If you are able to do so, that is keeping the ultimate *samaya*s with the Body, Speech, and Mind of the victorious ones. You can then truly be said to possess the sacred precepts of Vajrayana. Without doing so, understand that the *samaya*s of Secret Mantra hold extreme risk.

*Tulku Urgyen Rinpoche*

## THE SNAKE IN THE BAMBOO TUBE                    11.24

The practice of Vajrayana is said to entail great risk but also great advantage. The example for this is the proverbial snake in the bamboo tube, which can go only up or down; there is no other direction for the snake to go. Likewise, there is only up or down for the practitioner who enters the path of Vajrayana. Vajrayana is not like the lower vehicles where there is not that much risk but also not that much gain.

The snake cannot go right or left in the bamboo tube, only up or down. If one keeps one's *samaya*s well, remaining in awareness, it is certain that in this very body and lifetime, one can reach . . . the state of complete enlightenment. If one is unable to keep the sacred commitments of Vajrayana, one will definitely go down, plunging to what is called the Vajra Hell in Vajrayana or the Hell of Incessant Torment in the Sutra teachings. This is one extreme for a practitioner. The other is to go to the *dharmakaya* sphere, called in Dzogchen the "dissolved but unobscured state of inner brilliance."

*Tulku Urgyen Rinpoche*

## "ACCEPT EVERYTHING, BUT USE IT IN THE
## RIGHT WAY"                                        11.25

There is a story in the teachings of tantra about two close friends who both wanted to search for the truth. They went to a master, and the master said, "Do not abandon anything, accept everything. And once having accepted, use it in the right way." And the first one thought, "Well, this is wonderful. I can go on being just the way I am." So he set up hundreds of brothels and hundreds of butcher shops and hundreds of drinking places, which in India was regarded as something that only a lower-caste person would do. He began to run all these big businesses, and he thought this was what he was supposed to do. But the other friend thought this was not quite right and he began to examine himself; and by examining himself he came to the conclusion that he had had enough material already and did not have to collect any more. He did not have to do any particular practice of meditation, but by acknowledging the already existing heap, he achieved enlightenment, or at least a certain stage of realization. . . . Then one day they met each other and talked together and compared their experiences. The first one was not at all awakened; he was still struggling and collecting and doing all these things. In fact he had fallen into an even worse trap and had not even started to examine himself. But each of them was quite sure that he was right, so they both decided to go and consult the teacher. And the teacher said, "I am afraid your way is wrong" to the one who was running the businesses. And he was so disappointed that he drew his sword and murdered the teacher on the spot.

*Chögyam Trungpa Rinpoche*

## THE PRACTICE OF SADHANA                                    11.26

In Vajrayana, a *sadhana* is the act of manifesting what is originally present in the form of the threefold *mandala* of deity, mantra, and *samadhi*. When practicing a *sadhana*, we are not superimposing something artificial atop the natural state of things. Rather, it is a way of acknowledging our original state, in which the nature of all forms is the deity, the nature of all sounds is mantra, and the nature of mind is *samadhi*. This is the basic principle of development stage. And the differences in profundity between the teachings of sutra and tantra lie in how close the teachings are to the original nature. The closest, the most direct, are the Vajrayana teachings.

*Tulku Urgyen Rinpoche*

## RELYING ON THE DEITY AS OUR SOLE REFUGE                    11.27

When we have a strong sense of total reliance, it turns out much more favorable for us because it protects us from confusion. It protects us from second thoughts. It protects us from the ordinary leaks of our negative emotions filling up the pot of our good heart. Therefore, to have this kind of unshakeable trust, total faith and reliance, and one-pointedness in taking refuge in the deity as our sole refuge is essential. Having strong conviction in your relationship and being very direct in your heart connection with the deity is very important. Likewise, understanding what the deity's wisdom, power, and kindness or compassion mean to you personally is very important. If we do any practice with such conviction, trust, and understanding, it is going to be much more poignant. This is especially true in taking refuge, which is the beginning of developing our relationship with the deity or with Dharma practice in general.

*Dzigar Kongtrul Rinpoche*

## The Importance of Relying on the Tantric Deities 11.28

If we feel connected to one particular deity, then we have to learn how to rely on that deity completely. If we learn to devote ourselves to it full-heartedly, that deity becomes much more powerful for us. This is not because the deity is pleased by us. It is rather that, when we are able to rely on and find complete confidence in that deity, instead of feeling insecure and unable to take refuge in one deity, our own mind transforms in a favorable way for us. As the deity is the embodiment of all the enlightened ones, so all the enlightened ones' blessings become accessible to us.

*Dzigar Kongtrul Rinpoche*

## Visualization Is Seeing Things as They Actually Are 11.29

[The] development stage [*utpattikrama*] is usually understood as visualizing the support, which is the buddha field and the celestial palace, and what is supported therein—the form of the deity. The palace and the deity are considered to be the pure world and pure being. We may think that this is a product of our imagination, but in fact it is an exact replica of the original state of all things. It is how things already are

in actuality—also called the great *mandala* of the manifest ground.
Thus visualization is ultimately not a matter of imagining something
to be what it isn't, but rather of seeing it as it actually is. It is acknowledging things as they already are. This is the essential principle of
Vajrayana.

*Tulku Urgyen Rinpoche*

## UTPATTIKRAMA                                    11.30

In evolutionary-stage yoga, which some people prefer to call genera-
tion-stage yoga, we learn to identify ourselves as a Buddha, a deity, a
fully enlightened being. In intensive meditation, we develop the clear
and vivid appearance of ourselves as a deity and the divine pride of
actually being the deity.

*Lama Thubten Yeshe Rinpoche*

## MAINTAIN AWARENESS OF YOURSELF AS THE DEITY       11.31

Maintaining awareness of yourself as the deity . . . is extremely important. Don't think of yourself as an ordinary person who is just pretend-
ing to be the deity. Feel strongly that your body is the deity's body,
your speech is the deity's mantra, and your mind is great blissful wisdom. This stops the self-pity mind. Do not lose the divine pride of
being this illusory deity, nor your comprehension of yourself as nondual.

*Lama Thubten Yeshe Rinpoche*

## THE PURPOSE OF THE DEVELOPMENT STAGE             11.32

The purpose of the development stage is to purify our habitual tendencies as human beings. . . .

The main purpose of the development stage is to destroy our clinging to a solid reality. It is our fixation on concreteness that makes us
continue in samsaric existence. The development stage dismantles that.

How do we approach that? By imagining [ourselves as a buddha],
the world is a buddhafield, our dwelling place is the celestial palace, and
the beings in it are the divine forms of deities, visible yet intangible like
a rainbow in the sky.

*Tulku Urgyen Rinpoche*

## Why Do We Need to Visualize?                                    11.33

Until we are able to practice the ultimate development stage, we need
to visualize or mentally create pure images in order to approach that
absolute state. The ultimate development stage involves simply resting
in the essence of the mind of all the buddhas, out of which the two
form *kayas*—the *sambhogakaya* of rainbow light and the *nirmanakaya* of
a physical body—spontaneously manifest.

*Tulku Urgyen Rinpoche*

## Sampannakrama                                                    11.34

In *sampannakrama*, or the dissolution [of our visualization into empti-
ness], one cuts through the tendency of conceptualization. . . . We
may have the understanding that everything arises from the ground of
emptiness, yet at some point we become entertained by it. Again and
again the mind deviates and does not remember the innate nature.
Within *utpattikrama*, it forgets the innateness of what arises. Arrogance
about, and attachment to, practice occurs. We become possessive about
deities. One deity is better than the other. While you're doing one
practice, you cannot do the other practice. You copyright the deity and
the practices *(laughter)*. All of these unnecessary things happen because
the ground of emptiness is again lost. We call some practices the "basic
preliminaries." We call others "actual," and yet others "advanced." All
of these distinctions come about because of forgetting the ground of
emptiness.

Sampannakrama means dissolving it back into emptiness. In English,
it is called the "completion phase" or the the "dissolution phase." In
Tibetan it is *dzogrim*. Vajradhara dissolves into a mass of light, and dissolves into oneself. It was generated from within the expanse of one's
own mindstream, and quite similarly it reverts and goes back into one's
mindstream. Just as wisdom arises in the form of compassion, that compassion again dissolves within one's awareness, one's absolute nature of
mind. Just as thoughts arise and dissolve into oneself, the empty nature
of one's mind, similarly the creation of samsara comes about. At the
time of death it dissolves again within oneself. At the time of exhaustion
of creation, it dissolves into oneself. *Sampannakrama* allows the meditator to deepen and complete the confidence of knowing the indivisibility

of what is generated by the innate nature of mind, or the empty nature of mind. *Utpattikrama* is the first recognition of everything arising from within; completion [or *sampannakrama*] is confidently remaining within that understanding and realization. . . . Rest in the nature of *sampannakrama*. Prolong and familiarize yourself with the dissolution phase.

*Venerable Khandro Rinpoche*

## DEDICATION OF MERIT                                    11.35

After completion, we should dedicate the merit for the welfare of everyone. In this way the virtue is multiplied immensely, so that the effect is one million times greater than simply doing a virtuous action without much thought about it.

*Tulku Urgyen Rinpoche*

## MAHAMUDRA IS THE MOST EXCELLENT                        11.36

Of all the approaches taught by the Buddha, mahamudra is considered the most excellent. This was the approach followed by the early teachers of the Kagyü tradition, who achieved complete realization within a single lifetime, relying exclusively on the path of Mahamudra and its skillful means.

*The Third Jamgön Kongtrul Rinpoche*

## THE TIBETAN WORD FOR MAHAMUDRA                         11.37

The Tibetan word for *mahamudra* is *chak gya chenpo*. *Chak* refers to emptiness, which is perfect in every respect; *gya chenpo*, the great expanse, refers to the all-encompassing wisdom inherent in emptiness. The meaning of this gloss is that in its depth and breadth, Mahamudra encompasses everything.

*Chökyi Nyima Rinpoche*

## THE CORE OF MAHAMUDRA MEDITATION                       11.38

The core of Mahamudra meditation involves resting in the present moment of awareness without either altering, creating, or suppressing anything. [It] means remaining undistracted in the freshness of thoughts, relaxing without meditating on anything, and resting calmly in the primordial, unfabricated state. Composure [Mahamudra *shamatha*] and awareness [Mahamudra *vipashyana*] are essential to achieve this. Composure is needed to focus the mind and bring it to rest, whereas awareness is needed to perceive coarse and subtle thoughts or distractions of the mind. In maintaining composure and awareness, one should be neither too tight nor too loose, since this would give rise respectively to wildness and dullness of mind.

*The Third Jamgön Kongtrul Rinpoche*

## MAHAMUDRA SHAMATHA AND VIPASHYANA    11.39
The function of [Mahamudra] *shamatha* is to develop mental stability, or stillness. The function of [Mahamudra] *vipashyana*, or insight, is to look at the nature of your mind, and by doing so, to see the nature of phenomena or all things.

*Thrangu Rinpoche*

## THE BENEFITS OF MAHAMUDRA MEDITATION    11.40
Mahamudra meditation helps our meditation by reducing emotional confusion and creating more peace of mind. As the disturbing emotions are calmed, we will come to know the joy and peace deep within our mind. When we are free from disturbing emotions, then our actions become much more precise and helpful, and there is greater joy and meaning in life.

*Thrangu Rinpoche*

## THE RESULTS OF MAHAMUDRA SHAMATHA AND
## MAHAMUDRA VIPASHYANA    11.41
When the mind becomes stable through the practice of tranquility [Mahamudra *shamatha*] meditation, it doesn't go all over the place and things become clear; this is what is meant by "pure mind." So the first result of tranquility meditation is basically a pure mind. Emotional

confusion and emotional disturbance are reduced, and as a result the mind becomes stable and clear.

The principal result of insight practice [Mahamudra *vipashyana*] is the development of discriminating intelligence (Skt. *prajna*). This is very important because it is this kind of intelligence which can inform us of what is really going on. . . . The intelligence and understanding which develop through insight practice are very stable. This intelligence is the mind itself and the knowing that develops is always present. Particularly when insight takes place with a basis of tranquility meditation, that stability of mind invests the understanding which comes through the insight practice with a great deal of stability. Once this intelligence is developed, it is always present.

*Thrangu Rinpoche*

## THE FRUITION OF MAHAMUDRA    11.42

The fruition [of] Mahamudra is the realization that relative appearances and mind are, by their very nature, the three *kaya*s. . . . *Dharmakaya* is the fact that whether one is talking about relative external appearances or the internal mechanisms of mind, by their very nature these are devoid of true existence. *Sambhogakaya* means that manifestation is unobstructed, and *nirmanakaya* that appearances are numerous and manifold. In the same way that *dharmakaya* is inherent in mind, the light of *dharmakaya* is inherent in appearances. Mind and appearances are inseparable as the light of *dharmakaya* and its rays.

*The Third Jamgön Kongtrul Rinpoche*

## THE SPIRIT OF DZOGCHEN    11.43

The spirit of Dzogchen is very much an attitude, one which springs from a deep confidence and trust. The trust comes from the realization of the true meaning of the teaching of Dzogpachenpo and from our personal experience, through practice. It is a trust in your ultimate nature, that you have the buddha, the wisdom of Rigpa, which exists even in spite of all your confusion. It *is* there, self-present.

*Sogyal Rinpoche*

*The Third Jamgön Kongtrül Rinpoche*

## DZOGCHEN: TAKING THE COMPLETE FRUITION
## AS PATH                                                  11.44

There are three different approaches to actually applying Vajrayana in
practice: taking the ground as path, taking the path as path, and taking
the fruition as path. These three approaches can be understood by using
the analogy of a gardener or farmer. Taking the ground or cause as path
is like tilling soil and sowing seeds. Taking the path as path is like weed-
ing, watering, fertilizing, and coaxing crops forth. Taking the fruition
as path is the attitude of simply picking the ripened fruit or the fully
bloomed flowers. To do this, to take the complete result, the state of
enlightenment itself, as the path, is the approach of Dzogchen.

*Tulku Urgyen Rinpoche*


## THE MOMENT OF DZOGCHEN                                    11.45

It may be that the sky is always limpid, clear, vast, infinite, and so on,
but when the moment of Dzogchen arrives it is as if the sun has suddenly risen. It is not that the sky of our inherent nature has improved,
but something definitely does seem to happen. This metaphor of the
rising sun refers to *rangjung yeshe*, the spontaneous, self-born awareness
wisdom or innate wakefulness dawning within our nature. This is the
moment of Dzogchen, the dawn of the self-arisen awareness wisdom,
innate wisdom.

This is the meaning of what is called in Tibetan *nyur de dzogpa
chenpo*, meaning, "swift and comfy innate Great Perfection"—a path
that does not require austerities or arduous practices. It is direct, swift,
spacious, natural, and comfy. It is doable!

*Nyoshul Khenpo Rinpoche*


## IN ONE LIFETIME                                           11.46

In one lifetime, in one body, even in one instant of self-arisen awareness, this dawn of Vajrasattva—the self-born innate awareness wisdom—shines forth like a blazing inner sun. When you relate to this
self-arisen innate awareness wisdom, when you practice Dzogchen as it
actually is, this fleeting human condition is instantaneously made meaningful. And not just this life, but all our lives are made meaningful, as

well as the lives of all those who have been connected with us. The
experience of the natural state of the luminous innate Great Perfection
implies the annihilation, the crashing into dust, of all forms of self-cling-
ing and duality, of clinging to the concrete reality of things, to their
appearances. The inherent freedom of being is spontaneously, primordially present. All delusory perceptions are naturally nonexistent in this
dawn of innate awareness wisdom. . . . Everything "falls apart" because
it is inherently unborn from the very beginning; and the freedom of
perfect being, of *rigpa*, spontaneously present since the beginningless
beginning, is clearly and thoroughly realized in that very moment.

*Nyoshul Khenpo Rinpoche*

## RECOGNIZING THE PRIMORDIAL STATE                    11.47
The pure State of Enlightenment is our own mind . . . not some sort of
dazzling light coming from outside. If we recognize our primordial
State of pure presence, pure from the beginning, albeit temporarily obscured, and we stay present in this recognition without getting distracted, then all impurities dissolve: this is the essence of the path. Now
the nature of the primordial State as total purity truly manifests, and
recognizing it for what it is, we become its owner forever.

*Namkhai Norbu Rinpoche*

## SEND THE THINKING MIND ON HOLIDAY                    11.48
What hinders us from realizing the wisdom of our Rigpa is the obscuration perpetuated by our thinking mind. So you send the thinking mind
on holiday, or deport it, because it is an illegal immigrant. You don't
issue it a visa. If you just leave your mind quietly in its own natural
state, then out of that comes the real settling, calming, and clearing,
from which arises the nature of mind—whatever that may be!

*Sogyal Rinpoche*

## SHAMATHA AND VIPASHYANA IN DZOGCHEN                    11.49
The extraordinary *shamatha* here is to resolve and rest in the true emptiness itself. We do not merely get the idea of emptiness; in actuality, in

direct experience, we resolve emptiness and rest naturally in that state. Naturally resting is the genuine *shamatha* of not creating anything artificial whatsoever, of simply remaining in the experience of emptiness. And *vipashyana* means not to deviate from that state.

According to ordinary *shamatha* and *vipashyana*, *shamatha* is first cultivated and then *vipashyana* is pursued. Cultivating *shamatha* means to produce a state of mental stillness, and then to train in it. Pursuing or seeking the insight of *vipashyana* means to try to find who the meditator is; trying to identify what it is that remains quiet. It's evident that both of these practices are pretty much involved in conceptual thinking.

Only in the Essence Mahamudra and Dzogchen systems is emptiness resolved without fabrication. In Dzogchen, from the very first, emptiness is resolved without any need to manufacture it. It emphasizes stripping awareness to its naked state, and not clinging to emptiness in any way whatsoever. The true and authentic *vipashyana* is the empty and cognizant nature of mind.

*Tulku Urgyen Rinpoche*


## A SHORT COMMENTARY ON GARAB DORJE'S THREE STATEMENTS CONCERNING THE INHERENT NATURE       11.50

1. *One is introduced directly to one's own nature* (ngo rang).
2. *One definitely decides upon this unique state.*
3. *One continues directly with confidence in liberation.*


1. As for the direct introduction to one's own nature: This fresh, immediate awareness of the present moment, transcending all thoughts related to the three times, is itself the primordial awareness or knowledge (*ye-shes*) that is self-originated intrinsic Awareness (*rig-pa*). This is the direct introduction to one's own nature.

2. As for deciding definitely upon this unique state: Whatever phenomena of Samsara and Nirvana may manifest, all of them represent the play of the creative energy or potentiality of one's own immediate instrinsic Awareness (*rig-pa'i rtsal*). Since there is nothing that goes beyond just this, one should continue in the state of this singular and unique Awareness. Therefore, one must definitively decide upon this

unique state for oneself and know that there exists nothing other than this.

3. As for directly continuing with confidence in liberation: Whatever gross or subtle thoughts may arise, by merely recognizing their nature, they arise and (self-)liberate simultaneously in the vast expanse of the Dharmakaya, where Emptiness and Awareness (are inseparable). Therefore, one should continue directly with confidence in their liberation.

*Dudjom Rinpoche*

## MAHAMUDRA, DZOGCHEN, AND MADHYAMAKA          11.51
Is there any difference in the views of Mahamudra, Dzogchen, and Madhyamaka? Sometimes it is said that the ground is Mahamudra, the path is Madhyamaka, and the fruition is Dzogchen. Whether there is a difference or not depends on what aspect we are discussing.

### Madhyamaka

Please understand that Madhyamaka is not just Madhyamaka; you must define what aspect is under consideration. There are different kinds of Madhyamaka, such as Svatantrika Madhyamaka, the Prasangika Madhyamaka, and the Great Madhyamaka of the Definitive Meaning.

### Mahamudra

Within the Mahamudra system there is Sutra Mahamudra, Tantra Mahamudra, and Essence Mahamudra. Sutra Mahamudra is the same as the Mahayana system describing the progressive stages through the five paths and ten *bhumi*s. That definitely differs from Dzogchen, and therefore it is not simply called Mahamudra, but Sutra Mahamudra. Tantra Mahamudra corresponds to Maha Yoga and Anu Yoga, in which you utilize the "wisdom of example" to arrive at the "wisdom of meaning." Essence Mahamudra is the same as Dzogchen, except that it doesn't include Tögal. The Great Madhyamaka of the Definitive Meaning is no different from the Dzogchen view of Trekchö.

### Dzogchen

Within the Dzogchen system, there are likewise different levels. It is not enough to say "Dzogchen" without mentioning which particular aspect of it we are talking about. Dzogchen is not a single entity; there are four subdivisions. There is the outer Mind Section, which is like the body. There is the inner Space Section, which is like the heart, and the secret Instruction Section, which is like the veins within the heart. Finally there is the innermost Unexcelled Section, which is like the life-energy inside the heart, the pure essence of the life force. What is the difference between these four sections, since all four are Dzogchen? The outer Mind Section of Dzogchen emphasizes the cognizant quality of mind, while the inner Space Section emphasizes its empty quality, and the secret Instruction Section emphasizes the unity of the two. The innermost Unexcelled Section teaches everything—ground, path, and fruition, as well as Trekchö and Tögal.

*Tulku Urgyen Rinpoche*

## THE RAINBOW BODY                                                    11.52

[Realized Dzogchen practitioners attain] the rainbow body, the dissolution of the physical body at death into a state of rainbow light. Such practitioners leave behind only their hair and fingernails. . . . Among the three *kayas*—*dharmakaya*, *sambhogakaya*, and *nirmanakaya*—*sambhogakaya* manifests visually in the form of rainbow light. So, attaining a rainbow body in this lifetime means to be directly awakened in the state of enlightenment of *sambhogakaya*.

*Tulku Urgyen Rinpoche*

# → 12

# Making the Journey

THE FINAL CHAPTER in this part contains several teachings providing an overview of the journey to full realization and some practical suggestions of how we may handle its ups and downs. The terrain that we follow in the course of our practice can be described in several ways. It may be seen as moving from intellectual understanding (gaining a conceptual view), through experience (gaining deeper and deeper familiarity with what concepts point to), and realization ("when delusion has totally collapsed") (12.1). It may also be depicted in terms of the three stages of recognizing (the buddha nature within), training (nurturing this recognition so we can sustain it for longer and longer periods of time), and stability (when our nondistraction from the nature is uninterrupted) (12.2). And, finally, our journey may be marked by view, meditation, action, and fruition. Three of these items duplicate the preceding list (view = recognizing, meditation = training, and fruition = stability). New here is "action," taking one's "view," one's resting in the nature, into all sorts of activities, as an element of further training (12.3). The third element of "action" is given more detail in the final passage from this section, "Practice in the 'Marketplace.'" (12.4).

In our practice, we must not think we are meditating on the nature or imagining it. It is primordially already present and all we need to do is not depart from it (12.5). Practicing devotion and compassion will strengthen our recognition of the nature of mind (12.6). Realizing and relaxing in our "playmind" resolves many difficulties (12.7). Along the way, we may find surprising resources, such as a mate or lover (12.8). Our greatest resource is simply this raw and rugged world that we live in (12.9).

In our Vajrayana practice, how should we regard and relate to our thoughts? Thoughts seem powerful and real, but they lack true existence and are just like wind roaring in empty space (12.10). However solid and substantial they may seem, it is important not to be fooled by them; by remembering the unborn awareness pointed out by our teacher, we are able to realize that thoughts suddenly arise and then abruptly dissolve back into emptiness (12.11). We need to maintain the understanding that all phenomena, both inner and outer, are like a rainbow. They appear vividly but are empty of any substance, essence, or significance. In that way, we can remain in the state of simplicity and, when we encounter pleasure or pain, gain or loss, we will not be imprisoned by them (12.12). The way to deal with thoughts is to go to the source and realize their origin (12.13).

At the same time, while not being taken in by seemingly real thoughts, we must also not go to the other extreme and think that they are utterly nonexistent. Emptiness does not negate experience (12.14). In fact, thoughts—while empty—vividly appear as expressions of our own essence (12.15, 12.16). In the process of the liberation of thoughts, there are three stages (12.17). Our solidified, objectified version of reality is like ice frozen by the winter chill. Through our practice, we can "melt the ice of concepts into the living water of the freedom within" (12.18).

There are thus two ways to purify negativity: one is to perform *yidam* practice (the conventional tantric method), the other is to rest in the nature (*rigpa*, unborn awareness, or Mahamudra) (12.19). When we become tired in meditation, we should realize that the mind nature itself is beyond fatigue (12.20). Success and failure will challenge us along the way. When we encounter success, we should not take credit for it, but give it away, thanking the three jewels; when we are unsuccessful, we should think that we are burning up negative karma and be grateful (12.21).

In our meditation practice, sometimes emotions, especially the defiling emotions (passion, aggression, ignorance, etc.) arise in a powerful and compelling way. How should we regard and relate to them? In the Vajrayana, powerful emotions are not to be rejected, but can be used to enhance our experience of the awakened state. In the first place, we must realize what a tremendous resource they can be (12.22). Beyond this, specific techniques and methods are provided by which, at the very moment when we are completely caught up in despair, paranoia, or anger, we can apply our awareness to them in a certain way and liberate them (12.23).

In general, as we continue our practice, outer, inner, and secret obstacles of all sorts will present themselves. Our Vajrayana practice provides the means for working through these (12.24). There are signs of authentic progress along the way, but these are not the dramatic experiences that we usually imagine (12.25).

The final challenge is, of course, our own death. From the tantric point of view, death is not a real, objective experience, but rather just as much of a dream as any other phenomenon (12.26). This being so, there is no reason to feel sad or depressed when we are dying (12.27). We should die, remaining in the recognition of the nature and "leave this life like an eagle soaring up into the blue sky" (12.28). Realizing that death is on the horizon and that, when we die our experience will be choiceless, we should dedicate ourselves to practice while we still can (12.29). And we should know that, through training in our practice now, we will have the opportunity to attain liberation at the moment of death, when our innate nature is nakedly revealed (12.30).

The final selection in this chapter is a poem composed by Dilgo Khyentse Rinpoche at the tender age of thirteen for his parents, prior to his entering retreat. Although written in Tibet long before the Chinese invasion, I include it here because Rinpoche was later such an important teacher to Westerners. This poem shows the kind of humility and inspiration that moved him right at the beginning of his own journey and led him to become such an extraordinarily accomplished master. For all of us would-be practitioners of Tibetan Buddhism, it provides much food for reflection (12.31).

## INTELLECTUAL UNDERSTANDING, EXPERIENCE, AND REALIZATION                                    12.1

Intellectual understanding occurs when, for instance, we hear that emptiness, meaning empty cognizance, is our nature. The mental idea we get of this is called "understanding."

In the case of experience, we are told how to recognize emptiness so that we can see exactly how this empty cognizance is. We have a taste of it, maybe no more than a glimpse, but, nevertheless, an experience of what is called "recognizing mind essence." . . . When this glimpse is followed by training in repeatedly recognizing the nature of mind and avoiding being carried away by thoughts, we gradually grow more and more used to this experience. In this case, by recognizing the empty nature we are disengaging from its expression, the stream of deluded thinking. Each time the expression dissolves back into the state of awareness, progress is made, and realization finally occurs.

Ultimate realization is when delusion has totally collapsed and there is no recurrence of discursive thought whatsoever.

*Tulku Urgyen Rinpoche*


## STAGES OF MEDITATION—RECOGNIZING, TRAINING, AND STABILITY                                    12.2

Please understand that there are three steps: recognizing, training, and attaining stability.

### Recognizing

The first of these steps, recognizing, is like acquiring the seed of a flower. Once it is in your hands and you acknowledge it to be a flower [seed], it can be planted and cultivated. When fully grown, flowers will bloom; but the seed needs the right conditions. However, we must first acknowledge that it is a flower seed. In the same way, the naked awareness that has been pointed out by our master should be acknowledged as your nature.

### Training

This recognition must be nurtured by the right conditions. To cultivate a seed, it must have warmth and moisture and so on; then it will cer-

*Tulku Urgyen Rinpoche*

tainly grow. In the same way, after recognizing, we must train [through meditation] in the natural state: the short moment of recognition needs to be repeated many times. As a support for this training, have devotion to enlightened beings and compassion for unenlightened beings. . . . Training is simply short moments of recognition repeated many times and supported by devotion and compassion. . . . Repeatedly training in non-distraction is how to proceed in the practice of mind nature.

*Stability*

Finally comes the stage of stability. When this moment of non-distraction lasts unceasingly, day and night, what will that be like?

*Tulku Urgyen Rinpoche*

## VIEW, MEDITATION, ACTION, AND FRUITION            12.3

To recognize the buddha nature present in oneself is called the view. To sustain the continuity of that connection is called meditation or training. To mingle that with daily activities and act in accord with the dharma is called action or conduct. And to realize it as totally unobscured, like the sun shining with unchanging brilliance in the sky, is called fruition.

*Tulku Urgyen Rinpoche*

## PRACTICE IN THE "MARKETPLACE"            12.4

After the practitioner becomes stable to some extent in the recognition of the innate nature, the unadulterated awareness free from distraction, he goes "to the marketplace" to interact with other people. The practice then is to mingle awareness with the daily activities of eating, moving about, sitting, and sleeping. One tries to see whether one's stability is in any way influenced by external experiences. The best is if there is no effect, if nothing harms or benefits one's recognition.

*Tulku Urgyen Rinpoche*

## NOT BY MEDITATING!            12.5

We need to train in this thought-free wakefulness, but not by meditating on it or imagining it. It is primordially present already. Yet this present wakefulness gets caught up in thinking. To get free of thought, simply recognize; recognize your present wakefulness. Don't forget; don't get distracted. That doesn't mean to sit and force oneself to be undistracted and unforgetting. Trying like that only fouls it up. Simply allow your basic state to be undistracted nonmeditation.

*Tulku Urgyen Rinpoche*

## DEVOTION AND COMPASSION STRENGTHEN OUR RECOGNITION OF MIND NATURE                                    12.6

Devotion and compassion strengthen the recognition of mind nature. Other practices also further enhance mind essence; however, the Third Karmapa states the most essential point when he said: "In the moment of love, the empty essence dawns nakedly." In the moment that either devotion or compassion is felt sincerely, from the core of our heart, there is really nothing to obscure us any longer. The more we train in devotion to all enlightened masters, buddhas, and bodhisattvas, the more our progress in recognizing mind essence will be enhanced. In exactly the same way, generating loving kindness and compassion for all sentient beings will also help tremendously to enhance our realization of buddha nature.

*Tulku Urgyen Rinpoche*

## PLAYMIND                                                                                              12.7

Through play, spiritual energy can be sustained. . . . Whether or not our rigid, mature minds reject play, everything is still the display of the natural secret essence of the elements. If we are serious and rigid, our subtle elements become congested and cannot reflect this wisdom display. If our mind is calm and vast and playful, we can always recognize this essence display.

When we study, if we have an open playmind, we can absorb what we study. Flexibility comes from playmind, so when our mind is open we can accept what we are taught. With a rigid and serious mind, we cannot learn because our mind is tight and imbalanced. Our serious mind is always tired, while our playmind is always rested.

When we work, if we have an open playmind, we will not have

fears of losing anything so we can work continuously until we attain our goal. With the confidence that comes from playmind, we never hesitate and do not make mistakes.

If we have playmind, we can see through meditation that all phenomena are like magic. Wherever we go, we are comfortable.

*Thinley Norbu Rinpoche*

## YOUR MATE SPEAKS FOR THE REST OF THE WORLD    12.8
When you have a very close personal relationship with a person such as your mate, your husband or wife, that person becomes the spokesman for the rest of the sangha. When you live with somebody long enough, there is intense irritation and intense warmth. Often you regard each other as being very cute and sweet, but sometimes as a living devil or devilette. There are a lot of unexplored areas of experience, and you only get to use your microscope with your own mate. With others there's no time to use it. Nobody else will sit there and let themselves be scrutinized and take the trouble to scrutinize you. Only your mate will put up with that, which is a very generous thing, fantastic. So in that way, your mate becomes a spokesman for the rest of the world. That seems to be a very important part of one's life.

*Chögyam Trungpa Rinpoche*

## BEYOND EGO'S DREAMS    12.9
The real experience, beyond the dream world, is the beauty and color and excitement of the real experience of *now* in everyday life. When we face things as they are, we give up the hope of something better. There will be no magic, because we cannot tell ourselves to get out of our depression. Depression and ignorance, the emotions, whatever we experience, are all real and contain tremendous truth. If we really want to learn and see the experience of truth, we have to be where we are. The whole thing is just a matter of being a grain of sand.

*Chögyam Trungpa Rinpoche*

## "I" IS JUST A THOUGHT    12.10
If you vanquish ego-clinging today, tonight you will be enlightened. If you vanquish it tomorrow, you will be enlightened tomorrow night.

But if you never vanquish it, you will never be enlightened. Yet "I" is just a thought. Thoughts and feelings have no intrinsic solidity, form, shape, or color. When a thought of anger arises in the mind with such force that you feel aggressive and destructive, is anger brandishing a weapon? Is it the head of an army? Can it burn things like fire, crush them like a rock, or carry them away like a violent river? No. Anger, like any other thought or feeling, has no true existence—not even a definite location in your body, speech, or mind. It is just like the wind roaring in empty space.

*Dilgo Khyentse Rinpoche*

## WHAT MIND IS AND HOW NOT TO BE FOOLED BY IT 12.11

What we normally call the mind is the deluded mind, a turbulent vortex of thoughts whipped up by attachment, anger, and ignorance. This mind, unlike enlightened awareness, is always being carried away by one delusion after another. Thoughts of hatred or attachment suddenly arise without warning, triggered off by such circumstances as an unexpected meeting with an adversary or a friend, and unless they are immediately overpowered with the proper antidote, they quickly take root and proliferate, reinforcing the habitual predominance of hatred or attachment in the mind and adding more and more karmic imprints.

Yet, however strong these thoughts may seem, they are just thoughts and will eventually dissolve back into emptiness. Once you recognize the intrinsic nature of the mind, these thoughts that seem to appear and disappear all the time can no longer fool you. Just as clouds form, last for a while, and then dissolve back into the empty sky, so deluded thoughts arise, remain for a while, and then vanish in the emptiness of mind: in reality nothing at all has happened.

*Dilgo Khyentse Rinpoche*

## ALL PHENOMENA ARE LIKE A RAINBOW 12.12

All phenomena of samsara and nirvana arise like a rainbow, and like a rainbow they are devoid of any tangible existence. Once you have recognized the true nature of reality, which is empty and at the same time appears as the phenomenal world, your mind will cease to be under the power of delusion. If you know how to leave your thoughts free to dissolve by themselves as they arise, they will cross your mind as a bird crosses the sky—without leaving any trace.

Maintain that state of simplicity. If you encounter happiness, success, prosperity, or other favorable conditions, consider them as dreams and illusions, and do not get attached to them. If you are stricken by illness, calumny, deprivation, or other physical and mental trials, do not let yourself get discouraged, but rekindle your compassion and generate the wish that through your suffering all beings' sufferings may be exhausted. Whatever circumstances arise, do not plunge into elation or misery, but stay free and comfortable, in unshakable serenity.

*Dilgo Khyentse Rinpoche*

## How Is Samsara Created? How Is Realization Attained?

12.13

In order to conquer the high ground of the uncreated nature of mind, we must go to the source and recognize the origin of our thoughts. Otherwise, one thought gives rise to a second thought, the second to a third, and so on forever. We are constantly assailed by memories of the past and carried away by expectations for the future, and lose all awareness of the present.

It is our own mind that leads us astray into the cycle of existence. Blind to the mind's true nature, we hold fast to our thoughts, which are nothing but manifestations of that nature. This freezes awareness into solid concepts, such as I and other, desirable and detestable, and plenty of others. This is how we create samsara.

But if, instead of letting our thoughts solidify, we recognize their emptiness, then each thought that arises and disappears in the mind renders the realization of emptiness ever clearer.

*Dilgo Khyentse Rinpoche*

## Emptiness Does Not Negate Experience

12.14

While perceiving, buddha nature is empty of a perceiver; while being empty, there is still experience. Search for the perceiver; there is no "thing" to find. There is no barrier between the two. If it were one or

the other there should either be a concrete perceiver who always remains, or an absolute void. Instead, at the same time as vivid perception
takes place, that which perceives is totally empty. This is called the unity
of experience and emptiness, or the unity of awareness and emptiness.
The fact of experience eliminates the extreme of nothingness, while the
fact that it is empty eliminates the extreme of concrete existence.

*Tulku Urgyen Rinpoche*

## WHAT ARE THOUGHTS? 12.15

Thoughts occur as an expression of your essence, and not from anywhere else. They do not arise from the five elements, from the five
sense organs, from flesh, blood, temperature, the heat or breath of your
body—not at all. They are simply the expression of the primordially
pure essence.

*Tulku Urgyen Rinpoche*

## CONCEPTUAL THOUGHTS AND MIND ESSENCE 12.16

The essence itself is totally free of conceptual thinking. Yet, at the same
time, its expression *is* conceptual thinking. Do not focus your attention
on the expression. Rather, recognize the essence: then the expression
has no power to remain anywhere. At this point, the expression simply
collapses or folds back into the essence. As we become more stable in
recognizing the essence free from conceptual thinking, its expression
as conceptual thinking becomes increasingly baseless or unfounded. As
conceptual thinking diminishes and finally vanishes, what is left to cause
us to wander in samsara? The very basis for samsaric existence is none
other than conceptual thinking.

*Tulku Urgyen Rinpoche*

## THE LIBERATION OF THOUGHTS 12.17

[The] liberation of thoughts can be described as occurring in several
different ways. The great master Vimalamitra mentioned three types of
liberation. . . . The first example is said to be like meeting someone you

already know; the second is similar to a knot tied in a snake; and the third is the analogy of a thief entering an empty house.

Recognize the thought as it occurs so that it is liberated simultaneously with its arising. . . . In the beginning, if we have already recognized our nature even once, we have caught the scent of it. Once you get a "whiff" of your nature, it becomes familiar, like someone you already know: you do not need to doubt who your friend is when you meet him. At this point, thoughts are liberated upon recognition, like the vanishing of a drawing on water.

Once the practitioner gains an immediate recognition of buddha nature, there is no need to apply any additional technique at all. The same moment a thought starts to move, the thought is liberated by itself. It is like a knot tied in a snake that does not have to be untied by anyone because it unravels by itself. This exemplifies becoming more stable in the training.

Finally, the third analogy of the liberation of thoughts is described as being like a thief entering an empty house. This is called stability or perfection in training. A thief entering an empty house does not gain anything, and the house does not lose anything. All thought activity is naturally liberated without any harm or benefit whatsoever.

*Tulku Urgyen Rinpoche*

## TRANSCENDING THE IMPRISONMENT
## OF APPEARANCES                                           12.18

In the heart of winter, the chill freezes lakes and rivers; water becomes so solid that it can bear men, beasts, and carts. As spring approaches, earth and water warm up and thaw. What then remains of the hardness of the ice? Water is soft and fluid, ice hard and sharp, so we cannot say that they are identical; but neither can we say that they are different, because ice is only solidified water, and water is only melted ice.

The same applies to our perception of the world around us. To be attached to the reality of phenomena, to be tormented by attraction and repulsion, by pleasure and pain, gain and loss, fame and obscurity, praise and blame, creates a solidity in the mind. What we have to do, therefore, is to melt the ice of concepts into the living water of the freedom within.

*Dilgo Khyentse Rinpoche*

## How Is Negativity Purified?                                    12.19

There are two ways to purify one's obscurations: conventional and ultimate. The conventional way is to engage in the practices of visualizing,
chanting, engendering remorse, and making resolutions. The ultimate
practice is to purify the deluded state of mind by means of the "threefold purity," by simply resting in *rigpa*, in nondual awareness. At that
moment, what ties the whole of samsara together falls apart.

*Tulku Urgyen Rinpoche*

## Overcoming Fatigue in Meditation                              12.20

You should not become tired from alternately recognizing and forgetting mind nature. What is truly tiring is the state of deluded mind that
creates completely pointless activity from one moment to another. It is
a totally futile involvement that has been going on for untold lifetimes,
but it is so habitual that we don't realize how exhausting it is. In the
state of unfabricated naturalness, there is nothing to be tired of at all. It
is totally free and open. . . .

The antidote for exhaustion is, from the very beginning, to relax
from deep within; to totally let be. Training in the awakened state is not
something you must keep up in a deliberate way. Rather, recognizing
unfabricated naturalness is totally effortless. The best relaxation brings
the best meditation. If you are relaxed from deep within, how can that
be tiring?

*Tulku Urgyen Rinpoche*

## How to Relate with Success and Defeat                         12.21

When we have positive conditions and good fortune, and everything
seems to be working out, we should think, "This is thanks to the Three
Jewels!" . . . Likewise, when we are unsuccessful, disappointed, frustrated, or sick, or when things simply don't work out, we should think,
"Now my negative karma from the past is being used up. How nice!"
. . . Whatever good is happening is not because I am special or I did
something unique; it's more beneficial to think that it happens due to
the kindness of the Three Jewels. Thinking in that way multiplies our
merit. Conversely, when meeting with difficulties, instead of feeling

overwhelmed and saying, "How terrible! I can't take this!" just say, "How nice! Now my negative karma is being used up and I am rid of that!" and then rejoice in the difficulties. Training your mind in this way will help increase the merit and ensure that all negative karma is brought to an end.

*Tulku Urgyen Rinpoche*


## USING ONE'S NEUROSIS ON THE PATH                              12.22

It is said, I think in the Lankavatara Sutra, that unskilled farmers throw away their rubbish and buy manure from other farmers, but those who are skilled go on collecting their own rubbish, in spite of the bad smell and the unclean work, and when it is ready to be used they spread it on their land, and out of this they grow their crops. That is the skilled way. In exactly the same way, the Buddha says, those who are unskilled will divide clean from unclean and will try to throw away samsara and search for nirvana, but those who are skilled bodhisattvas will not throw away desire and the passions and so on, but will first gather them together. . . . When the time is right one scatters them and uses them as manure. So out of these unclean things comes the birth of the seed which is realization. . . . [Thus] one should first recognize and acknowledge them, and study them and bring them to realization.

*Chögyam Trungpa Rinpoche*


## EMOTIONAL UPHEAVALS AND RECOGNIZING THE
## NATURE OF MIND                                                12.23

It is a fact that at the very moment we are strongly caught up in thought forms or in the surging waves of emotions, of anger, for instance, it is much easier to recognize the naked state of awareness. This of course is not the case when one has trained in the very tranquil, placid state of meditation where there are no thoughts and negative emotions. . . . Conversely, experiencing great despair, great fear, and intense worry can be a much stronger support for practice. . . . It is the intensity of emotion that allows for a more acute insight into mind essence. . . .

When we are really angry, so enraged we feel as though we are one big flame of blazing, focused anger, if we recognize our natural face and just let go, at that moment the state of wakefulness is laid utterly bare, in a much brighter and more vivid fashion that would normally be. Or, if we are suddenly frightened, as when we are pursued by a pack of vicious dogs and the mind becomes petrified, if we can remember, difficult as it may be, to recognize mind essence at that time, the insight will surpass our normal state of insight generated in meditation practice.

*Tulku Urgyen Rinpoche*

## OBSTACLES                                                   12.24

Generally speaking, there are three types of obstacles: the outer obstacles of the four elements; the inner obstacles of the channels, winds, and essences; and the secret obstacles of dualistic fixation.

To dispel outer obstacles there are the three aspects of approach, accomplishment, and the activities, which are connected to the *sadhanas* of guru, *yidam*, and *dakini*. . . . To clear away the inner obstacles of imbalances in the channels, winds, and essences, *tummo* practice is the most eminent. To overcome obstacles of clinging to subject and object, there is no better remedy than simply maintaining the correct view.

The outer obstacles of the four elements are defined as earth, water, fire, and wind. For example, we can understand the obstacle of earth to be an earthquake, the obstacle of water to be flooding, the obstacle of fire our house catching fire, and the obstacle of wind to be a hurricane. These types of destruction do occur and they can be averted by certain *sadhanas* to pacify the four outer elements.

The inner obstacles involve the channels, winds, and essences of our physical body. . . . Inner obstacles occur when the balance between the channels, winds, and essences is disturbed. The circulation is somehow blocked, giving rise to all different kinds of sickness. These imbalances, the inner obstacles, can be cleared up through the . . . practices of channels, winds, and essences.

Secret obstacles are grasping at objects outwardly and fixating on the perceiver inwardly, and are therefore called "grasping and fixation." . . . In the moment of recognizing nondual awareness, grasping and fixation both dissolve into the innate space of *dharmadhatu*.

The only things that truly prevent enlightenment are the secret obstacles of grasping and fixation. Certainly outer obstacles of the four elements can be problematic. Earthquakes, floods, fires, and hurricanes do take people's lives, as do the inner obstacles of sickness. But it is most essential to clear away the secret obstacles. Only the secret obstacles can really prevent buddhahood.

As long as we haven't reached enlightenment we are always keeping company with these obstacles.

*Tulku Urgyen Rinpoche*


SIGNS OF AUTHENTIC PROGRESS                                    12.25

[The signs of authentic progess] are an acute feeling that life is imperma-nent and that there is no time to waste; that the Dharma is unfailing; that there is genuine benefit from training in *samadhi*; and that it is truly possible to overcome conceptual thinking.

While these are taught to be the most wonderful signs of progress, a materialistic type of person will not see them as being so wonderful. He wants a flabbergasting meditation experience. If something astound-ing happens that he can see or hear or maybe even touch, he thinks, "Wow! I am really getting somewhere now! This is completely different from what I am used to—such a beautiful experience. Such bliss! Such clarity! Such emptiness! I feel totally transformed! This must really be it!"

On the other hand, when you reach the "even plains" of non-thought, the simple quiet after conceptual thinking dissolves, there is nothing very exceptional to see or hear or grasp. . . . [Such] nondual awareness is the most effective way, but the materialistic practitioner does not appreciate this.

*Tulku Urgyen Rinpoche*


AT THE MOMENT OF DEATH                                        12.26

At the moment of death, "time does not change, experiences change." Time here means that there is no real death that occurs, because our innate nature is beyond time. It is only our experiences that change. All these experiences should be regarded as nothing but a paper tiger.

*Tulku Urgyen Rinpoche*

## OUR ATTITUDE AT DEATH                                    12.27

The most important thing to remember is not to feel sad or depressed about anything—there is no point in that. Instead, have the attitude of a traveler who is returning home while joyfully carrying the burden of the suffering of all sentient beings.

*Tulku Urgyen Rinpoche*

## HOW TO DIE                                               12.28

Even if death were to strike you today like lightning, be ready to die without any sadness or regret, without any residual clinging for what is left behind. Remaining in the recognition of the view, leave this life like an eagle soaring up into the blue sky. When an eagle takes flight into the immensity of the sky, he never thinks, "My wings won't be able to carry me. I won't be able to fly that far." Likewise, when dying, remember your teacher and his instructions, and adhere to them with utter confidence.

*Dilgo Khyentse Rinpoche*

## AFTER DEATH, OUR EXPERIENCE WILL
## BE CHOICELESS                                            12.29

The time before death is more comfortable than what follows. No matter how bad our situation may be while we are alive, we can always try to improve it through our ingenuity. At this time we have free will and the opportunity to change our circumstances. But the events that occur after death depend totally on our personal karma. We are absolutely powerless and choiceless regarding the experiences that will arise.

*Tulku Urgyen Rinpoche*

## EXPERIENCING THE DHARMAKAYA AT THE MOMENT
## OF DEATH                                                 12.30

The dualistic mind . . . becomes the Dharmakaya. It is the fundamental truth in which all dualities merge into transcendent oneness and is beyond sensual perception. The Dharmakaya is Wisdom Beyond Joyfulness. It is beyond conceptualization, more profound and indestructible.

At that moment, one does not have to make an effort to meditate; it comes spontaneously and naturally. If you are unable to realize the essence of the mind of all the Buddhas, then you fall back into Samsara. However, if [because of previous practice] you are able to have this realization, then you will attain enlightenment and have no need to wander further in the Bardo.

*Lama Lodö*


## A RETREATANT'S PARTING THOUGHTS TO
## HIS PARENTS                                              12.31
Kyema! Kyema! My dearest parents,
You gave me birth with all the freedoms and advantages of human life,
And you have cared for me with love, from my infancy till now.
Since you introduced me to an authentic teacher,
It is thanks to your kindness that I have encountered the path
    to liberation.

After hearing, thinking about, and meditating on
The life of my perfect teacher,
I have resolved to slip quietly away from all this life's concerns
And roam through empty, uninhabited valleys.

Father and mother, stay in your handsome, lofty house;
I, your young son, long instead for empty caves.

Thank you for the fine, soft clothes you gave me;
Yet I don't need them—I would rather dress in plain white felt.

I leave my valuable belongings behind—
A begging bowl, a staff, and Dharma robes are all I need.

I've cast aside this luxury and wealth with no regrets;
A handbook of profound advice is all I wish to collect.

I need no attendants, who just fuel anger and attachment:
Birds and wild animals are the only company I long for.

Earlier, in the presence of my sovereign teacher,
As he bestowed the Secret Heart Essence empowerment,
I vowed to abandon all the activities of this life
And practice in accord with the Dharma.
In my heart that promise is as clear as if engraved in stone—
I cannot but leave for a secluded mountain retreat.

Although for now your son will hide away in mountain glens,
Your smiling faces will be with me always,
Nor shall I forget your loving care;
And if I reach the citadel of experience and realization,
I shall repay your kindness, of that you can be sure!

*Dilgo Khyentse Rinpoche, at age thirteen*

*Part Five*

# CONCLUSION

# ✣ 13

# Tibetan Buddhism in the West

THE PASSAGES IN THIS CONCLUSION all revolve around the topic of Tibetan Buddhism in the West. There are several factors behind the spread of Buddhism in the West (13.1). Among Asian teachers there are questions about Westerners' capacity to receive the dharma (13.2). In any case, the transplantation will not be accomplished within a single generation (13.3). At least, we Westerners would do well to learn accurately and deeply (13.4).

At the same time, we can't become Tibetans: our path must be based on our own Western social context, history, and identity. We must become American buddhas; there is no other choice (13.5). Can Western Buddhism be authentic? Yes, but only if the Buddha's view is preserved (13.6). Can Westerners have true spiritual lineage? Yes, if we define that in a profound, rather than a superficial, cultural sense (13.7). It is clear, however, that changes in the way Buddhism is transmitted may need to occur (13.8). Certainly the traditional Tibetan custom of renouncing the world and living as a monk or hermit, supported by a religious community, may not work very well in the West (13.9). Will modern technology be an impediment to the spread of the dharma? Not if it is used in the right way (13.10).

There are serious obstacles facing the Western assimilation of Buddhism. One serious impediment is the Western shopping mentality

(13.11). Another is our tendency to accept only those aspects of Buddhism that fit in with our immediate preconceptions and convenience (13.12). Such an approach could leave us with an ego version of the dharma (13.13). This does not mean Westerners should not test the dharma thoroughly (13.14). Western students, in fact, have certain qualities to recommend them (13.15, 13.16).

## WHY BUDDHISM IS EXPANDING IN THE WEST          13.1

One can find three reasons for the expansion of Buddhism in the West.

1. Some people, having heard about Tibet and Tibetans, conceived a favorable opinion and went to India, where they were able to meet Tibetan masters. Observing how the teachings benefited them, they invited many lamas and tulkus to come to the West.
2. The values shared by Christianity and Buddhism have prepared favorable ground: devotion (for God or the Three Jewels), the love and the compassion for beings, the respect for ethics, and so on.
3. For the most part, Westerners have been studying a lot, and have developed their intelligence. They can understand the deep aspects of Buddhism more easily.

*Kalu Rinpoche*

## TRANSPLANTING THE BUDDHA-DHARMA IN THE WEST          13.2

Transplanting anything from a foreign culture is a difficult process which may corrupt what is being imported. Buddhism is certainly no exception; in fact, among imported foreign goods, dharma is perhaps the most prone to corruption.

For this reason, most Oriental teachers are very skeptical about exporting dharma to the Western world, feeling that Westerners lack the refinement and courage to understand and practice properly the buddhadharma. On the other hand there are some who try their best to work on the transmission of the dharma to the West.

*Dzongsar Khytense Rinpoche*

## TRANSPLANTING THE DHARMA IS NOT AN EASY PROCESS          13.3

It is important to remember that a thorough transplantation of dharma cannot be accomplished within a single generation. It is not an easy process, and as when Buddhism was brought from India to Tibet, it will undoubtedly take time. There are enormous differences between the attitudes of various cultures and different interpretations of similar phenomena. It is easy to forget that such supposedly universal notions as "ego," "freedom," "equality," "power," and the implications of "gender" and "secrecy," are all constructions that are culture-specific and differ radically when seen through different perspectives. The innuendoes surrounding a certain issue in one culture might not even occur to those of another culture, where the practice in question is taken for granted.

*Dzongsar Khytense Rinpoche*

## WE NEED THE HUMILITY . . .     13.4

Surely no culture should claim to have the deep appreciation and understanding necessary to produce a thorough and justified critique of an important aspect of another's culture (especially when the topic is as sophisticated and complex as Buddhism) without having the humility to make the effort to accurately and deeply learn about that topic on that culture's own terms.

*Dzongsar Khytense Rinpoche*

## BECOMING AN AMERICAN BUDDHA     13.5

You can't reject your history. You can't say that your hair is black if it is blond. You have to accept your history. Those wanting to imitate Oriental culture might go so far as to become 100 percent Hindu or 100 percent Japanese, even to the point of undergoing plastic surgery. But somehow denying your existence—your body, your makeup, your psychological approach—does not help. In fact, it brings more problems. You have to be what you are. You have to relate with your country, the state of your country, its politics, its cultures. That is extrmely important, since you cannot become someone else. And it is such a blessing. . . . That represents our relationship to the earth as a whole, our national karma, and all the rest of it. That seems to be the starting point for attaining enlightenment, becoming a buddha, an American buddha.

*Chögyam Trungpa Rinpoche*

## WILL MODERNIZATION LEAD TO THE LOSS OF THE
## OLD BUDDHIST TRADITION?                                    13.6

As long as the fundamental view of Buddhism is not lost, there is no problem. We may try for sentimental reasons to preserve the traditional aspects as much as possible, but they will eventually change. Don't forget that the customs and traditions that we are trying to preserve today were once modern and progressive.

I have met people in the West who are excessively attached to the external trappings of Buddhism. There is all this sentimental attachment to Tibetan customs and culture, and the actual Buddhist view is overlooked. In fact, I have heard that in creating a so-called "American Buddhism," some people are saying, "Okay, maybe the Buddha's view should be changed, now that Buddhism is in America." And that's not good.

I would prefer that Americans really stick with the Buddha's view, the emptiness of inherent existence, that everything composite is impermanent, and so on. It doesn't matter if they leave out Tibetan culture. The really important thing is that they should accept the dharma. They should not worry about trying to design something better suited to Americans. The Buddha was an omniscient being. What he said was good for all sentient beings, and that includes us 2500 years later. Nothing additional is necessary now.

*Dzongsar Khytense Rinpoche*


## CAN WESTERNERS HAVE TRUE SPIRITUAL LINEAGE?         13.7

Some Easterners, or Westerners who think like Easterners, believe that Westerners cannot have lineage because they have no tradition. If we believe that Westerners are too materialistic to have any spiritual lineage, we are disrespectful to pure Buddhist lineage. If we are not concerned with true spiritual qualities but are superficially seduced by Eastern customs and manners because we associate the East with Buddhist lineage, we are also disrespectful to pure Buddhist lineage. If we think that only priests, lamas, and gurus have lineage, then we have title lineage conception and padlock and key lineage conception which is disrespectful to pure spiritual lineage. . . . If we do not acknowledge those who hold pure lineage regardless of where they come from, we are disrespectful to vast omniscient spiritual lineage.

*Thinley Norbu Rinpoche*

## POINTING-OUT INSTRUCTIONS: THE TRADITIONAL WAY AND THE MODERN WORLD                                    13.8

The traditional way of receiving the instruction on how to realize the nature of mind involves first going through the training of the preliminary practices of the "four times hundred thousand." After that, you would carry out the *yidam* practice, staying in retreat and completing the set number of recitations. Finally, after all this, the teaching would be given.

But nowadays we live in different times. People are so busy that they have no time to actually sit down and go through all this training. We might call it progress in material development, but doesn't it just make us all so much more busy? . . .

My root guru told me once that different times were coming. He said, "If you happen to be in front of people who ask about and want to hear about the nature of mind, explain it to them. If they have the karmic readiness, they will understand, and if they do understand, they are benefited. To benefit beings is the purpose of the Buddha's teachings. It's all right."

*Tulku Urgyen Rinpoche*

## RENOUNCING THE WORLD IN THE WEST?                         13.9

Actually, spiritual practice and worldly aims are like two irreconcilable enemies that will never get along. . . . The Buddha demonstrated that one embraces spiritual training by leaving worldly concerns behind.

On the other hand, if one has already submerged oneself in the maya or illusion of family life, one can't just leave that. One has to take responsibility for one's family. As the West lacks the tradition of renunciant life, it is admittedly difficult for Westerners to forsake everything—career, luxuries, and social standing. In Tibet, certain individuals could give up everything and focus one hundred percent on practicing the Dharma, and somehow, they would still get by. . . .

I don't think it's like that in the West. . . . One has to take responsibility for one's personal livelihood: that's the Western way, so that's what has to be followed. Try to make the best of it so that you can carry on your mundane life and at the same time not give up the Dharma. . . . Try to do both at the same time.

*Tulku Urgyen Rinpoche*

## Is Modern Technology Detrimental to the Dharma?                    13.10

Modern technology is not a threat to so-called traditional Buddhism. . . . We can no longer go to any place where there is no modern technology. We cannot avoid technology—it's already at the doorstep, if not already inside our house. So instead of allowing these things to influence us, the wise thing to do is to make use of their power and speed—to be the influence rather than the influenced. We can use the telephone, the web, and television to teach, instead of them teaching us. We can use their power and speed.

*Dzongsar Khytense Rinpoche*

## The Dharma and the Western Shopping Mentality                    13.11

If people could put some effort into being respectful and open-minded, there is so much knowledge available that could liberate them from all kinds of suffering and confusion. It is only now that I have come to realize the significance of the great respect that the Tibetan translators and scholars of the past had toward India, their source of dharma and wisdom. Instead of being critical or even resentful of their source, they called it "The Sublime Land of India." This kind of attitude is very different from the Western shopping mentality that regards the dharma as merchandise and our own involvement as an investment—only wanting to accept what sits well with our habitual expectations and rejecting what we don't find immediately gratifying.

*Dzongsar Khytense Rinpoche*

ON THE SELECTIVE APPROPRIATION OF THE DHARMA    13.12

I find heartbreaking the imperialist attitude that arrogantly isolates one aspect of Eastern culture, analyzing it at a careful distance, manipulating and sterilizing it to fit Western agendas, and then perhaps concluding that it is now suitable for consumption.

*Dzongsar Khytense Rinpoche*


WE COULD END UP WITH EGO'S OWN VERSION    13.13

This is cherishing of ego. For even if we think we want to practice the Buddhist path, to give up our ego-clinging is not easy, and we could well end up with our own ego's version of dharma—a pseudo-dharma which will only bring more suffering instead of liberation.

*Dzongsar Khytense Rinpoche*


WESTERNERS SHOULD BE CRITICAL OF THE
BUDDHIST TEACHINGS    13.14

This is not to say that Westerners should not be critical of the Buddhist teachings. On the contrary, as the Lord Buddha himself said, "Without melting, beating, weighing, and polishing a yellow substance, one should not take it for gold. Likewise, without analysis one should not accept the dharma as valid." Logical analysis has always been encouraged in the Buddhist tradition, and Buddhism has always challenged the promotion of blind faith.

The difference lies in the attitude you take towards the criticism. In the process of analyzing that "yellow substance," the analyzer must not only maintain an open mind, but also acknowledge that he/she may not have an adequate knowledge of the subject matter. That is the whole point of analysis. Otherwise we are just seeking confirmation of what we already believe. Being skeptical and seeking faults are two completely different things.

*Dzongsar Khytense Rinpoche*


IT IS MORE DIFFICULT TO TEACH
WESTERN STUDENTS    13.15

It is more difficult to teach Western people than Tibetans. If Tibetans ask me whether they can purify all their negative karma by reciting the

Vajrasattva mantra, I can simply answer by giving a relevant quotation from Shakyamuni Buddha or Lord Tsongkhapa. I don't have to think much about my answer. I can just cite some words from a text, and they will be satisfied. If you quote the right words, Tibetans will stay quiet. A Westerner, on the other hand, would demand, "Lama Je Tsongkhapa said what? Why did he say that? How can he say that? Does it work?" This is good.

*Lama Thubten Yeshe Rinpoche*

## WESTERN STUDENTS AND THEIR TEACHERS    13.16

I think the relationship between Western students and their teachers is better than that between Eastern students and their teachers, because no formal customs are involved. Westerners question everything, and I find this a very honest approach. If something does not make sense to you, you say so openly. If something makes sense to you, you say, "Yes, this is helpful. I will use it." There is no custom obliging you to answer or behave in a certain way. If you like or don't like something, you simply say so. This is very difficult for Eastern students to do, because they feel a social obligation to behave in a certain way. I feel the Western way is more realistic.

*Lama Thubten Yeshe Rinpoche*

# GLOSSARY

Spelling, italicization, and capitalization of foreign terms are not always consistent throughout the book because the preferred treatment of these words in individual selections has been preserved. This glossary makes note of alternative spelling of key terms.

*abhisheka* (Skt., "empowerment"). The ritual of initiation in Vajrayana Buddhism. Most commonly, the *abhisheka* authorizes the practitioner to carry out the practice of one of the great tantric buddhas or deities, or *yidam*. Each *yidam* and the associated cycles of practices requires a specific *abhisheka,* and therefore, in the Vajrayana, many different *abhishekas* are known.

*anuyoga* (Skt.). The eighth in the Nyingma stages of the path to enlightenment known as the nine *yanas,* or vehicles. *Anuyoga* is particularly known for its practices of the inner yogas of the winds (*prana*), channels (*nadi*), and consciousness (*bindu*).

*Avalokiteshvara* (Skt.). "The Lord who looks down from on high (with compassion)." Considered the essence of compassion, Avalokiteshvara is one of the three most important celestial bodhisattvas in Tibetan Buddhism (Manjushri and Vajrapani are the other two). Certain high lamas, such as the Dalai Lamas and the Karmapas, are considered to be human embodiments of Avalokiteshvara.

*bardo* (Tib.). "The state in-between." Most commonly, *bardo* refers to the state after death through which the consciousness, now separated from the body, journeys on its way to a new birth.

*bhumis* (Skt.). "Levels," "stages," or "grounds." In the practice of Mahayana Buddhism, the development of the bodhisattva is described in a sequence of ten (sometimes expanded to thirteen) *bhumis,* with the final one representing the complete and perfect enlightenment of a buddha. The *bhumis* all describe quite elevated levels of spiritual maturity.

*bodhisattva* (Skt.). "Being destined to enlightenment." The term originally referred to Shakyamuni Buddha, beginning when he first made the vow to attain complete and perfect enlightenment, through three incalculable eons of rebirths in which he developed wisdom and compassion, down to the moment in his final birth when he attained awakening. Subsequently, *bodhisattva* came to indicate the Mahayana practitioner. All Mahayanists, like the Buddha, have made the vow to follow the path to complete and perfect enlightenment, one day becoming a world-redeeming buddha like Shakyamuni and thereby accomplishing the maximum possible benefit to sentient beings.

*bodhi* (Skt.). "Enlightenment."

*bodhichitta* (Skt.). "Mind (or heart) of enlightenment." *Bodhichitta* is the essence of enlightenment that, according to the Mahayana, exists in the heart of all sentient beings. Understood in Tibetan Buddhism as another name for the buddha-nature, it is gradually brought to the full maturity of buddhahood through the various Mahayana practices.

*buddha* (Skt., "awake"). A fully and completely enlightened being. All the historical Buddhist traditions—Theravada (Hinayana), Mahayana, and Vajrayana—enumerate many such beings, both preceding and following the buddha of this world age, Shakyamuni Buddha. Mahayana Buddhism counts the buddhas as limitless in number, appearing throughout endless time and space. In the Mahayana and Vajrayana, many celestial buddhas are known and become the objects of meditation and worship.

*buddha-dharma* (Skt.). The teachings and heritage of Shakyamuni Buddha. This term is preferred by many Asian and Western Buddhists, rather than the Western designation "Buddhism," because the latter term implies an "ism," a fixed entity, while "buddha-dharma" implies a living and ever-changing body of teaching, practice, and realization.

*buddha-field* (Skt. *buddhakshetra*). The sphere of a buddha's activity. In Mahayana cosmology, world systems—of which there are an infinite number throughout time and space—are typically presided over by a buddha. Buddha-fields are of two types, pure and impure; our world system is a representation of the latter.

*buddha-nature*. The most commonly used rendering of the Sanskrit *tathagata-garbha*, which means, more precisely, the embryo or the womb of the *tathagata*, or buddha. The concept of buddha-nature points to the fact that all sentient beings possess within them, at their core, the essence or essential nature of a buddha, which is wisdom united with compassion. The Mahayana path is understood as the gradual shedding of the adventitious defilements that cover the buddha-nature and hide it from our experience. A fully enlightened buddha is a person from whom all the defilements have been removed.

*chitta, citta* (Skt.; Tib. *sems*). Mind or heart. One of the many terms for "mind" in Buddhism, *chitta* is a general word for mind that includes all its aspects, although most often in Tibetan Buddhism it designates the conditioned or unenlightened mind.

*dakini* (Skt.; Tib. *khandroma*). "Sky goer." *Dakinis* are female beings of power and insight. They may be either "wisdom *dakinis*," who are embodiments of the reality and message of enlightenment, or "worldly *dakinis*," who can be either helpful or harmful to the practitioner on the path. Sometimes *dakinis* are human women, and sometimes they appear in visions and dreams in a vivid but nonphysical form.

*dana* (Skt.). "Generosity," one of the six perfections (*paramitas*).

*dharma* (Skt.). "Truth" or "reality." Buddhism speaks of an outer dharma, namely, the teachings of the Buddha, and an inner dharma, reality when we see it as it truly is. From this latter point of view, all phenomena are expressions of dharma.

*dharmachakra* (Skt.). "Wheel of dharma" or, more loosely, "promulgations of major cycles of Buddhist teaching." According to Tibetan Buddhism, Buddha Shakyamuni turned the wheel of dharma three times, first at the Deer Park in Varanasi where he taught the four noble truths, second on Vulture Peak Mountain near Rajagriha where he taught emptiness, and finally in a celestial palace where he taught the buddha-nature.

*dharmakaya* (Skt.). The "body of truth" or "body of reality." *See* three bodies of the buddha.

*Dzogchen* (Tib.). The "great perfection"; according to the Nyingma lineage, the highest of the nine *yanas,* or vehicles, of practice and realization. Dzogchen contains two major facets, *trekchö,* "cutting through," and *tögel,* "crossing over." *Trekchö* refers to the cultivation of a mind that is utterly empty and without any constraints, limitations, or preoccupations. *Tögel* refers to the practice of relating to appearance as a vehicle of immediate liberation.

*eight worldly dharmas.* The eight worldly ways of judging and discriminating experience that create karma and perpetuate our entrapment in samsara. These include gain and loss, fame and ill-repute, praise and blame, and pleasure and pain. Each of the eight worldly dharmas arises as a function of belief in a "self" that we are trying to maintain and protect.

*five aggregates* (Skt. *skandhas*). These are the five types or "heaps" into which all human experience can be exhaustively grouped: form, feeling, impulse, karmic formations, and consciousness. According to Buddhism, in our experience there is no substantial or continuous "self," only the five *skandhas*. No self is to be found within the five *skandhas*, nor do the five *skandhas* as a group make up a self, nor is a self found outside of them. This is one of the proofs of "no-self," the realization of which brings liberation.

*four immeasurables*. Practices through which one develops compassion toward others and fearlessness in relation to one's own experience. These include (in Sanskrit) *maitri* (loving-kindness), *karuna* (compassion), *mudita* (sympathetic joy), and *upeksha* (equanimity).

*four mind changings*. The four thoughts that turn the mind (from samsara). These are (1) the preciousness of human birth (in this human life we have an opportunity to practice and attain realization); (2) impermanence (death is real and comes without warning); (3) the pain of samsara (there are six realms of existence, and inescapable suffering occurs within and as a result of each of them); and (4) karma (everything we do produces an effect that we will have to live with, producing happiness or suffering for us in the future).

*four reminders*. *See* four mind changings.

*Gampopa* (1079–1153 CE). One of the two principal students of Milarepa (the other being Rechungpa). When Gampopa met Milarepa, he was a Kadam monk, and subsequently he combined Milarepa's meditative and eremitical approach with the settled monasticism of his Kadam training. Through his disciple, Tusumkhyenpa, he was instrumental in the formation of the Kagyü sublineage, the Karma Kagyü, presided over by the Karmapa line of incarnations.

*Garab Dorje*. An Indian siddha and first human progenitor of the Dzogchen teachings of the Nyingma lineage of Tibetan Buddhism.

*Gautama*. The clan name of Buddha Shakyamuni prior to his enlightenment.

*Gelug, Geluk* (Tib.). One of the four main schools of Tibetan Buddhism, founded by Tsongkhapa in the fourteenth century. Developing as a reform movement within the Kadam sect of Atisha (eleventh century), it has maintained its primary seat in Central Tibet and is the lineage of the Dalai Lamas.

*guru* (Skt.; Tib. *lama*). "Teacher." The guru is simply the person from whom one receives Buddhist instruction. While commonly one or a few teachers may play principal teaching roles in a person's life (functioning as "root guru," or "primary teacher"), Tibetans may have several individuals whom they think of as their lamas or gurus.

*Guru Rinpoche* (Skt.). *See* Padmasambhava.

*guru yoga* (Skt.). One of the four "preliminary practices" (Tib. *ngöndro*) carried out by practitioners aspiring to receive *abhisheka*, or full initiation into the Vajrayana.

*Hinayana* (Skt.). "Little," "immediate," or "direct" vehicle. *See* three yanas.

*jewels*. *See* three jewels.

*Kadampas*. The early lamas of the Kadam lineage, founded by the Indian master Atisha, after he arrived in Tibet in 1042. *See also* Gelug.

*Kagyü* (Tib.). The lineage deriving from the Indian *siddha* Tilopa (988–1069) and his Indian disciple Naropa (1016–1100). It was passed on to the first Tibetan holder of the lineage, Marpa (1012–1096), to his disciple Milarepa (1040–1123), and then on to Rechungpa, Gampopa, the Karmapas, and other Kagyü masters.

*karma* (Skt.). "Action." One of the central teachings of the Buddha and of Buddhism, expressed in the second noble truth, which details how suffering comes about. There are two principal types of karma, the karma of result and the karma of cause. The karma of result refers to the fact that our current circumstances and the events of our present life are the result of causes and conditions laid down by us in previous times. The karma of cause indicates that whatever we do in the present will contribute toward the circumstances and events that we will experience in the future.

*Karmapa* (Skt.). "Man of (enlightened) action." The line of incarnations (*tulkus*) that has reigned as the supreme head of the Karma Kagyü lineage. The Karmapa incarnations began with Gampopa's disciple Tusumkhyenpa in the twelfth century and continue down to the present in the person of the seventeenth Gyalwang Karmapa.

*kaya* (Skt., "body"). *See* three bodies of the Buddha.

*kleshas*. The primary "defiling emotions" or "emotional obscurations" that lead to demeritorious actions, the creation of negative karma, and ongoing bondage and suffering within samsara. The *kleshas* are listed in a threefold group—passion, aggression, and ignorance—and in a fivefold grouping, the three mentioned plus pride and jealousy or paranoia. In the Hinayana the *kleshas* are abandoned; in the Mahayana, they are transformed; and in the Vajrayana, their essence is realized to be nothing other than the immaculate wisdom of a buddha.

*kshanti* (Skt.). "Patience," one of the six *paramitas*. *See* paramitas.

*lhagthong* (Tib.). Insight practice. *See* vipashyana.

*Madhyamaka* (Skt.). "School of the middle way." The Madhyamaka is the most important Mahayana philosophical school in Tibet. Founded by Nagarjuna (ca. second century), the Madhyamaka is a commentarial tradition on the *Prajnaparamita Sutra* (a collection of sutras on the "perfection of wisdom") that involves the study and, eventually, the experiential understanding of emptiness (Skt., *shunyata*). Within Tibetan Buddhism, the most important Madhyamaka line has been that of the Prasangika Madhyamaka, which seeks to show the fallacy (or emptiness) of any position that may be advanced without, however, advancing any position of its own.

*Mahayoga* (Skt.). The seventh of the nine *yanas* of the Nyingma path. Mahayoga emphasizes the visualization of tantric deities and the practice of the liturgies and meditations associated with them.

*Mahamudra* (Skt.). The "great symbol," the epitome of realization in the schools (Sakya, Kagyü, Gelug) that arose during the second spreading of Buddhism in Tibet (from the tenth to the end of the twelfth century). Mahamudra points to the union of appearance and emptiness in the realized state: *mudra* indicates appearance, the phenomena that arise within awareness, while *maha* indicates their utter emptiness—the fact that they are utterly beyond any formulation or conceptualization. Mahamudra is often divided into Ground Mahamudra (the inherent purity of awareness within all beings), Path Mahamudra (the practices through which the realization of Mahamudra is cultivated), and Fruition Mahamudra (enlightenment).

*Mahasandhi* (Skt.). *See* Dzogchen.

*mahasiddha* (Skt.). "Completely perfected one," the designation given to those Vajrayana practitioners in India who were considered to have attained the complete perfection of enlightenment. The *mahasiddhas* were people from all castes and walks of life who followed a tantric guru, practiced meditation intensively, attained realization, and themselves became gurus to others. In the tradition, a group of eighty-four *mahasiddhas* was especially well known, all of whom are reputed to have lived in India between the eighth and the twelfth centuries.

*Mahayana* (Skt.). The "great vehicle," the genre of Buddhism practiced in Tibet. *See* three yanas.

*mandala* (Skt.). The *mandala,* or "sacred circle," is a central image within the Vajrayana Buddhism of Tibet. In Vajrayana rites, the *mandala* is a geometrically delineated circle or three-dimensional "palace" that represents the cosmos when seen from an enlightened viewpoint. The principal tantric deity of the ritual is depicted at the center of the *mandala,* while his or her retinue are typically stationed at the four primary and four intermediate directions, and in other locations, around the periphery.

*Manjushri, Manjuśri* (Skt.). One of the three principal celestial bodhisattvas in Tibet (including also Avalokiteshvara and Vajrapani). Manjushri is thought to be the essence of wisdom, and great scholars or teachers may be said to be the human incarnations of this bodhisattva.

*mantra* (Skt.). Sanskrit words or syllables, sometimes with conceptual meaning, often without, that embody the energy of particular deities (*yidams*), who in turn embody aspects of the awakened state. Mantras are uttered in the context of ritual

Vajrayana practice, during which one also carries out visualizations and performs various hand gestures (*mudras*).

*Mantrayana* (Skt.). "The vehicle of mantras," another term for Vajrayana Buddhism.

*Mara* (Skt.). The "evil one" who attempted, at the last minute, to dissuade Shakyamuni Buddha from completing his quest for enlightenment. Mara is the personification of the forces of ignorance that keep sentient beings enmeshed in samsara. In the developed tradition, Mara is said to have four primary forms: He manifests as the five *skandhas*; the lord of death; the defiling emotions (*kleshas*); and as divine beings who carry out his biddings.

*Milarepa* (1040–1123). The best-known and perhaps most well-loved hermit and *yogin* in Tibetan Buddhist history. He was the principal disciple of the translator Marpa (1012–1097), Tibetan founder of the Kagyü lineage received in India from the *siddha* Naropa (1016–1100). After an extraordinarily difficult youth filled with suffering and much evildoing, Milarepa met Marpa, studied under him, and finally received Vajrayana transmission. Then, at Marpa's direction, Milarepa entered solitary retreat in the mountains and spent the rest of his life meditating and training disciples. His principal students were Rechungpa and Gampopa.

*Nagarjuna* (ca. second–third century). The founder of the Madhyamaka, or "middle way school."

*Naropa* (1016–1100). Originally a highly accomplished Buddhist scholar and eventually abbot at Nalanda, the renowned Buddhist monastic university in northern India, Naropa one day realized that, in spite of all his learning, he did not really understand or embody the Buddhist teachings. He left his position at Nalanda and wandered through the jungles looking for a teacher who could train him and open his eyes. Eventually he met an apparently mad *yogin* named Tilopa (989–1069), who was a *mahasiddha* (an enlightened tantric master). Studying with him for twelve years, Naropa finally achieved realization and began teaching and accepting disciples of his own. One of these was Marpa, who took the lineage of Tilopa and Naropa to Tibet, where it became famed as the Kagyü lineage.

*New Translation schools.* The Sakya, the Kagyü, and the Kadam/Gelug schools.

*ngöndro* (Tib.). "That which comes before." The *ngöndro* are the four (in the Nyingma, five) Vajrayana "preliminary practices" that are commonly done in preparation for full initiation into the *vajra,* or tantric, vehicle. The *ngöndro* include one hundred thousand repetitions each of: full-body prostrations, including refuge formula; the 108-syllable mantra of the deity Vajrasattva; offerings of one's body, speech, and mind to the lineage; and the mantra of one's guru known as *guru yoga.* In the Nyingma, the first of the four *ngöndro* may be divided into two separate practices of prostrations and recitations of the refuge formula, making five *ngöndro* in all. Each of the practices is accompanied by a visualization, *mudras*, and *mantras* or other utterances.

*nine yanas* (Skt.). In the Nyingma lineage of Tibetan Buddhism, the path is described in terms of nine stages, or *yanas* (lit., "vehicles"). The first three represent the pretantric vehicles (*shravaka-yana, pratyekabuddha-yana, bodhisattva-yana*); the second three include the three "outer *yanas*" (*kriyayoga-yana, upayoga-yana,* and *yoga-yana*), while the final three comprise the "inner yogas" (*mahayoga-yana, anuyoga-yana,* and *atiyoga-yana*, also known as Dzogchen). These final three of the nine *yanas* represent the characteristic and advanced Nyingma tantric practices.

*nirmanakaya* (Skt.). The "created body." *See* three bodies of the buddha.

*nirvana* (Skt., lit., "blown out," "extinguished"). The extinction of craving and its resulting grasping and fixation. Nirvana marks full realization or enlightenment in Buddhism.

*no-self* (Skt. *anatman*). The teaching that while in ordinary experience there appears to be a substantial "self" at the root of our human person, when such a truly existing self is sought for, it cannot be found. Realization of no-self is described as the hallmark of enlightenment in the early Buddhist teachings. In the Mahayana, the doctrine of no-self is further developed: first is the no-self of the individual, and second, the no-self of all phenomena. This latter "selflessness of the dharmas" points to the fact that any aspect or element of our experience is also, itself, without a self.

*Nyingma* (Tib.). The "lineage of the ancients" or "Old Translation school," one of the four principal schools of Tibetan Buddhism and the only one to emerge from the first spreading of Buddhism to Tibet in the seventh to ninth centuries. It is understood to have been founded by Guru Rinpoche (Padmasambhava) with the help of Guru Rinpoche's consort Yeshe Tsogyal, twenty-five great disciples, and numerous other devoted practitioners.

*Old Translation school.* *See* Nyingma.

*Padmakara* (Skt.). *See* Padmasambhava.

*Padmasambhava.* Also known as Guru Rinpoche and Padmakara. The Indian *siddha* who brought Vajrayana Buddhism for the first time to Tibet, in the eighth century CE. His traditional biography says that he was miraculously born in a lotus, adopted by king Indrabhuti in Northwest India, and brought up as a prince. His unconventional behavior led to banishment, and he spent the rest of his life roaming the charnel grounds, jungles, and wastelands, learning from *dakinis* both human and superhuman, and practicing the tantric teachings. During his wanderings, he met and trained many disciples. At the request of the Tibetan king Trisong Detsen, Padmasambhava went to Tibet and was instrumental in the establishment of Buddhism there. He is considered the founder of the Nyingma tradition and also its principal guru, and many liturgies and meditations invoke his presence and request his blessings.

*paramita* (Skt., "perfection"). The *paramitas* are Mahayana practices carried out by bodhisattvas for the benefit of others on the long road (through three incalculable eons of rebirths) to the complete and perfect enlightenment of a world-redeeming buddha. In the most common listing, they include generosity, discipline, exertion, patience, meditation, and *prajnaparamita,* or transcendent knowledge. The first five *paramitas* are considered relative practices that one carries out, while the sixth is the ultimate *paramita* of the realization of emptiness, or *shunyata.*

*Patrül (Paltrül, Petrul) Rinpoche* (1808–1887). A great Nyingma scholar, practitioner, teacher, and author who lived in eastern Tibet. Although a high incarnation (*tülku*), he abjured the customary pomp and circumstance associated with his station and spent most of his life meditating in lonely places, wandering abroad, begging for his food, sleeping in caves and ditches, and helping the common people wherever he could. He is especially renowned for his instruction on the Mahayana and Vajrayana, and his "Teaching on the Three Words that Strike the Heart" is a much-loved Dzogchen classic.

*perfections.* See paramita.

*prajna* (Skt., knowledge; Tib. *sherab*). In Buddhism, the term appears frequently and can have any one of a number of different meanings, depending on context. *Prajna* can indicate ordinary, worldly knowledge. More commonly, it is given in a set of "three *prajnas,*" indicating three progressively deeper states of understanding: (1) study or learning ("hearing"), in which one gains a conceptual knowledge of a certain teaching; (2) contemplating, in which one reflects on a particular teaching to understand its fuller meaning and ramifications; and (3) meditation, in which one sees the inner, nonconceptual meaning. In the Hinayana, *prajna* refers to the kind of knowledge known as *vipashyana.* In the Mahayana teachings, *prajna,* as in *prajnaparamita,* "transcendent knowledge," refers to the understanding of *shunyata,* or emptiness.

*prajnaparamita.* The last and highest of the six *paramitas,* or perfections.

*Prajnaparamita Sutra.* A collection of Mahayana sutras or text in which the Buddha gives teachings on the meaning of *shunyata,* emptiness. The earlier *Prajnaparamita Sutras* are among the earliest Mahayana compositions and later became the basis for the Madhyamaka school through Nagarjuna's influential commentaries on them.

*preliminary practices.* See *ngöndro.*

*rigpa* (Tib.; Skt. *vidya,* "knowledge"). While *rigpa* can refer to ordinary, worldly knowledge, in the Nyingma lineage it is the primary term designating the inherent wisdom within, the awakened state itself.

*root guru.* One's principal teacher. *See also* guru.

*roots, the three.* The three special refuges of Vajrayana practitioners. These include the guru who is the root of blessings; the *yidam* who is the root of accomplishment; and the dharma protectors (*dharmapalas*) or *dakinis* who are the root of enlightened action.

*sadhana* (Skt.). A Vajrayana text that includes various meditations and ritual practices that one carries out in association with a particular *yidam* or tantric deity after receiving *abhisheka* into that deity's *mandala*. The primary tantras of each deity contain material that is similar, but in an often random or cryptic fashion, whereas in the *sadhana* the same practices are presented in a structured, accessible, and understandable way.

*Sakya* (Tib.). One of the four schools of Tibetan Buddhism. The Sakya school has origins in the teachings of the Indian *mahasiddha* Virupa (ninth or tenth century) and was brought to Tibet by the Tibetan Drokmi (993–1077). The Sakya school is particularly renowned for its *lamdre* (path and fruit) teachings that combine Mahayana and Vajrayana into a unified synthesis.

*samadhi* (Skt., meditation). *Samadhi* is most often a general term comprising all forms of meditation. In this context, Buddhist texts speak of the Buddhist path as threefold, including *shila* (ethical conduct), *samadhi* (meditation), and *prajna* (knowledge).

*Samantabhadra.* The "all-good," ultimate, *dharmakaya* buddha in the Nyingma tradition, depicted as naked and dark blue in color, often in union with his consort Samantabhadri, who is depicted as white in color.

*samaya* (Skt., "sacred bond"). Each of the three *yanas* has its characteristic vow: refuge in the Hinayana, the bodhisattva vow in the Mahayana, and the *samaya* vow in the Vajrayana. The ultimate meaning of *samaya* is the commitment to maintain one's view of the sacredness of all of reality and always to act in accord with that. This translates into many much more specific *samaya* commitments, such as the vow to carry out one's practice for the rest of one's life, to respect one's teacher, and never to malign or harm one's companions on the tantric path. Since it is impossible for ordinary practitioners to keep *samaya* for very long, many practices are given in the Vajrayana to repair one's *samaya* breaches and cleanse one's being.

*sambhogakaya* (Skt., "enjoyment body"). *See* three bodies of the buddha.

*sampannakrama* (Skt., "stage of completion"). One of the two stages of *yidam* practice. *See also* yidam.

*samsara* (Skt., "cyclical existence"). The condition of humans and other sentient beings who have yet to achieve enlightenment. Samsara is based in ignorance; is characterized by endless, repetitive suffering; and is perpetuated through intentional actions that create karma. Buddhist tradition describes six kinds of samsaric destiny: the six realms of hell-beings; hungry ghosts; animals; humans; jealous, warring gods; and gods. (Sometimes the gods and jealous gods are put together, yielding five realms.) The Buddhist path leads to nirvana or liberation, a state in which the causes of samsara are gradually eliminated and its ignorance, suffering, and creation of karma cease.

*Saraha.* One of the eighty-four *mahasiddhas* or enlightened tantric masters. Saraha is known in Tibetan Buddhism as the "grandfather of the *siddhas*," indicating a belief that his life falls rather at the beginning of the tradition of *mahasiddhas*. He is particularly known for his instruction on Mahamudra, given in *dohas* (collections of realization songs).

*sangha* (Skt.). The Buddhist community. In the strictest and probably earliest sense, *sangha* refers to the group of highly realized beings whom we may supplicate in our practice. The term also refers to specific monastic communities and their ordained membership. Next, *sangha* can indicate the members of a particular community of disciples of a certain teacher. Finally, and most broadly, *sangha* indicates the entire collection of those who have taken refuge and are considered Buddhists.

*Shakyamuni Buddha* (ca. 563–483 BCE). The historical individual who founded the Buddhist tradition in this world.

*shamatha* (Skt., "calm abiding"; Tib. *shi-ne*). A group of meditation practices, with and without a specific object of mindfulness, that bring the mind into a state of quiescence. The breath is most usually taken as the primary object of meditation in the practice of *shamatha*. *Shamatha* is practiced in all the Buddhist meditation traditions and is commonly considered the preliminary to *vipashyana*, or insight. *See also* vipashyana.

*shastras.* "Commentaries." Commentaries, composed by renowned Buddhist authors, on teachings given by Shakyamuni Buddha.

*shila* (Skt., "discipline"). One of the "three trainings," *shila* includes various codes of conduct that Buddhists follow as part of the path to awakening. Laypeople typically follow the five precepts (to refrain from taking life, stealing, false speech, sexual misconduct, and intoxicants that cloud the mind), while monks and nuns adhere to a collection of several hundred rules of monastic restraint divided into categories of varying severity.

*shi-ne, shi-nay* (Tib.). *See* shamatha.

*shunyata* (Skt.). Emptiness. In the Mahayana, *shunyata* is said to be the ultimate nature of "what is." Phenomena are "empty" in the specific sense that they have no enduring essence that can be objectified, conceptualized, or named. What they inherently are is, thus, utterly beyond language and the ability of the mind to grasp.

This "ineffability" of things is experienced by the thinking mind as utterly empty, but by the nonconceptual, inherent wisdom of our buddha-nature as "inseparable appearance and emptiness." In other words, while things are empty in the way stated, they continue to appear, "beyond thought."

*six classes of beings.* The beings who live in the six realms of samsara. *See also* samsara.

*six realms.* The various possible states of existence within samsara.

*skillful means* (Skt. *upaya*). Enlightenment in the Mahayana is understood to be composed of two inseparable facets, wisdom (realizing emptiness) and compassion (reflected in skillful means). A buddha, whose mind is identified with emptiness, sees with perfect clarity what sentient beings need and also how that need may best be fulfilled. A buddha can be perfectly accurate (or skillful) in his or her actions (or means) precisely because, having realized emptiness, he or she has no self-serving agendas to promote.

*sutra* (Skt.). Discourse of the Buddha. The Buddha is held to have given two sorts of teachings, sutras and tantras. Sutras are discourses on the conventional vehicles of Hinayana and Mahayana and include teachings on ethical conduct, the practice of meditation, Buddhist philosophy and psychology, and the like.

*Sutrayana* (Skt., "vehicle of the sutras"). All the practices of Hinayana and Mahayana that are taught in the sutras of these two conventional, pretantric vehicles.

*svabhavikakaya* (Skt.). The "self-existing body," understood as a fourth "body of the buddha," in which the three bodies of the buddha are unified. *See* three bodies of the Buddha.

*tantra* (Skt.). A text containing the Vajrayana teachings of the Buddha. The tantras contain teachings, visualizations, and various ritual practices reflecting the Vajrayana, or diamond vehicle, and are typically geared to one or another of the great tantric *yidams*. Most Tibetan Vajrayana practice is grounded in one or another of the classical tantras.

*Tantrayana* (Skt.). "The vehicle of the tantras," another name for Vajrayana.

*tathagata-garbha* (Skt.). "Embryo" (*garbha*) of the buddha (*tathagata*), more commonly translated into English (somewhat incorrectly) as "buddha-nature." The term refers to the embryonic enlightenment that is within each sentient being.

*three bodies of the Buddha* (Skt. *trikaya*). Shakyamuni Buddha and all other buddhas are held to possess three bodies of enlightenment, the *trikaya*. The *nirmanakaya*, "the transformational body," is a buddha's physical body of flesh and blood, visible to ordinary sentient beings. The *sambhogakaya*, the enjoyment body, is the form of the buddha seen through the medium of spiritual vision. This body has form but no material substantiality. The *dharmakaya*, the body of truth or reality, is the ultimate nature of the buddha, the enlightened mind, the awakened state itself. All three bodies are united in a fourth body, the *svabhavikakaya*, the essential body.

*three jewels* (Skt. *triratna*). In order to become a Buddhist, a person takes refuge in the three jewels of Buddha, dharma, and sangha. Each of the three jewels has an outer and an inner meaning. The outer buddha is Shakyamuni Buddha, the historical founder of the tradition and the lineage he left; the inner buddha is the buddha-nature within. The outer dharma is the body of Buddhist teachings, while the inner dharma is the experience of the practitioner. The outer sangha is the community of practitioners; the inner sangha is the quality of integrity and mutual respect among dharma practitioners.

*three poisons*. The three primary *kleshas* of greed, hatred, and ignorance.

*three trainings*. The three basic domains of Buddhist practice: *shila*, or discipline; *samadhi*, or meditation; and *prajna*, or wisdom.

*three yanas*. The three "vehicles," Hinayana, Mahayana, and Vajrayana.

*Tilopa* (989–1069 CE). One of the Indian *mahasiddhas*. Tilopa was the founder of the Kagyü lineage. His primary disciple was Naropa, who taught the Tibetan Marpa. From Marpa, the lineage passed to Milarepa and an array of subsequent teachers and sublineages.

*tögal* (Tib.). "Crossing over." The second stage of Dzogchen.

*tonglen* (Tib.). "Sending and taking," an important Mahayana contemplative practice to develop compassion for others. In the practice, one visualizes oneself taking in the suffering of others on the in-breath and sending them relief, peace, and happiness on the out-breath.

*trekchö* (Tib.). "Cutting through," the first stage of Dzogchen.

*trikaya* (Skt.). *See* three bodies of the Buddha.

*Tsongkhapa* (1357–1419 CE). The founder of the modern Gelug lineage. Trained as a Kadam monk, Tsongkhapa was troubled by the laxity and abuses he saw in the Buddhism of his time. To rectify this, he instituted reforms in monastic discipline (requiring greater fidelity to the monastic codes), in scholarship (upgrading the rigor of monastic scholarly training), and in Vajrayana practice (restricting tantric practice to monks who had proven ability in monastic discipline and scholarship). He was a brilliant scholar, a powerful teacher, and a prolific author, and his innovations and interpretations of Buddhism set the standard for the Gelug order down to the present day.

*tummo* (Tib.). The "inner fire" that is aroused in the practice of the inner yogas, an important domain of practice in Tibetan Buddhism.

*utpattikrama* (Skt., "stage of generation"). One of the two stages of *yidam* practice.

*Vajradhara* (Skt.). The ultimate, *dharmakaya* buddha in the New Translation schools.

*Vajrapani* (Skt.). One of the three most important celestial bodhisattvas in Tibetan Buddhism (along with Avalokiteshvara and Manjushri). Vajrapani is considered to embody the enlightened quality of spiritual power.

*Vajrayana* (Skt., "diamond vehicle"). *See* three yanas.

*vipashyana* (Skt.; Tib. *lhagthong*). Insight practice. *Vipashyana* literally means "extraordinary seeing" and refers to the experience of "seeing things as they are." At the Hinayana level, *vipashyana* refers to seeing that there is no substantial and continuous "self," only the five *skandhas*. At the Mahayana level, *vipashyana* refers to the direct, nonconceptual experience of the emptiness of all phenomena. *Shamatha* (tending to mental stabilization) provides the ground for the arising of *vipashyana*.

*virya* (Skt.). "Exertion," one of the six *paramitas*.

*wheel of dharma*. *See* dharmachakra.

*wish-fulfilling jewel* (Skt. *chintamani*). A fabulous mythological gem that was reputed to produce for its owner any benefit desired. In Buddhism, the wish-fulfilling gem came to symbolize the buddha-nature itself, which, once realized, brings through its wisdom, compassion, and power any and every fulfillment desired by the practitioner.

*yana* (Skt.). "Vehicle." *See* nine yanas; three yanas.

*yeshe* (Tib.; Skt. *jnana*, "wisdom"). The wisdom of enlightenment. In the Vajrayana, "five wisdoms," taken together, represent the enlightened mind like five facets of a jewel.

*yidam* (Tib.). The meditational tutelary deity that embodies a practitioner's enlightened being. Through meditating on the *yidam*, the practitioner is enabled gradually to disengage from his or her illusory, personal "self" and identify more and more fully with the buddha-nature within. Each Tibetan school has its most characteristic *yidams*, upon which most members of the school will meditate at one time or another. In addition, practitioners are often given a specific *yidam* that most closely reflects their own as yet hidden enlightened qualities.

Tantric meditation on the *yidam* typically contains two phases, *utpattikrama* (the stage of generation) and *sampannakrama* (the stage of completion). In the first, one visualizes the deity with all of his or her accoutrements and performs various ritual activities, including refuge, generation of *bodhichitta*, confession of misdeeds, offerings, and praises, culminating in visualizing oneself as the *yidam* and reciting his or her mantra. In the completion stage, one dissolves the visualization and rests one's mind in emptiness, realizing the inborn wisdom that is immaculate and out of which all phenomena arise.

# ABOUT THE TEACHERS

## CHAGDUD TULKU RINPOCHE (1930–2002)

A meditation master, artist, and Tibetan physician, Chagdud Tulku Rinpoche was born in East Tibet in 1930 and recognized as the latest in the line of Chagdud tulkus, or incarnate lamas. His primary early teacher was his mother, Delog Drolma, known throughout East Tibet as a realized practitioner, teacher, *tertön* (treasure finder), and *delog* (a visionary who is able to visit the realms beyond death). Chagdud Tulku Rinpoche received extensive instructions in all aspects of Tibetan Buddhism, completed two three-year retreats, and studied with some of the greatest Vajrayana masters of his time. He fled Tibet at the time of the Chinese Communist occupation in 1959 and helped to establish and administer several refugee camps in both India and Nepal. He came to the United States in 1979 and, through the Chagdud Gonpa Foundation, established centers for the study and practice of Vajrayana Buddhism in the United States, Canada, and Brazil.

## CHÖGYAM TRUNGPA RINPOCHE (1940–1987)

Chögyam Trungpa Rinpoche was born in East Tibet and was recognized at the age of eighteen months as the eleventh in the line of Trungpa Tulkus. During his youth, he was trained in the Nyingma and Kagyü lineages of Tibetan Buddhism and studied with some of the most eminent masters in East Tibet, most notably his primary teachers Jamgön Kongtrül of Sechen, Dilgo Khyentse Rinpoche, and Khenpo Gangshar Rinpoche. He fled Tibet in 1959 and spent a period of time first in India and subsequently in England, studying at Oxford University and teaching. In 1970 he came to North America, where he remained for the rest of his life. A meditation master, teacher, author, poet, and visual artist, he was a pioneer in bringing the Buddhist teachings of Tibet to the West and is credited with introducing many important Buddhist concepts into the English language and psyche in a fresh and unique way. He started the first Buddhist-inspired university in

North America, Naropa University; founded more than one hundred meditation centers throughout the world; established Shambhala Training, a secular curriculum of teachings on meditation; authored some two dozen popular books on meditation, Buddhism, poetry, art, and the Shambhala path of warriorship; brought many of the great Tibetan lineage holders to North America for the first time; and attracted several thousand students who have continued to spread his teachings and his legacy into the new millennium.

## CHÖKYI NYIMA RINPOCHE

Chökyi Nyima Rinpoche was born the eldest son of Tulku Urgyen Rinpoche, a renowned meditation master of the Barom Kagyü lineage. At the age of eighteen months, he was recognized as the seventh incarnation of the Drikung Kagyü Lama, Gar Drubchen. Shortly before the Chinese invasion of Tibet in 1959, Chökyi Nyima fled to Sikkim with his family and subsequently entered the monastic training program at Rumtek Monastery. There he was trained under the guidance of such eminent masters as His Holiness the sixteenth Gyalwa Karmapa, His Holiness Dilgo Khyentse Rinpoche, and his own father, Tulku Urgyen Rinpoche. After completing his studies and at the special request of the sixteenth Karmapa, Chökyi Nyima Rinpoche settled in Nepal with his family, helped establish the Ka-Nying Shedrub Ling Monastery in Boudhanath, and began teaching Westerners. In 1981 Chökyi Nyima Rinpoche founded the Rangjung Yeshe Institute for Buddhist Studies, and later he established Rangjung Yeshe Publishers, which has produced many transcripts of his teachings and commentaries. Rinpoche possesses an excellent command of English and continues to include in his teaching activities instruction to Western students both in Nepal and in the West.

## DESHUNG RINPOCHE (1906–1987)

At the age of five, at Deshung Rinpoche's own request, his family allowed him to enter monastic life. At this time, he became the student and attendant of his uncle Ngawang Nyima, a monk who spent most of his life in retreat. At age ten Deshung Rinpoche met the great Sakya lama Ngawang Legpa Rinpoche and became his disciple. At the age of eighteen he was recognized by the officials of the Deshung Monastery to be the third rebirth of the Sakya master Deshung Lungrig Nyima and was accorded the appropriate wealth, position, and quarters in the monastery. He remained in residence at the Thaglung Monastery, however, rather than interrupt the precious teachings he was receiving from Legpa Rinpoche. Through his many years of intense education, Deshung Rinpoche was trained in both the scholarly and meditative traditions of the Sakya and other lineages. Fleeing Tibet at the time of the Chinese invasion, he came to the United States in 1960 and lived there until his death. Initially a participant in a University of Washington research project on Tibetan culture and religion, Rinpoche began teaching dharma to Westerners and in subsequent years gave countless teachings and empowerments at centers across the United States and Canada. He founded Sakya centers in New York City, Minneapolis, and Boston. Members of Sakya Monastery in Seattle have been most fortunate to receive extensive teachings from Rinpoche and to be inspired by his great compassion. Rinpoche established a monastery in Nepal in 1981 and subsequently divided his time between teaching in the United States and at his monastery in Nepal.

## DILGO KHYENTSE RINPOCHE (1910–1991)

His Holiness Dilgo Khyentse Rinpoche, head of the Nyingma school of Tibetan Buddhism, was universally revered as an outstanding master of the Dzogchen teachings and a foremost upholder of the unbiased (Ri-me) spirit within the Buddhist tradition of Tibet. He was one of the principal lineage holders of the Dzogchen Longchen Nyingthik tradition and a highly acclaimed *tertön*, a discoverer of spiritual treasures concealed by Padmasambhava. As such, he became the teacher of many of the important lamas of today, of countless Tibetan laypeople, and of many devoted Western students. Born in East Tibet, he was recognized by the great Mipham Rinpoche as the wisdom-mind emanation of Jamyang Khyentse Wangpo (1820–1892), the extraordinary visionary master and scholar who helped shape modern Tibetan Buddhism. Dilgo Khyentse Rinpoche spent many years at Shechen with his guru, Shechen Gyaltsap and, in addition, studied with many other great meditation masters and scholars. Through some twenty years in solitary retreat, his understanding and realization gradually came to fruition. He spent his life traveling throughout India, the Himalayas, Southeast Asia, and the West, transmitting the pure essence of the teachings to his countless disciples. In addition to teaching, Rinpoche engaged in the preservation of Tibet's sacred texts, established the great living tradition of Shechen Monastery in Boudhanath, Nepal, constructing a new monastery, Shechen Tennyi Dargyeling, and personally supervised the education and training of the young lamas destined to continue the tradition there. Upon his death, the Dalai Lama remarked, "We all, his disciples, should repay his kindness with our practice."

## DRUBWANG TSOKNYI RINPOCHE

Tsoknyi Rinpoche was recognized by His Holiness the sixteenth Gyalwang Karmapa as a reincarnation of Drubwang Tsoknyi, a renowned master of the Drukpa Kagyü and Nyingma traditions. Born in 1966 and raised by Khamtrül Rinpoche, he also studied under Kyabje Dilgo Khyentse Rinpoche; his late father, Kyabje Tulku Urgyen Rinpoche; Adhi Rinpoche; and Nyoshul Khenpo Rinpoche. Tsoknyi Rinpoche heads the Drukpa Heritage Project devoted to the preservation of works of the literature of the Drukpa Kagyü lineage. He is also the abbot of Ngedön Ösel Ling in the Kathmandu Valley of Nepal, and of Gekchak Gompa, one of the largest nunneries in Tibet. Since 1991, he has been engaged in teaching students from around the world.

## DUDJOM RINPOCHE (1904–1987)

His Holiness Dudjom Rinpoche was born in the Puwo region of Tibet. He studied under the greatest masters of the Nyingma tradition and held the lineages of all the major Nyingma transmissions. He acted as the supreme head of the Nyingma lineage until his death. He was renowned for the depth of his practice and scholarship. Rinpoche was also an accomplished *tertön* who uncovered many cycles of teachings that are widely practiced among Nyingmapas today. Dudjom Rinpoche was a prolific author whose collected works span some nineteen Tibetan volumes. In the West, his best known publication is probably his *Nyingma School of Tibetan Buddhism: Its Fundamentals and History*, an encyclopedic work published in two volumes with extensive indices and notes. During his life, he taught widely in Tibet, Bhutan, and the Tibetan cultural areas of Nepal and India; in his later years he also taught in several countries in the West and South Asia.

## DZIGAR KONGTRUL RINPOCHE

Venerable Dzigar Kongtrul Rinpoche was born in 1964 to Tibetan parents in the North Indian state of Himachal Pradesh, where he grew up in a monastic environment. Recognized as an incarnation of Jamgön Kongtrül Lodrö Thaye, he received extensive training in all aspects of Buddhist doctrine. In particular he received the teachings of the Nyingma lineage, especially that of the Longchen Nyingthik from his root teacher, H. H. Dilgo Khyentse Rinpoche. Rinpoche also studied extensively under Tulku Urgyen Rinpoche, Nyoshul Khenpo Rinpoche, and the great scholar Khenpo Rinchen. In 1989 Rinpoche moved to the United States with his family and in 1990 began a five-year tenure as a professor of Buddhist philosophy at Naropa University. Rinpoche also founded Mangala Shri Bhuti at that time, an organization with the aim of furthering the wisdom and practice of the Longchen Nyingthik lineage. Later, Rinpoche moved to southern Colorado and established a mountain retreat center, Longchen Jigme Samten Ling. He currently spends much of his time there in retreat and guides students in long-term retreat practice. When not in retreat, Rinpoche travels widely throughout the world, teaching and furthering his own education.

## THE DZOGCHEN PÖNLOP RINPOCHE

The Seventh Dzogchen Pönlop Rinpoche is acknowledged as one of the foremost scholars of his generation in the Kagyü and Nyingma traditions. Born at Rumtek

Monastery in Sikkim, India, he was recognized as the rebirth of the sixth Dzogchen Pönlop Rinpoche by the sixteenth Karmapa, enthroned at Rumtek Monastery in 1968, and trained in the traditional monastic curriculum. Rinpoche's main gurus include the sixteenth Karmapa, Dilgo Khyentse Rinpoche, and Khenpo Tsultrim Gyamtso Rinpoche. He holds traditional Tibetan degrees from the Karma Shri Nalanda Institute at Rumtek and Sampurnanant Sanskrit University in Varanasi, India. As the abbot of Dzogchen Monastery, Rinpoche is a high-ranking Nyingma master. His Holiness the sixteenth Gyalwa Karmapa formally empowered the Seventh Dzogchen Pönlop Rinpoche as one of the lineage holders of the Karma Kagyü school and heart son of His Holiness Karmapa. Since 1980, Rinpoche has taught extensively in North America, where he resides, and also in Europe. Pönlop Rinpoche is the founder of Nitartha International, an organization dedicated to preserving the ancient literature of Tibet in computerized formats. He helped establish Nitartha Institute in the United States and is the director of the Kamalashila Institute of Germany. In 1997, Rinpoche founded Nalandabodhi to preserve the genuine lineage of the Nyingma and Kagyü schools of Tibetan Buddhism. Fluent in English and well versed in Western culture, Pönlop Rinpoche is known for his sharp intellect, his humor, and the lucidity and skill of his teaching style. Rinpoche is also an accomplished calligrapher, visual artist, and poet.

## DZONGSAR KHYENTSE RINPOCHE

Dzongsar Khyentse Rinpoche was born in Bhutan in 1961 and was recognized as the main incarnation of the Khyentse lineage of Tibetan Buddhism, the incarnation of Jamyang Khyentse Chökyi Lodrö. Rinpoche is considered to be an emanation of Vimalamitra, King Trisong Deutsen, and the bodhisattva Manjushri. His grandfather is His Holiness Dudjom Rinpoche, his father is Dungsay Thinley Norbu Rinpoche, and his mother is Jamyang Choeden. Rinpoche was first recognized by His Holiness the Sakya Trizin, who gave him the name Jamyang Thubten Chokyi Gyatso (Khyentse Norbu). This was confirmed by H. H. the sixteenth Gyalwa Karmapa and the Sakya Dagchen Rinpoche. He has studied with some of the greatest contemporary masters, particularly H. H. Dilgo Khyentse Rinpoche, Dudjom Rinpoche, the sixteenth Gyalwa Karmapa, and the Sakya Trizin. From a young age he has been active in preserving the Buddhist teachings, establishing centers of learning, supporting practitioners, publishing books, and teaching all over the world. Dzongsar Khyentse Rinpoche supervises his traditional seat of Dzongsar Monastery and its retreat centers in East Tibet, as well as his new colleges in India and Bhutan. He also has established centers in North America, Australia, and Asia.

## GEN LAMRIMPA

Gen Lamrimpa, Venerable Jampal Tenzin, was born in Tibet in 1934. A close disciple of His Holiness the fourteenth Dalai Lama, he has been living in meditative solitude in the mountains high above Dharamsala, India, since 1971. There he has gained a reputation for his deep experience of the "stages of the path" practices. He is also renowned as an accomplished practitioner of meditative stabilization and *tummo* (psychic heat) as well as other tantric meditations. Gen Lamrimpa teaches meditation to both Tibetans and Westerners.

## JAMGÖN KONGTRÜL THE THIRD (1954–1992)

Jamgön Kongtrül was born in East Tibet to a prominent Lhasa family. He was recognized as an important tulku and was brought up and trained by His Holiness the sixteenth Gyalwang Karmapa. He was one of the "four princes" of the Kagyu-pas and, after the death of His Holiness, became one of the principal leaders of the Kagyü lineage. Rinpoche traveled and taught extensively throughout Asia, Europe, and North America and gathered many disciples. He was founder of the Paramita Charitable Trust in India and also the Rigpe Dorje Foundation, an international network of organizations dedicated to furthering educational, medical, and social development in India and Nepal. Rinpoche was tragically killed in a car accident in India in 1992.

## KALU RINPOCHE (1905–1989)

Rinpoche was born in East Tibet. During his early years, he was tutored by his father at home in the meditative and ritual traditions of Tibetan Buddhism. At the age of fifteen he entered Palpung monastery, the foremost center of the Karma Kagyü school, for ten years of higher study of the Buddhist philosophical traditions. He also completed two three-year retreats. Rinpoche's principal gurus included the fifteenth Gyalwa Karmapa, Khakhyap Dorje; Situ Pema Wangchuk Gyalpo, the abbot and foremost teacher of Palpung monastery; Zhechen Gyaltsab Byurme Namgyla, the great Nyingma master and disciple of Mipham Rinpoche; and the great meditation master Drupon Norbu Donrdrup. At age twenty-six, Rinpoche left Palpung to pursue the life of a solitary yogi in the woods of the Khampa countryside. For nearly fifteen years he strove to perfect his realization of all aspects of the teachings, and he became renowned in the villages and among the nomads as a true representative of the bodhisattva's path. Subsequently, he returned to Palpung to receive final teachings from Drupon Norbu Dondrup, including the rare transmission of the teaching of the Shangpa Kagyu. In Kham, Rinpoche became the abbot of the meditation center associated with Palpung and the meditation teacher of His Holiness the sixteenth Gyalwa Karmapa. He remained in that position until the situation in Tibet forced him into exile in India. Kalu Rinpoche taught extensively in America and Europe, and during his three visits to the West he founded teaching centers in over a dozen countries. In France he established the first retreat center ever to teach the traditional three-year retreats of the Shangpa and Karma Kagyü lineages to Western students. At his death, he left behind many devoted disciples in Asia and the West, as well as a considerable body of teaching, much of which appears in his numerous books in European languages.

## VENERABLE KHANDRO RINPOCHE

Venerable Khandro Rinpoche, the daughter of His Holiness Mindrolling Tichen, was born in 1967 in Kalimpong, India. In 1969 she was recognized by the sixteenth Gyalwa Karmapa as the reincarnation of a famous retreatant, the Great Khandro of Tsurphu, consort of the fifteenth Karmapa and an emanation of the yogini Yeshe Tsogyal. Khandro Rinpoche's root teachers have been His Holiness Mindrolling Tichen, His Holiness Dilgo Khyentse, and His Holiness the sixteenth Gyalwa Karmapa. Besides a traditional Tibetan education, she also completed a Western education at St. Joseph's Convent, Wynberg Allen, and St. Mary's Convent, all in India. Rinpoche has lived in the Mindrolling monastery in Dehra Dun all of her life. In addition, she supervises Samten Tse Retreat Centre for Nuns in Mussoorie, Uttaranchal, northern India. Rinpoche speaks fluent English, Tibetan, and Hindi, and has been teaching internationally since 1987. She now regularly teaches in North America and Europe. A teacher in both the Kagyü and Nyingma traditions of Tibetan Buddhism, Khandro Rinpoche is particularly known for the brilliance and clarity with which she presents traditional Buddhist teachings in English.

## KHENPO KÖNCHOG GYALTSEN

Könchog Gyaltsen was born in Tsari, Tibet, in 1946. He fled to India with his family in 1959 and in 1967 began nine years of study in the Central Institute of Higher Tibetan Studies in Varanasi. His studies included Madhyamaka, Abhidharma, Vinaya, the Abhisamayalankara, and the Uttaratantra, as well as history, logic, and Tibetan grammar. In early 1968 he took full monastic ordination from Kalu Rinpoche and, after graduating from the Institute, received teachings from the sixteenth Gyalwa Karmapa and other masters of the Kagyü and other lineages. Rinpoche began a three-year retreat in 1978 and subsequently practiced both Mahamudra and the Six Yogas of Naropa. In 1982 Rinpoche traveled to the United States and founded the Tibetan Meditation Center in Washington, D.C. In November 1991 Rinpoche moved along with the Center to Frederick, Maryland. In more recent years, Khenchen Rinpoche has spent a great deal of his time traveling in order to give teachings and lead retreats. He has established centers throughout the United States and in Chile, and he frequently visits Europe, especially Germany and Austria, as well as Southeast Asia.

## KHENPO TSULTRIM GYAMTSO RINPOCHE

Khenpo Rinpoche was born to a nomad family in East Tibet in 1934. Drawn to spiritual practice, he left home at an early age to train with his root guru, the yogin Lama Zopa Tarchin. After completing this early training, Tsultrim Gyamtso embraced the life of a yogi-ascetic, wandering throughout East and Central Tibet, undertaking solitary retreats in caves to realize directly the teachings he had received. He often lived in charnel grounds in order to practice and master *chö*, a skillful means to cut ego clinging, develop compassion, and realize deeper levels of emptiness. Subsequently he took up retreat in the caves above Tsurphu, the seat of the Karmapas, where he received instructions on the six yogas of Naropa, the *Hevajra Tantra*, and other profound teachings from Dilyak Tenzin Drupon Rinpoche and other masters. Escaping to India at the time of the Chinese invasion, he was able to continue his training, studying the sutras, the tantras, and all four schools of Tibetan Buddhism He became renowned for his skill in logic and debate, and received a khenpo degree from H. H. the sixteenth Karmapa, and the equivalent *geshe lharampa* degree from H. H. the fourteenth Dalai Lama. In 1975 Khenpo Tsultrim established the Thegchen Shedra in Athens, Greece, and for the next ten years taught throughout Europe. Since 1985 he has traveled widely, completing annual world tours in response to invitations from Europe, the United States, Canada, South America, Southeast Asia, Africa, and Australia. In 1986 he founded the Marpa Institute for Translators, in Boudhanath, Nepal, to offer intensive courses in language and scripture. Khenpo Rinpoche continued to supervise this annual event when it moved to Pullahari Monastery above Boudhanath. While Khenpo Tsultrim Gyamtso unites prodigious intellect with great compassion, he also embodies the training and temperament of a true yogi. In fact, Rinpoche is often compared to the great yogi Milarepa, whom he resembles in both substance and style.

## LAMA LODÖ

Lama Lodö was born in Sikkim in 1939. At the age of eight, he entered a monastery to study the traditional subjects of the Karma Kagyü lineages: reading, writing, the study of Buddhist texts, and religious singing and dancing. At fifteen, he met Drupon Tenzin Rinpoche and subsequently, under his direction, entered a three-year retreat. Both teacher and disciple became ill at this time; Drupon Tenzin Rinpoche helped Lama Lodö to recover but died himself. Through the agency of H. H. the sixteenth Karmapa, Lama Lodö then became a disciple of Kalu Rinpoche and completed his three-year retreat. In 1974, on the instruction of H. H. the Karmapa and Kalu Rinpoche, Lama Lodö began teaching in Europe and North America. Since 1976, he has been in residence as the Senior Spiritual Teacher at Kagyü Droden Kunchab Center in San Francisco.

## LAMA THUBTEN YESHE RINPOCHE (1935–1984)

Lama Thubten Yeshe was born in Tibet and subsequently recognized as the reincarnation of a certain abbess in the Gelug tradition. At age six he received his parents' permission to join Sera Je, a college at one of the three great Gelug monastic centers in the vicinity of Lhasa. There, under the strict supervision of his uncle, he began training in the Gelug monastic curriculum. This phase of his education came to an end in 1959 when he was forced to flee to India. At the settlement camp of Buxaduar, Tibet, he resumed his studies, receiving full monk's ordination at age twenty-eight from Kyabje Ling Rinpoche. Lama Yeshe accepted as his principal disciple a young monk named Zopa Rinpoche, putting him through rigorous scholarly and spiritual training. Subsequently, master and disciple traveled and taught together. Lama Yeshe and Zopa Rinpoche's contact with Westerners began in 1965. The lamas, with permission from H. H. the Dalai Lama, and their first Western student, American Zina Rachevsky, took up residence near the Boudhanath stupa several miles from Kathmandu. There they founded the Nepal Mahayana Gompa Centre in 1969. The lamas began teaching extensively throughout the West, inspiring many to become devoted students of the dharma. Lama Yeshe passed away in Los Angeles at the age of forty-nine.

## NAMKHAI NORBU RINPOCHE

Chögyal Namkhai Norbu, born in East Tibet in 1938, is one of the primary living masters of Dzogchen. At the age of three he was recognized as the incarnation of a great Dzogchen master. He received the full traditional education of a *tulku* or reincarnated lama, and went on to study and practice with several great masters in Tibet, before political events forced him to relocate in India. After having taught for more than twenty years as Professor of Tibetan and Mongolian Language and Literature at the Oriental Institute, University of Naples, he is at present fully dedicating his time to the transmission and preservation of Dzogchen teachings and Tibetan culture. Rinpoche is the founder of the Dzogchen Community, which has major centers in the United States and Italy. He continues to travel and teach all over the world. He is the author of books and scholarly articles not only on Dzogchen but on all the main branches of Tibetan culture, including history, medicine, astrology, and Bön.

## NYOSHUL KHENPO RINPOCHE (1932–1999)

Nyoshul Khenpo Rinpoche, Jamyang Dorje, was one of the most eminent contemporary Tibetan Buddhist masters. He was a Dzogchen master and an upholder of the non-sectarian Rime Practice Lineages. Khenpo Rinpoche was a major lineage holder of the Longchen Nyinthig ("Heart Essence") Dzogchen tradition. He lived in Bhutan and passed away at the Nyingmapa retreat center of Chateloube in the Dordogne, France.

## RINGU TULKU RINPOCHE

Ringu Tulku Rinpoche is a Kagyü master who is recognized as the incarnation of the Abbot of Rigul Monastery in Tibet. Gyalwa Karmapa and Dilgo Khyentse Rinpoche were his root gurus, and he has studied and practiced with distinguished lamas from all the traditions of Tibetan Buddhism. Born in East Tibet in 1952, he took his formal education at Namgyal Institute of Tibetology in Gangtok and Sampurnananda Sanskrit University in Varanasi. He served as Professor of Tibetology in Sikkim for seventeen years. Since 1990 he has been traveling and teaching in Europe, North America, Australia, and Asia. He also participates in various interfaith dialogues. He is a visiting faculty person at Naropa University and is the author of several books in Tibetan and English. He founded Bodhicharya, an organization created to preserve and transmit Buddhist teachings and to promote intercultural dialogues and educational and social projects in Tibet.

## SAKYONG MIPHAM RINPOCHE

Sakyong Mipham Rinpoche is the primary lineage holder of the Shambhala Buddhist school established by his father, the late Chögyam Trungpa Rinpoche. Born in 1962 in Bodhagaya, India, he spent his early years with his mother in a Tibetan refugee village in northwestern India, later joining his father in the West. His primary teachers include his father and other respected lamas of the Karma Kagyü and Nyingma lineages, including H. H. Dilgo Khyentse Rinpoche and H. H. Penor Rinpoche, head of the Palyul Nyingma lineage. In recent years, the Sakyong has brought the many activities of his father's students under the umbrella of Shambhala International, which now includes Vajradhatu, a path of traditional Buddhist teachings; Shambhala Training, a secular program of meditation and warriorship; and Nalanda Foundation, dedicated to educational, social, and artistic programs. In 1995, then known as Sawang Ösel Rangdröl Mukpo, he was formally installed by H. H. Penor Rinpoche as Sakyong, leader of both the spiritual and secular aspects of Shambhala. His Holiness also recognized him as Mipham Rinpoche, a descendant of the revered nineteenth-century Tibetan meditation master and scholar Mipham Jamyang Namgyal. The enthronement formalized Sakyong Mipham Rinpoche's lifelong commitment to work with others toward creating an enlightened society.

## SOGYAL RINPOCHE

Born in East Tibet, Sogyal Rinpoche was recognized as the incarnation of Lerab Lingpa Tertön Sogyal, a teacher to the thirteenth Dalai Lama, by Jamyang Khyentse Chöky Lödro, one of the most outstanding masters of the twentieth century. Jamyang Khyentse raised Sogyal Rinpoche and supervised his training. Rinpoche went on to study with many other masters of all schools, especially Kyabje Dudjom Rinpoche and Kyabje Dilgo Khyentse Rinpoche. First as translator and aide to these masters, and then teaching in his own right, he traveled to many countries, exploring how to attune the teachings to modern life. Rinpoche continues to travel widely in Europe, America, Australia, and Asia, and is a frequent speaker at major conferences.

## TARTHANG TULKU RINPOCHE

Lama Tarthang Tulku, a reincarnate Nyingma master who came to America in 1968, is one of the pioneers in the meeting of East and West. Born, raised, and educated in Tibet, he has combined his comprehensive training in Tibetan Buddhism with a knowledge of Western philosophy, psychology, and cultural dynamics. Tarthang Tulku is widely appreciated for his accomplishments in preserving traditional Buddhist texts, art, and architecture by founding Dharma Publishing in Berkeley, California, in 1971; for his innovative work in creating *sangha* among his followers; for supporting Buddhists of many traditions with books, funds, and meditation practice necessities; for his writings on personal development, work, and meditation; for establishing work/study centers; and also for creating long-term retreat facilities.

## THINLEY NORBU RINPOCHE

His Holiness Dungse Thinley Norbu Rinpoche, the eldest son of H. H. Dudjom Rinpoche, former head of the Nyingma lineages, is considered to be an emanation of Longchen Rabjam (Longchenpa), the great Nyingma scholar and siddha. He is a preeminent teacher of the Nyingma lineage and a patron of the Vajrayana Foundation. In his youth in Tibet he studied for nine years at Mindroling Monastery. Since his exile in the West, he has written many influential books and trained numerous disciples in the Nyingma traditions.

## THRANGU RINPOCHE

Khenchen Thrangu Rinpoche is the ninth in the line of Thrangu tulkus. He was recognized at the age of four in 1937 by the Gyalwa Karmapa and Palpung Situ Rinpoche. After preliminary training in various subjects, at the age of sixteen he began his studies in Buddhist philosophy, psychology, logic, debate, and scriptures with Lama Khenpo Lodrö Rabsel. At the age of twenty-three he received full monastic ordination along with Garwang Rinpoche and Chögyam Trungpa Rinpoche from the Gyalwa Karmapa. Following this, Thrangu Rinpoche engaged in a period of intense practice and retreat, and was introduced to the Absolute Nature by Lama Khenpo Gyangshar Wangpo. At the age of thirty-five he was given the degree of *geshe rabjam* with honors and was appointed Vice Chancellor of the Principal Seat of the Kagyü Vajra Upholder of the Three Disciplines of His Holiness Karmapa. He is full holder and teacher of all the Kagyü Vajrayana lineages and has a special, very direct transmission of the Shentong philosophical tradition handed down by Jamgön Kongtrül the Great. As one of the most learned lamas of his generation, he was subsequently chosen to educate the four great Kagyü regents. Thrangu Rinpoche has traveled extensively in Europe, the United Sates, Canada, and Asia. He is now the abbot of Rumtek Monastery and Nalanda Institute for Higher Buddhist studies. He founded his own *shedra* (school), Thrangu Tashi Choling, and the retreat centrer Namo Buddha in Nepal. He is in charge of long retreats at Samye Ling, Scotland, is abbot of Gampo Abbey, and offers yearly Namo Buddha Seminars for beginning and advanced students of Buddhism.


## TRALEG KYABGON RINPOCHE

The Venerable Traleg Kyabgon Rinpoche is the president and spiritual director of E-Vam Buddhist Institute, New York, and Kagyu E-Vam Buddhist Institute, Melbourne, Australia. Born in 1955 in East Tibet, Traleg Rinpoche was recognized by His Holiness the sixteenth Gyalwa Karmapa, head of the Kagyü lineage, as the ninth incarnation of the Traleg lineage. Rinpoche was enthroned at the age of two as the supreme head of Tra'gu Monastery. Following the Chinese invasion in Tibet, he continued his rigorous training abroad, including five years at the Sanskrit University in Varanasi, India, and several years at Rumtek Monastery in Sikkim, the main seat of the Kagyü Lineage. In 1980 Rinpoche went to Australia as the official representative for the Kagyü lineage and established Kagyu E-vam Buddhist Institute in Melbourne. He holds a master's degree in Comparative Philosophy from La Trobe University, Melbourne.


## TULKU THONDUP RINPOCHE

Tulku Thondup Rinpoche was born in Gelok, East Tibet, in 1939. At the age of five he was recognized as the tulku or reincarnation of Könme Khenpo, a celebrated scholar and saint of the renowned Nyingma monastery Dodrupchen. Rinpoche took up residence at Dodrupchen, where he underwent the traditional training in study and practice, eventually being given the title of Dorje Loppön (Vajracharya). At the time of the Chinese invasion of Tibet, he settled in India, where he subsequently taught at Lucknow and Vishva-Bharati universities. From 1980 to 1983 he was a visiting scholar at Harvard University. He has continued to live in Cambridge, Massachusetts, engaging in translation and research on Tibetan Buddhism, particularly of the Nyingma tradition, under the auspices of the Buddhayana Foundation. Tulku Thondup has also been affiliated with Mahasiddha

Nyingmapa Center of Massachusetts and Chorten Gonpa (monastery) of Sikkim, India. He travels throughout North America and Europe teaching Buddhism and leading healing meditation workshops. For many years, he has been dedicating his resources to rebuilding the main temple of Dodrupchen Monastery, which was destroyed over several decades beginning in the late 1950s.

## TULKU URGYEN RINPOCHE (1920–1996)

Tulku Urgyen Rinpoche's family has, for many generations, held the now rare Baram Kagyü lineage. He was a Dzogchen guru of the sixteenth Karmapa and also held the Chogyur Lingpa lineage. Tulku Urgyen was an exponent of the nonsectarian Ri-me movement in Tibetan Buddhism. After the Chinese invasion, Rinpoche's seat became Ka-Nying Shedrup-Ling near the stupa of Boudhnath, Kathmandu. In 1980 Tulku Urgyen and his son, Chökyi Nyima Rinpoche, toured Europe, the United States, and Southeast Asia, where they gave Dzogchen and Mahamudra teachings and empowerments to numerous people.

## LAMA ZOPA RINPOCHE

Lama Zopa Rinpoche was born in Nepal in 1946 and became a disciple of Lama Thubten Yeshe beginning in 1960. Together they were the founders and spiritual directors of the Foundation for the Preservation of the Mahayana Tradition, a worldwide network of Buddhist centers, monasteries, and affiliated energies including some seventy centers in seventeen countries. They toured the West for the first time in 1974. After the death of Lama Yeshe in 1984, Lama Zopa Rinpoche has continued to carry on the work of the Foundation.

# SOURCES

## CHAGDUD TULKU RINPOCHE

From *Gates to Buddhist Practice*. Junction City, Calif.: Padma Publishing, 2001. Reproduced by permission of the publisher.

10.8, The Guru Is the Buddha, the Dharma, and the Sangha: p. 230

10.9, The Guru Embodies the Three Kayas: p. 233

10.14, The Need for Commitment and Diligence: pp. 56–57

10.16, We Have to Realize the Truth Ourselves: p. 234

# CHÖGYAM TRUNGPA RINPOCHE

From *Born in Tibet*. Boston: Shambhala Publications, 1977.

1.1, A Vivid Moment of Recollection: pp. 48–49

From *Cutting Through Spiritual Materialism*. Boston: Shambhala Publications, 1973. © 1973 by Diana J. Mukpo. Reprinted by arrangement with Shambhala Publications, Inc., Boston, www.shambhala.com.

1.8, The Buddha's Method: Meditation: p. 9

8.4, The Fundamental Characteristic: p. 213

8.5, Compassion Is an Attitude of Wealth: p. 99

8.6, How Compassion Evolves Naturally from Meditation: pp. 97–99

8.7, Skillful Means: p. 210

8.9, Peace on Earth: p. 102

10.15, It Is Not Enough to Imitate Your Guru: p. 17–19

11.2, Prostrations: A Gesture of Surrender: p. 26

11.16, You Must Accept Yourself as You Are: p. 64

12.9, Beyond Ego's Dreams: p. 70

From *Glimpses of Shunyata*. Halifax: Vajradhatu Publications, 1993.

7.14, A Terrifying Prospect: pp. 17–18

From *The Heart of the Buddha*. Boston: Shambhala Publications, 1991. © 1991 by Diana J. Mukpo. Reprinted by arrangement with Shambhala Publications, Inc., Boston, www.shambhala.com.

8.24, What Is Implied by the Bodhisattva Vow?: pp. 108–9

8.25, What Is the Bodhisattva Vow Based On?: pp. 109–10

8.26, The Power of the Bodhisattva Vow: p. 108

From *Illusion's Game*. Boston: Shambhala Publications, 1994. © 1994 by Diana J. Mukpo. Reprinted by arrangement with Shambhala Publications, Inc., Boston, www.shambhala.com.

4.15, To Understand Pain Is the Ground of Tantra: p. 56

7.19, The Real Definition of Shunyata: p. 90

9.1, Vajrayana as the Final Stage: p. 55

9.5, *Tantra* Means "Continuity": p. 64

9.8, Beyond Shunyata: pp. 100–101

9.10, Naropa's "Sanity" Is Not Adequate to Vajrayana: p. 16
9.13, Giving Up Hope: p. 32
10.25, Is the Guru an External Person?: p. 34
13.5, Becoming an American Buddha: p. 25

From *Meditation in Action*. Boston: Shambhala Publications, 1996. © 1969, 1991 by Diana J. Mukpo. Reprinted by arrangement with Shambhala Publications, Inc., Boston, www.shambhala.com.
1.4, The Buddha Was a Great Revolutionary: p. 5
1.5, The Buddha's Discovery: pp. 6–7
11.25, "Accept Everything, but Use It in the Right Way": pp. 23–24
12.22, Using One's Neurosis on the Path: p. 21

From *The Myth of Freedom*. Boston: Shambhala Publications, 1988.
1.6, The Buddha's Insignificance: p. 59

From *Orderly Chaos*. Boston: Shambhala Publications, 1991
8.3, Compassion Is Open Space: p. 89

From *The Path Is the Goal*. Boston: Shambhala Publications, 1995.© 1995 by Diana J. Mukpo. Reprinted by arrangement with Shambhala Publications, Inc., Boston, www.shambhala.com.
2.4, The Three Yanas Are an Evolutionary Process: p. 87
5.24, Commitment to Mindfulness and Awareness Is Critical: p. 120
5.25, Meditation Involves Constant Challenge: p. 136
5.26, Is Meditation Therapeutic?: p. 32
5.36, Awareness Is Totality: p. 21
5.39, Vipashyana in Our Experience: p. 108
5.40, Mindfulness and Awareness: pp. 105–6
5.41, Awareness and Mindfulness: p. 119
5.48, Letting Awareness Come to Us: p. 116
5.49, Boredom in Vipashyana: p. 111
5.50, The Challenge of Boredom: p. 107
5.51, Vipashyana Awareness Is Just Being: pp. 118–19
5.52, The All-Pervasiveness of Vipashyana: p. 108
10.11, The Teacher Should Be a Traveler Too: p. 144
10.13, What Is Involved in Relating to a Teacher?: pp. 128–29
10.22, The Sangha: p. 130
12.8, Your Mate Speaks for the Rest of the World: pp. 148–49

From "Commentary" in *The Tibetan Book of the Dead: The Great Liberation Through Hearing in the Bardo*. Translated and Commentary by Francesca Fremantle and Chögyam Trungpa. Boston: Shambhala Publications, 1987.
11.18, The Peaceful Deities: p. 13
11.19, The Wrathful Deities: pp. 14 and 26

From *Training the Mind and Cultivating Loving-Kindness*. Boston: Shambhala Publications, 1993.

 8.2, Emptiness and Compassion: pp. 13–14 and 150

From *Transcending Madness: The Experience of the Six Bardos*. Boston: Shambhala Publications, 1992.

 8.8, Genuine Compassion and the Warrior: p. 119.

## CHÖKYI NYIMA RINPOCHE

From "Introduction," in Tulku Urgyen Rinpoche, *Repeating the Words of the Buddha*. Boudhanatha: Ranjung Yeshe Publications, 1991. Reproduced with permission from Rangjung Yeshe Publications, www.rangjung.com.

 3.17, The Two Approaches in More Detail: pp. 10–11
 11.37, The Tibetan Word for Mahamudra: p. 16

From *Song of Karmapa*. Boudhanatha: Rangjung Yeshe Publications, 1996. Reproduced with permission from Rangjung Yeshe Publications, www.rangjung.com.

 11.11, The Four Empowerments of the Abhisheka: p. 50
 11.12, The First Part of the Abhisheka: The Vase Empowerment: pp.
   50–51
 11.13, Part Two of the Abhisheka: The Secret Empowerment: p. 52
 11.14, Part Three of the Abhisheka: The Wisdom-Knowledge
   Empowerment: p. 52
 11.15, Part Four of the Abhisheka: The "Word" Empowerment: p. 53

## DESHUNG RINPOCHE

From *Three Levels of Spiritual Perception*. Somerville, MA: Wisdom Publications, 1995.

 6.25, Ultimate Bodhichitta: p. 340

## DILGO KHYENTSE RINPOCHE

From "Heart Treasure of the Enlightened Ones" in *Essence of Buddhism: Teachings at Tibet House*. New Delhi: Tibet House, 1986.

 6.28, One Begins with Relative Bodhichitta: p. 122
 6.32, How Absolute Bodhichitta and Relative Bodhichitta Support
   Each Other: p. 123

From *The Wish-Fulfilling Jewel: The Practice of Guru Yoga According to the Longchen Nyingthig Tradition.* Boston: Shambhala Publications, 1988.

> 11.5, The Importance of Guru Yoga: p. 3
> 11.6, Outer, Inner, Secret, and Most Secret Methods of Guru Yoga:
> > p. 9
> 11.22, Who Is Guru Rinpoche?: p. 14

## DRUBWANG TSOKNYI RINPOCHE

From *The Dzogchen Primer: Embracing the Spiritual Path According to the Great Perfection.* Compiled and edited by Marcia Binder Schmidt. Boston: Shambhala Publications, 2002.

> 10.4, Blessings Are Contagious: p. 163
> 10.32, One Should Not Be Overdependent on Spiritual Teachers:
> > p. 162

## DUDJOM RINPOCHE

From John Myrdhin Reynolds, *The Golden Letters* (Ithaca, NY: Snow Lion Publications, 1996.

> 11.50, A Short Commentary on Garab Dorje's Three Statements
> > Concerning the Inherent Nature: p. 41

From Sogyal Rinpoche, *The Tibetan Book of Living and Dying.* San Francisco: HarperSanFrancisco, 1992.

> 10.28. The Ultimate Lama: p. 44

## DZIGAR KONGTRUL RINPOCHE

From "Bodhicitta." Unpublished transcripts. Printed with permission.

> 6.11, The Bodhisattva's Aspiration to Leave the Cocoon Behind
> 6.12, The Bodhisattva's Commitment
> 6.21, Bodhichitta Is the Essence of Buddhism
> 8.13, We Have to Cultivate the Sense of Big Heart
> 8.14, We Must Care for Others as We Care for the Parts of Our Own
> > Bodies

From "Heart Treasure." Unpublished transcripts. Printed with permission.

From "To Be Free of Mind's Illusions." Unpublished transcripts. Printed with permission.

# THE DZOGCHEN PÖNLOP RINPOCHE

From "Vipashyana." *Shambhala Mirror*, April 2002. Printed with permission.

Excerpts from talks, edited by Cindy Shelton. © The Dzogchen Pönlop Rinpoche and Nalandabodhi. Printed with permission.

From *Hinayana View: The Nalandabodhi Study Curriculum*, Introduction to Hinayana (Seattle). Printed with permission.

# DZONGSAR KHYENTSE RINPOCHE

From "Buddhism in a Nutshell: The Four Seals of the Dharma." *Shambhala Sun*, March, 2000. Reprinted with permission from the *Shambhala Sun*, www.shambha-lasun.com.

From "Approaching the Guru." *Shambhala Sun*, November 2000. Reprinted with permission from the *Shambhala Sun*, www.shambhalasun.com.

From "Distortion." *Shambhala Sun*, September, 1997. Reprinted with permission from the *Shambhala Sun*, www.shambhalasun.com.

# Gen Lamrimpa

From *Calming the Mind: Tibetan Buddhist Teachings on Cultivating Meditative Quiescence*. Ithaca, NY: Snow Lion Publications, 1992.

   10.23, Seeing the Guru as Buddha: p. 36

# The Third Jamgön Kongtrul Rinpoche

From *Cloudless Sky: The Mahamudra Path of the Tibetan Buddhist Kagyu School*. Boston: Shambhala Publications, 1992.

   11.36, Mahamudra Is the Most Excellent: p. 13
   11.38, The Core of Mahamudra Meditation: pp. 70–71
   11.42, The Fruition of Mahamudra: p. 71

# Kalu Rinpoche

From *Excellent Buddhism*. San Francisco: ClearPoint Press, 1995.

   3.5, The Three Prajnas and an Example: p. 148
   13.1, Why Buddhism Is Expanding in the West: p. 98

From *Foundations of Tibetan Buddhism*. Ithaca, NY: Snow Lion Publications, 1999.

   2.2, All Three Yanas Are Authentic: p. 14
   2.11, From the Point of View of Individual Practice: p. 13

From *Gently Whispered*. Barrytown, NY: Station Hill Press, 1994.

   5.4, In Taking Refuge, One Is Creating Open Space in One's Mind:
      p. 45

From *Luminous Mind: The Way of the Buddha*. Somerville, MA: Wisdom Publications, © 1997 by Wisdom Publications. Reprinted with permission of Wisdom Publications, 199 Elm St., Somerville, MA, 02144, U.S.A., www.wisdompubs.org.

   3.13, The Third Prajna, Meditation: p. 132
   4.19, Karma Is Conditioned Activity: p. 31
   4.20, How the Process of Karma Works: p. 31
   4.21, Karma Does Not Imply Fatalism: p. 41
   5.20, The Sweeper Arhat: p. 104

## VENERABLE KHANDRO RINPOCHE

From unpublished transcripts. Printed with permission.
    1.9, The Buddha Did Not Intend to Create a New "Ism"
    2.9, The Sequential Way of Buddhist Practice
    4.22, Why Is the Teaching on Karma So Important?
    5.17, On the Necessity of Meditation Practice
    5.18, Why Do Study and Contemplation Come First?
    5.21, Meditation Helps Us Live a Good Life
    5.22, Buddhist Meditation Is Not Just for Oneself Alone
    5.29, Shamatha Instructions
    5.32, Thoughts
    8.21, How Can We Use Our Own Sadness to Benefit Others?
    11.34, Sampannakrama

## KHENPO KÖNCHOG GYALTSEN

From *In Search of the Stainless Ambrosia*. Ithaca, NY: Snow Lion Publications, 1988.
    6.27, Relative Bodhichitta: Aspiring and Entering (or Action): p. 76

## KHENPO TSULTRIM GYAMTSO RINPOCHE

From *Progressive Stages of Meditation on Emptiness*. Oxford: Longchen Foundation, 1986.
    5.47, The "Self": p. 31

## LAMA LODÖ

From *Bardo Teachings: The Way of Death and Rebirth*. Ithaca: Snow Lion Publications, 1982.
    12.30, Experiencing the Dharmakaya at the Moment of Death: pp. 6–7

From *The Quintessence of the Animate and the Inanimate: A Discourse on the Holy Dharma*. San Francisco: KDK Publications, 1985. Reprinted with permission of Lama Lodö Rinpoche.
    5.2, Refuge Is the Essential Teaching: p. 33
    5.6, Why We Need Refuge: pp. 34–35
    5.9, The Three Jewels in More Detail: pp. 36–39
    5.11, Refuge Is Not Giving Up Independence: p. 34

# LAMA THUBTEN YESHE RINPOCHE

From *The Bliss of Inner Fire: Heart Practice of the Six Yogas of Naropa*. Somerville, MA: Wisdom Publications, © 1998 by Wisdom Publications. Reprinted with permission of Wisdom Publications, 199 Elm St., Somerville, MA, 02144, U.S.A., www.wisdompubs.org.

    4.17, Desire Itself Is Not the Problem: p. 87

    7.28, We See Ourselves as Impure: p. 70

    9.12, If We Want to Engage in Tantric Practice: p. 61

    9.16, Desire in Sutrayana and Tantrayana: p. 21

    10.24, Seeing the Guru as Vajradhara: p. 60

    11.10, What Is Abhisheka?: p. 49

    11.30, Utpattikrama: p. 67

    11.31, Maintain Awareness of Yourself as the Deity: p. 98.

    13.15, It Is More Difficult to Teach Western Students: pp. 38–39

    13.16, Western Students and Their Teachers: p. 58

From *Introduction to Tantra: The Transformation of Desire*. Rev. ed. Somerville, MA: Wisdom Publications, © 2001 by Lama Zopa Rinpoche. Reprinted with permission of Wisdom Publications, 199 Elm St., Somerville, MA, 02144, U.S.A., www.wisdompubs.org.

    10.26, All Realization Comes from the Guru: p. 96

    10.27, Ordinarily, We Do Not Listen to the Voice of Inner Wisdom:
        p. 97

    10.30, The Relative Guru Is Vitally Important: pp. 97–98

From *The Tantric Path of Purification*. Somerville, MA: Wisdom Publications, 1995.

    4.27, Is Karma Only for Buddhists?: p. 9

    5.19, Reflection on Karma Is Also Meditation: pp. 9–11

    9.9, A Word of Caution to the Intellectual: p. xxiii

# LAMA THUBTEN YESHE RINPOCHE AND ZOPA RINPOCHE

From *Wisdom Energy*. Somerville, MA: Wisdom Publications, 1976.

    3.2, Mere Words Themselves Are of Little Importance: p. 25

    6.17, Bodhichitta: p. 101

    6.18, Bodhichitta Is the Gateway: p. 101

    6.35, The Great Benefits of Bodhichitta: p. 102

## NAMKHAI NORBU RINPOCHE

From *The Mirror: Advice on the Presence of Awareness.* Translated by Adriano Clemente and Andrew Lukianowicz. Barrytown, NY: Station Hill Openings, n.d.
    11.47, Recognizing the Primordial State, p. 29.

## NYOSHUL KHENPO RINPOCHE

From *Natural Great Perfection.* Ithaca, NY: Snow Lion Publications, 1995.
    11.45, The Moment of Dzogchen: pp. 59–60
    11.46, In One Lifetime: p. 60

## RINGU TULKU RINPOCHE

From *Buddhist Meditation.* Lanarkshire, Scotland: Bodhicarya Publications, 1998.
    5.23, The Importance of Learning Just to Be: p. 9

From *Refuge: Finding a Purpose and a Path.* Lanarkshire, Scotland: Bodhicarya Publications, 2000.
    3.15, The Scriptural Dharma and the Dharma of Actual Experience: pp.
        18–19
    10.21, Devotion Is a Mark of Our Practice: p. 25

From unpublished transcripts. Printed with permission.
    4.16, The Cause of Suffering Is Our Way of Perceiving and Reacting

## SAKYONG MIPHAM RINPOCHE

From "Refuge." *Shambhala Sun,* March 2002. Reprinted with permission.
    5.1, The Ceremony for Officially Entering the Path of Meditation: p. 13
    5.3, The Commitment Involved in Taking Refuge: p. 13
    5.10, Our Three Objects of Refuge: p. 13

From "Contemplation." Unpublished transcripts. Printed with permission.
    8.12, One of the Greatest Teachings
    9.14, Bodhichitta Is Essential to Vajrayana Practice

From "Contemplative Practice." Unpublished transcripts. Printed with permission.

    6.3, Mahayana

    8.44, 1. Loving-Kindness: "May all sentient beings enjoy happiness and the root of happiness."

    8.45, 2. Compassion: "May they be free from suffering and the root of suffering."

    8.46, 3. Joy: "May they not be separated from the great happiness devoid of suffering."

    8.47, 4. Equanimity: "May they dwell in the great equanimity free from passion, aggression, and prejudice."

    9.4, The Skillful Means of the Vajrayana

    9.11, Before We Go into Vajrayana

From "Being Human." Unpublished transcripts. Printed with permission.

    4.1, The Importance of View

    4.2, We Need to Understand the "View"

    4.3, Our Human Lives Are Exceedingly Precious

    4.10, The Basic Landscape We're Living In

    4.11, When Someone Close to Us Dies

From "Practice of Contemplation." Unpublished transcripts. Printed with permission.

    5.30, Shamatha Helps Us to Become Calm

    5.31, The Need for Focus

    5.34, As We Continue to Practice

    5.37, The Higher Seeing of Vipashyana

    5.42, From Shamatha to Vipashyana

    6.16, A Definition

    6.26, The Two Aspects of Relative Bodhichitta

    7.13, Sensing Emptiness

    8.18, Being About to Go

    8.48, Tonglen: Sending and Taking

    9.3, The Relation of Vajrayana to Mahayana

From Public Talk, March 8, 2002. Printed with permission.

    4.12, People Say, "Buddhists Believe in Death"

From "Taming the Mind." Unpublished Transcripts Printed with permission.

    4.5, It Is Very Hard to Find a Human Birth

From *Teachers' Sourcebook*. Halifax: Vajradhatu Publications, 1999 (private publication).

    3.11, In Contemplation, We Individualize the Teachings: pp. 149–50

    3.12, How to Practice Contemplation, the Second Prajna: pp. 145–46

## SOGYAL RINPOCHE

From *Dzogchen and Padmasambhava*. California: Rigden Fellowship, 1990.
    11.43, The Spirit of Dzogchen: p. 17.
    11.48, Send the Thinking Mind on Holiday: p. 17


## TARTHANG TULKU RINPOCHE

From *Crystal Mirror*, vol. 3. Berkeley: Dharma Press, 1974.
    2.5, The Buddha Taught the Three Yanas: pp. 3 and 50.
    2.7, Buddhism Has Many Different Techniques: pp. 1 and 112
    3.1, Studying the Dharma Is Very Different: pp. 3 and 114


## THINLEY NORBU RINPOCHE

From *Magic Dance: The Display of the Self-Nature of the Five Wisdom Dakinis*. Boston: Shambhala Publications, 1999.
    1.11, The Buddha Is Beyond Eternalism and Nihilism: p. 29
    1.12, The Buddha's Omniscience: p. 44
    2.12, The Yanas in a Nutshell: p. 31
    4.25, The Origin of Ego from Clear Space: p. 39
    11.20, The Five Elements pp. 7–8
    12.7, Playmind: p. 48
    13.7, Can Westerners Have True Spiritual Lineage?: p. 35


## THRANGU RINPOCHE

From *Introduction to Mahamudra Meditation*. Boulder: Namo Buddha Publications, 2000.
    11.39, Mahamudra Shamatha and Vipashyana: p. 25

From *Moonbeams of Mahamudra*. Boulder: Namo Buddha Publications, 1992.
    11.40, The Benefits of Mahamudra Meditation: p. 7
    11.41, The Results of Mahamudra Shamatha and Mahamudra
        Vipashyana: pp. 14–15

From *The Four Foundations of Buddhist Practice*. Boulder: Namo Buddha Publications, 2001.

4.4, Precious Human Birth: p. 18

From *The Middle-Way Meditation Instructions of Mipham Rinpoche*. Boulder: Namo Buddha Publications, 2000.

6.20, What Is the Essence of Bodhichitta?: pp. 25–27
6.36, Bodhichitta Generates the Qualities of Buddhahood: p. 29.
7.5, How Nagarjuna Shows Emptiness: pp. 28–29

From *The Practice of Tranquility and Insight*. Ithaca: Snow Lion Publications, 1993.

5.53, The Four Types of Vipashyana: pp. 69–71

From *The Three Vehicles of Buddhist Practice*. Boulder: Namo Buddha Publications, 1998. Reprinted by permission of Namo Buddha Seminar.

2.1, The Three Vehicles of Tibetan Buddhism: p. 13
2.6, Why Are There Three Yanas?: pp. 13–14
2.8, The Hinayana: pp. 14–15
3.4, The Three Approaches: p. 68
6.5, The Motivation of the Bodhisattva: p. 51
6.6, The Bodhisattva's Unbiased Love: p. 48
6.7, The Bodhisattva's Concern For All Beings: p. 48
6.34, The Natural Radiance of Bodhichitta: p. 51.
7.8, Emptiness Is Interdependent Origination: pp. 54–55
8.29, The First Paramita Is Generosity: p. 65
8.31, The Second Paramita Is Virtuous Conduct: p. 66
8.33, The Third Paramita, Patience: p. 66
8.35, The Fourth Paramita, Diligence: p. 67
8.37, The Fifth Paramita, Mental Stability: pp. 67–68
8.39, The Sixth Paramita, Wisdom: p. 68
8.42, The Four Immeasurables, p. 49
8.43, Why Impartiality Is First: p. 48
9.6, The Vajrayana Works with the Changeless: p. 73

From *The Twelve Links of Dependent Origination*. Boulder: Namo Buddha Publications, 2001. Reprinted by permission of Namo Buddha Seminar.

7.1, Nagarjuna's Contribution: pp. 28–29
7.6, How an Understanding of Interdependence Leads to Realizing Emptiness: p. 28
7.7, The Interdependence of Phenomena Reveals Their Emptiness: p. 28
7.9, Some Examples of Emptiness: p. 30

From *The Uttara Tantra: A Treatise on Buddha Nature*. Boulder: Namo Buddha Publications, 1989. Reprinted by permission of Namo Buddha Seminar.

# TRALEG KYABGON RINPOCHE

From *The Essence of Buddhism*. Boston: Shambhala Publications, 2001. © 2001 by Traleg Kyabgon Rinpoche. Reprinted by arrangement with Shambhala Publications, Inc., Boston, www.shambhala.com.

## TULKU THONDUP RINPOCHE

## TULKU URGYEN RINPOCHE

From *Repeating the Words of the Buddha*. Boudhanatha: Ranjung Yeshe Publications, 1991. Reprinted by permission of Ranjung Yeshe Publications.